FROM SEMINARY TO UNIVERSITY

An Institutional History of the Study of Religion in Canada

From Seminary to University

An Institutional History of the Study of Religion in Canada

AARON W. HUGHES

UNIVERSITY OF TORONTO PRESS
Toronto Buffalo London

Toronto Buffalo London
utorontopress.com

ISBN 978-1-4875-0497-7 (cloth)
ISBN 978-1-4875-3127-0 (EPUB)
ISBN 978-1-4875-3126-3 (PDF)

Library and Archives Canada Cataloguing in Publication

Title: From seminary to university : an institutional history of the study of religion in Canada / Aaron W. Hughes.
Names: Hughes, Aaron W., 1968–, author.
Description: Includes bibliographical references and index.
Identifiers: Canadiana (print) 2020018203X | Canadiana (ebook) 20200182056 | ISBN 9781487504977 (hardcover) | ISBN 9781487531270 (EPUB) | ISBN 9781487531263 (PDF)
Subjects: LCSH: Religion – Study and teaching (Higher) – Canada – History. | LCSH: Theology – Study and teaching (Higher) – Canada – History. | LCSH: Theological seminaries – Canada – History. | LCSH: Universities and colleges – Curricula – Canada – History.
Classification: LCC BL42.5.C2 H84 2020 | DDC 200.71/171 – dc23

This book has been published with the help of a grant from the Federation for the Humanities and Social Sciences, through the Awards to Scholarly Publications Program, using funds provided by the Social Sciences and Humanities Research Council of Canada.

University of Toronto Press acknowledges the financial assistance to its publishing program of the Canada Council for the Arts and the Ontario Arts Council, an agency of the Government of Ontario.

Canada Council for the Arts
Conseil des Arts du Canada

Funded by the Government of Canada
Financé par le gouvernement du Canada
Canada

For Gabriel,
la raison avant la passion

Contents

Acknowledgments

Addressing the Press Club in Washington, DC, on 25 March 1969, then current prime minister Pierre Trudeau spoke of the relationship between the United States and Canada in the following terms: "Living next to [the United States] is in some ways like sleeping with an elephant. No matter how friendly and even-tempered is the beast, if I can call it that, one is affected by every twitch and grunt." Canadian schoolchildren regularly learn about American history (in addition, of course, to Canadian history) at school and are exposed regularly to American popular culture through American television channels and radio stations. While this means that the border between the two countries is rather fluid (albeit with ideas generally moving in one direction, from south to north), the flip side of this is the increasing danger that Canadians mistake events in American history for their own.

The impetus for the present volume is related to this confusion. I recall a conversation I had with Canadian graduate students at the American Academy of Religion (AAR) about nine years ago. We talked about the history of religious studies in Canada, and several in that group mentioned the *Schempp* Supreme Court ruling in the United States that helped create the non-denominational study of religion in American state universities. I still remember how they tried to tell me that the Canadian model was also influenced by the US Supreme Court decision since, after all, departments of religious studies began to flourish in Canada at around the same time. While I did not object to the chronological convergence, the underlying cause did not seem right to me. So I have spent roughly the past decade trying to provide an accurate and informed response to this group. I trust my response will be of value to more than just them. Since my training is largely in premodern Islamic studies, however, I have had to move outside of my comfort zone to learn a new discourse that has involved Canadian history and the sociology of knowledge in Canada. It has been a thrilling journey, and I have learned much in the process and supplemented what I found out in hindsight was but a rudimentary knowledge of my own history as a Canadian. I have no intention of stepping on the toes of historians of Canada; rather, this volume hopes to contribute to understanding further one particular aspect of Canadian history.

I would like to thank the following people for joining me on my conversation and indulging my questions: Willi Braun, Jennifer Hall, Liliana Leopardi, Russell T. McCutcheon, Harold Remus, Leif Sternberg, Will Sweetman, Don Wiebe, Elliot R. Wolfson, and Philip Wood. I am grateful for the anonymous readers at the University of Toronto Press, whose comments further helped me streamline the argument. I would also like to acknowledge the professionalism and guidance of Len Husband, my editor at UTP. Finally, this book has been published with the help of a grant from the Federation for the Humanities and Social Sciences, through the Awards to Scholarly Publications Program, using funds provided by the Social Sciences and Humanities Research Council of Canada. I would like to thank them for allowing this volume to see the light of day.

Timeline

1763	France cedes New France to Great Britain (Treaty of Paris)
1776	American War of Independence
1791	Creation of Upper Canada and Lower Canada
1802	Royal Charter establishes King's College in Nova Scotia (founded in 1789)
1812–15	War of 1812
1821	Royal Charter establishes McGill College (Montreal)
1826	Royal Charter establishes King's College in Toronto (officially opens in 1843)
1827	Royal Charter establishes King's College, NB (founded in 1785)
1836	Creation of Upper Canada Academy
1837	Lower Canada Rebellion Lord Russell's Act of Union
1838	Canada Baptist College established in Montreal
1840	Upper Canada Act establishes Queen's at Kingston (superseded by Royal Charter in 1841)
1841	Union of Lower Canada and Upper Canada (now Canada West and Canada East) as the new Province of Canada (Capital in Kingston) Victoria College (Methodist) established in Cobourg (moves to Toronto in 1892)
1844	Capital of Canada moves from Kingston to Montreal Free Church Succession (Presbyterianism)
1846	King's College, NB, becomes University of New Brunswick (with new Charter)
1849	Baldwin Act establishes University of Toronto Secularization of the public school system in Ontario
1851	Trinity College (Anglican) created in Toronto

1852 St. Michael's College (Catholic) created in Toronto
1853 Hincks Act creates University College at University of Toronto
1860 Canadian Literary Institute established
1867 British North America Act creates Canada
1877 Wycliffe College (Anglican) created in Toronto
University of Manitoba created
1879 Emmanuel College (Anglican) created in Prince Albert, SK (University of Emmanuel College in 1883)
1884 Knox College (Free Presbyterian) created in Toronto
1887 Federation Act at University of Toronto (affiliates church-related colleges with the university)
McMaster University established out of Toronto Baptist College
1899 Vancouver College (BC) incorporated as McGill College, BC (becomes UBC in 1915)
Brandon College (Man) affiliates with McMaster
1906 McGill College of BC created
1907 Alberta College (Edmonton) affiliates with McGill
University of Saskatchewan created
1908 University of Alberta created
University of British Columbia created
1924 First issue of *Canadian Journal of Religious Thought* published
1925 Creation of United Church of Canada
Queen's Theological College becomes affiliated with United Church
1930 McMaster moves from Toronto to Hamilton
1931 Canada receives legislative autonomy from Great Britain
1932 Last issue of *Canadian Journal of Religious Thought* published
1949 Faculty of Divinity created at McGill
1955 First issues of *Canadian Journal of Theology* published
Canadian Theological Society (CTS) established
1960 Department of Religious Studies created at McMaster
Canadian Society of Church History (CSCH) established
1963 Société canadienne de théologie (SCT) established
1964 Department of Religious Studies created at UBC
1965 Canadian Society for the Study of Religion / Société canadienne pour l'étude de la religion (CSSR/SCÉR) established
1967 Département des sciences religieuses created at Université de Montréal

1968	Department of Religious Studies created at University of Manitoba
1969	"Combined Departments of Religious Studies" created at University of Toronto
1970	Canadian Corporation for Studies in Religion / Corporation canadienne des sciences religieuses (CCSR) created by federal charter
	Last issues of *Canadian Journal of Theology* published
	Faculty of Divinity changed to Faculty of Religious Studies at McGill
1971	Federal policy of multiculturalism established
	Studies in Religion / Sciences religieuses first published
1972	Département des sciences religieuses created at Université du Québec à Montréal
1973	Department of Religious Studies created at University of Alberta
	Department of Religious Studies created at Dalhousie University
1974	University of Saskatchewan–Regina becomes University of Regina
	Department of Religious Studies created at University of Regina
1975	Canadian Society of Patristic Studies / Association canadienne des études patristiques (CSPS) established
	Department of Religious Studies created at University of Toronto
1976	Department of Religious Studies created at University of Calgary
1982	Canada Act (Canadian constitution repatriated, along with the new Charter of Rights and Freedoms)
1984	Department of Religious Studies created at University of Saskatchewan
1988	Canadian Multiculturalism Act
1989	Société québécoise pour l'étude de la religion (SQÉR) established

FROM SEMINARY TO UNIVERSITY

An Institutional History of the Study of Religion in Canada

Introduction

The academic study of religion, for all intents and purposes, began in Germany in the nineteenth century.[1] Its goal was, as indeed it still is, to understand the religions of the globe from an ostensibly scientific (*wissenschaftliche*) perspective.[2] It was an endeavour that, to be sure, had a number of contradictory aims. It absorbed elements of historicism and so-called higher criticism, for example, yet it also tended to privilege Protestant religious forms.[3] If the former sought to account for the historical and sociological production of religious texts, the latter made certain assumptions about the scope and nature of "true" or "authentic" religion. The new and ostensibly more secular study thus drew upon several millennia of thinking about religion in what we might call a decidedly theological register. The line separating the two activities has by definition been opaque since both share the same subject matter, to wit, religion, and the more secular religious studies, as will be clear in the pages that follow, genealogically emerged out of theology. This was certainly the case in Europe, just as it was the case in North America. However, as this study seeks to show in detail, despite such similar developments, the study of religion – whether of the theological or the more secular variety – has always been understood in various nationalist or other regional contexts.

On account of its investment in method – that is, in how to understand properly both the category "religion" and its deployment in non-Christian traditions – a concomitant activity of religious studies has always been to distance itself from what it regards as a more confessional or theological approach. If the latter has been based on the articulation and subsequent defence of truth-claims, the more secular orientation of the former desires to illumine the human and cultural elements of religion using the tools of cognate disciplines such as anthropology, sociology, and history. There would seem to be clear differences between the two approaches; even so, it is safe to say that the line separating the theological and the secular approaches has been a very fine one ever since the emergence of the latter out of the former.

In order to firm up this line, it has become fashionable in the present day to debate the merits and utility of the very term "religion."[4] If theologians are in the business of procuring "good" religion, their more academic and secular cousins see themselves as engaged in the very discourses that bring religion into focus as a category of analysis.[5] This usually entails a quasi-"meta" and a quasi-historical analysis to show how "religion" is a Western construct that is invested in European intellectual and imperial hegemony. Rather than help us understand other cultures, it is now argued, the Western discourses created by the field of religious studies actually misread and distort other cultures, shaping them to fit problematic Western terms of analysis.[6] Because of this, as many have well argued, the axioms and first principles of religious studies need to be systematically rethought, if not actually dismantled.

There is much merit to this argument, and I like to think that I have indeed contributed to this rethinking and dismantling in a number of publications.[7] My goal here, however, is to come at this rethinking from a somewhat different angle. While I certainly want to reinforce the above position, I now go further and suggest that this could not have been otherwise because there can be no Archimedean point from which to adequately describe or analyse religion *on account of the study of religion's investment in the modern nation-state*. In other words, the study of religion – and, for the moment, I am not differentiating between theology and religious studies – in every Western country, is ultimately dependent upon, reflected in, and complexly intertwined with decidedly non-academic contexts. Religion is thus imagined, constructed, and situated in specific national frames of reference.[8] To show this, the following study examines in considerable detail how the study of religion came to be constructed in one particular country, Canada. So while my data are region-specific, the conclusions drawn will, I trust, be of value to those working both inside and outside of Canada. To this end, and to accommodate such a broader readership, at several junctures I shall provide what some might consider to be more introductory explanations of certain key events in Canadian history (e.g., Confederation, formation of the United Church of Canada) that, though hopefully familiar to scholars of religion in Canada, will certainly not be to those outside. The challenge here is to strike a delicate balance between providing a sweeping survey of the *longue durée* while simultaneously going into considerably greater detail when it comes to the major questions and themes that wind their way through this book.

What follows, then, provides a test case to illumine some of the intellectual and extra-intellectual contexts – the material conditions, if you will – that went into the production of a national discourse about the place, role, and function of religion as both a category and a set of discourses.[9] I work on the assumption that no discipline or field of study that has as its subject matter "religion" can escape being influenced by a complex set of demographic, social, political, legal, and other debates about the public and political understanding of religion. Such debates, I suggest, help structure the way religion is imagined nationally and subsequently reflected in how it is studied institutionally. Rather than speak about the study of religion as a generic field, then, it might be more profitable to think of various national (and nationalist) fields. This is not to say that transnational concerns do not exist; but it is to claim that every country has an often idiosyncratic set of anxieties that structure – legally, socially, pedagogically, and so on – issues about, for example, what gets to count as a religion, how religion is discussed in the public sphere, and ultimately what the appropriate institutional setting or settings are wherein religion should be taught, and, of course, to whom it should be taught.

I focus on Canada not only because I am a Canadian and a product of its system but also because the Canadian context is frequently ignored or bypassed. When one thinks about the academic study of religion in North America, it is the American context that is privileged. Given its history, and reinforcing my point, the overwhelming focus of this topic has been on the legal rulings that made the secular study of religion possible in the United States. More often than not this has involved an examination of the *School District of Abington Township, PA v. Schempp* Supreme Court case of 1963.[10] This ruling forbade public school readings of the Bible as a violation of the establishment clause of the American Constitution, but significantly, it also ruled in favour of teaching *about* religion as part of a general humanistic education. This ruling led directly to the founding of the American Academy of Religion (AAR) in the same year and the subsequent creation of departments of religion or religious studies in state universities throughout the country. That ruling, for all intents and purposes, made the secular study of religion possible in the United States.

It would be a mistake to assume, however, that the American story was standard, let alone normal. Instead, I would suggest that the American story is precisely that, a story that developed out of a set of idiosyncratic concerns unique to that country. We could similarly argue that how the study of religion came to be – indeed, how it continues to be configured in places such as Britain, France, Italy, Germany, Belgium,

Switzerland, Austria, Greece, and so on – is the direct product of those countries' own distinct and often idiosyncratic legal, theological, denominational, judicial, and social frameworks, all of which have been, and continue to be, forced to deal in some way, shape, or form with religion broadly conceived.

The present study seeks to provide the first historical, social, political, and institutional examination of the emergence, transformation, and florescence of the study of religion in Canada. While there have clearly been precursors (discussed below), what follows situates this study within the length and breadth of the history of Canada from the eighteenth century to the present. I certainly do not have the space or time to survey every seminary, university, or department in the country.[11] My goal is more modest, namely, to provide the context in which such institutions can be located. While I mention UBC, for example, I largely ignore the University of Victoria; and while I focus on the University of Alberta, which had the first Department of Religious Studies in that province, I treat only briefly the University of Calgary and bypass altogether the University of Lethbridge. Such omissions are certainly not political but are based solely on heuristic utility.

Though the narrative I provide is, in many ways, specific to Canada, I would hope that it is but one chapter of a much larger story that will encourage other scholars working in other national contexts to examine similar relevant questions. In this context, the story of the study of religion in Canada is, in many ways, the story of Canada itself. Its unfolding reveals the gradual movement from religious exclusion to secularism, from Christocentrism to multiculturalism, and from theology to secular religious studies. It is, simultaneously, the story of geographic expansion and growing national confidence in the face of British and subsequent American imperialism and influence. Finally, it is the story of institutional tensions, legal battles, and constitutional repatriation over the course of the long twentieth century. The story of the study of religion in any country is, after all, the story of how that country imagines itself, of its ability to deal (or not) with difference, religious or otherwise, and, in the final analysis, of how it situates itself in the world and in the community of nations. Canada is certainly not unique in this respect, but merely, as the present study shows, exemplary.

Most universities in Canada, especially in the east, began as theological schools or seminaries established by Royal Charter. This immediately alerts us to the fact that the study and teaching of religion, in the earliest years in this country, took place at the intersection of theology and British imperialism. Attempts to establish Anglicanism as the official religion of Canada, and the exclusionary principles of the earliest seminaries, gradually produced rival seminaries, since other denominations needed to train their own clergy to administer local flocks. Many of these seminaries – located in places like Toronto, Kingston, Hamilton, Saint John, and Halifax – would subsequently go on to become major secular research institutions.

It should be clear by now that a history of the study of religion cannot deal simply with the secular and academic. Although I had first intended to produce such a study, it became quite clear quite quickly that this would tell only a small fraction of the story – the veritable "tip of the iceberg." How the academic study of religion came to be, I am convinced, only makes sense when situated against the larger backdrop of ecclesiastic control and its gradual diminution. There were, in other words, many social, demographic, economic, and legal reasons underlying the gradual creation of religious studies in Canada – all of which must be taken into account.

The goal of these seminaries-cum-universities, for example, was to educate a Canadian clergy, albeit under the tutelage of British or American teachers, who would engage in the task of civilizing the inhabitants of the new colony, be they immigrant or Indigenous. Only gradually could secular universities emerge from the ashes of religious seminaries, and only at that point could a more secular and non-denominational study of religion develop. I want to make it clear, however, that this is by no means a straightforward or evolutionary narrative. Because my interest is in the gradual transition from seminary to university, I freely acknowledge that theology is still being taught in many places outside of the context of the secular university, as it should be. But that is not my concern here. Central to my story are the theological polemics between denominations – something that would be mitigated, to some extent, by the creation of the United Church in the early twentieth century – and those who opposed the promotion of one religion at the expense of others. The latter individuals included the businessman and civic leader James McGill (1744–1813) in Montreal and the reform-minded Robert Baldwin (1804–1858) and the Friends of Religious Liberty in Toronto. These men fought hard to exclude sectarian tests and preferences for both students and faculty at the newly forming colleges and universities. Their critics, such as John Strachan (1778–1867), the Anglican Bishop of Toronto, accused them of "godlessness" and were determined to make religion (i.e., their own religion) an essential component of university education. However, it was the vision of people like McGill and Baldwin, though certainly not the regnant one at the time, that would eventually carry the day. Their vision was universal in spirit and secular in outlook. It was they and other like-minded individuals who created the first non-denominational universities in Canada, at McGill and the University of Toronto, thus setting an important precedent for higher education in the rest of the young country.

While departments of religious studies would not emerge until the 1960s and '70s, the teaching of religion – under the guise of divinity, theology, the Old and New Testaments, moral philosophy, and the like – was omnipresent for much of the country's history, and such teaching only makes sense when contextualized within that history. The transformation from the teaching of religious truths at denominational theological colleges to the non-denominational and secular study of religion (i.e., *all* religions of the globe) was long and gradual, and cries out for documentation and analysis. This transformation was not based simply on academic whim or on changing ecclesiastical interest; rather, it was the result of many overlapping social, political, legal, and intellectual circumstances. The present volume is an attempt to unpack those circumstances and to begin unravelling them from one another. My goal, then, is to write an important chapter in the history of Canada and, more generally, in the history of religions. This volume, in other words, seeks to contribute to two distinct yet mutually overlapping areas: Canadian history, and how the study of religion is carried out in specific contexts.

In the inimitable words of former prime minister Pierre Elliott Trudeau, which I invoked in my acknowledgments, "living next to [the United States] is in some ways like sleeping with an elephant. No matter how friendly and even-tempered is the beast, if I can call it that, one is affected by every twitch and grunt." There is a danger – and here I am rephrasing Trudeau's remarks to suit my own interests – of assuming that the story of how the academic study of religion came about in the United States – to wit, that country's separation of Church and State, its constitutionalism, its monumental court case mentioned above, which legalized academic study *about* religion – was mirrored in Canada. As this volume clearly shows, it was not. While the academic study of religion in the United States and Canada may well look similar today, as it must with the migration of scholars and ideas in both directions, my aim here is to show that *historically* the Canadian context is far different from the American one, not to mention those found in various European countries.

What follows, however, is certainly not meant to be an exercise in comparison. I am not interested in showing where or how the study of religion in Canada is similar to or different from what is found in the United States, or in any other country for that matter. The Canadian story, on my reading, is significant in and of itself, and it does not need to be footnoted to any other. Instead, when it is told contextually we see clearly how the study of religion, broadly conceived, mirrors a host of anxieties and concerns about religion that are frequently specific to this country. It is a story, then, that does not need to be measured against the yardstick provided by another.

Religion, Politics, Individuals

The history of the study of religion in Canada, as should now be apparent, takes place against a much broader backdrop than might be expected or even imagined. It is not just the history of secular departments of religious studies scattered across the nation. It is, much more importantly, also the story of the decidedly non-academic forces that made those departments possible in the first place. These include, but are certainly not limited to, the secularization of education after Confederation; the creation of the United Church of Canada in 1925; the formation of the Department of Citizenship and Immigration in 1950, which gradually encouraged immigration from other parts of the globe; the adoption of multiculturalism as an official Act of Parliament in 1971; and the introduction of the Charter of Rights and Freedoms in 1982. All of these events, to be explored in greater detail in the pages that follow, both contributed to and coincided with an increased openness to the study of other religions and cultures as a matter of both national and civic policy.

The study of religion in Canada, then, is intimately connected to the history of seminaries and universities in Canada, to Acts of Parliament, and to other momentous events in Canadian religious history. In like manner this study was imagined, constructed, and disseminated by a host of individuals, many now forgotten. Certainly there are important names – such as George Monro Grant (1835–1902) at Queen's; Robert H.L. Slater (d. 1984) at Huron College in London, Ontario, then at McGill, who would subsequently become the inaugural director of the Center for the Study of World Religions (CSWR) at Harvard; Wilfred Cantwell Smith (1916–2000), who among other things established the Institute of Islamic Studies at McGill; and McMaster's George P. Grant (1918–1998) – but there are also many unsung heroes, like those who contributed to interfaith theology before these individuals and those who aided in the consolidation and florescence of departments of religious studies across the country shortly thereafter. Their stories must also be told. Yet the study of religion in Canada, be it theological or secular, is not just the story of individuals. It is also the story of social forces, political expedience, and legal battles over the role and function of religion in higher education. It is in this triangulation of Canadian religious history, legal acts of Parliament, and individuals and individual scholars who sought to create a Canadian field of study that, I maintain, is ultimately where the story of the study of religion unfolds.

Precursors to the Present Volume: The State-of-the-Art Reviews

Before proceeding, a word is in order for precursors to the present volume. In 1969, Charles P. Anderson, then of UBC, published a *Guide to Religious Studies in Canada/Guide des sciences religieuses au Canada*. The 1972 expanded volume, from which I here quote, was subsequently published under the auspices of the newly formed Corporation for the Publication of Academic Studies in Religion,[12] which had come into existence in 1971 through a federal charter and was charged with the task of "publishing a journal and other materials to serve the needs of scholars working in both the French and English languages in Canada in all fields of the academic study of religion."[13] Immediately the corporation was responsible for the publication of the newly formed *Studies in Religion / Sciences religieuses* (*SR*), the bilingual and more secular replacement for the *Canadian Journal of Theology* (*CJT*), which had begun publication in 1955.

The purpose of Anderson's guide was to provide a "survey and analysis of the state of religious studies in Canada," both anglophone and francophone.[14] It should be appreciated that 1972 represents the beginning of the florescence of religious studies, with departments springing up across the length and breadth of the country. Anderson, however, is most interested in showing this florescence not by accounting for its history, as I am, but by listing relevant programs found in universities, theological colleges, and community and/or junior colleges, complete with "descriptions and requirements of, and enrolments in various degree programs in religion."[15] His guide, then, is not meant to be a historical work. Indeed, at the beginning of his introductory essay, Anderson writes that

> if and when the history of religious studies in Canada comes to be written, its contours presumably will be portrayed against a backdrop of the appropriate cultural, religious, educational, economic, and other factors. Such an undertaking is far beyond the scope of this essay. Yet, such factors cannot be entirely ignored, and passing notice of some of them will be made. However, the main purpose of this essay is not to relate Canadian religious studies to its context, but to identify recent developments and trends within the discipline.[16]

The present volume attempts to do precisely what Anderson defines here as a desideratum. While his work offers in one convenient location a snapshot of what the academic study of religion looked like in Canada in the late 1960s and early 1970s, the present volume, among other things, seeks to show how things got to be the way that Anderson recounts them in his important volume.

Following on the heels of the guide is the Canadian Corporation for Studies in Religion (CCSR)–sponsored and Social Sciences and Humanities Research Council (SSHRC)–funded State-of-the-Art Review of the academic study of religion in Canada, which began in the early 1980s under the general editorship of Harold Coward. The series' goal was to provide a history, description, and comprehensive analysis of religious studies as conceived and practised in its Canadian context. It has five volumes, each devoted to a particular region. They are listed here by order of appearance: Alberta,[17] Quebec,[18] Ontario,[19] Manitoba and Saskatchewan,[20] British Columbia,[21] and Atlantic Canada.[22]

Like Anderson's volume, this series, except for Remus's excellent opening chapter to the Ontario volume, is not meant to be historical. These volumes provide exhaustive and detailed accounts of specific regions, but missing is a synthetic and comparative overview to pull them all together. Why, when, and where, for example, did the study of religion (be it theological or secular) emerge, and where, in particular, did and does religious studies fit into Canadian post-secondary education?

These individual volumes are important and extremely useful. I allow them to do much of my practical legwork, at least where the creation of individual departments is concerned.[23] There is no need, for example, to retell those stories here, especially when these volumes do that so ably and competently. What is lacking in the volumes, however, and what this volume seeks to provide, is an overarching history of a field, as opposed to just departments. Indeed, on another level, the present volume provides the larger historical context in which these State-of-the-Art volumes can be read and appreciated.

Coward, the general editor, stated that his intent was eventually to write a concluding volume to the series wherein he could provide an overarching analysis of the field in Canada. Such a volume unfortunately never transpired. He did, however, produce a memoir in 2014 titled *Fifty Years of Religious Studies in Canada*.[24] That the subtitle refers to this book as a memoir is revealing. In it, he frequently mentions the need for what he calls a "formal history" of the academic study of religion in Canada.[25] Indeed, he repeatedly acknowledges that that history remains to be written. "What I offer," he writes, "is not a formal history (a task that remains for someone else), but my own retrospective."[26]

The present volume seeks to provide this so-called formal history. However, unlike Coward and the authors of the regional volumes,

I take a much broader view of the academic study of religion. For me, the study of religion did not begin out of the blue with the rise of religious studies departments in the 1960s. On the contrary, I argue that that decade was but the endpoint of a much larger set of developments dating back to pre-Confederation days. Nor is the present volume, as I have stated several times already, simply an academic or disciplinary narrative. On my reading, the academic study of religion as it has come to be carried out in the Canadian context is the result of numerous extra-academic, not to mention theological, developments.

English versus French Canada?

The reader will soon notice that anglophone Canada is privileged over its francophone counterpart. While I had originally intended a broader-reaching project, it soon became clear that such an undertaking would be difficult, if not impossible, to bring to fruition. The differences between English and French Canada – their histories, their legal cultures, their demographics, their educational institutions – are so different that a study that paid equal attention to both would be either too voluminous or, alternatively, too superficial. As Hillary Kaell notes, Quebec poses a number of unique challenges to religious history, for the province "occupies a rather unique position between two primary models in the West: unlike many European countries, it never had an established church paid for directly through taxes; unlike the rest of North America, it never developed a pattern of voluntary denominationalism."[27]

When France formally ceded New France in 1763, the former French territory found itself under a Protestant Crown with which it had formally been at war. The British passed the Quebec Act of 1774 to guarantee the region's French inhabitants liberty of language and religion; this paved the way for the creation of a Québécois Church that would consolidate power and influence in the British colony and that would subsequently control education, hospitals, and even local politics.[28] This meant that Quebec would always develop its own course, which would depend heavily on its unique religious identity, one that was distinct from the rest of Canada. As a result of this strongly Catholic influence, especially on theological institutions and those of post-secondary education, Quebec society is very different from that of English Canada. For this reason, I have opted to deal primarily with the latter.

This is not to say that I ignore Quebec, however. I pay particular attention, for example, to anglophone institutions in that province, most notably McGill University, whose Faculty of Divinity and subsequent

Faculty of Religious Studies (as of 2016, the School of Religious Studies) played an important role in shaping discourses about religion in Canada. Moreover, I also mention other relevant and significant developments in Quebec, including, among other things, the founding of Laval University in 1852 (its precursor, the Séminaire de Québec, had been founded in 1663), the rise of "la religiologie" or "sciences des religieuses" in Québécois universities in the 1960s and '70s, and the creation of learned societies devoted to the study of religion in that province, such as the Société canadienne de théologie (SCT) and the Société québécoise pour l'étude de la religion (SQÉR). Beyond this, however, the primary focus of this study, for reasons stated above, will be on English Canada.[29]

Definition of "the Study of Religion"

Though I imagine this study as contributing to what is often called "theory and method" in the academic study of religion, I have no interest in providing a definition of what religion is or in articulating a correct way of engaging in its study. It is not incumbent on me to opine on what the proper study of religions should be or should look like. I treat theological and academic approaches to religion equally, and while I certainly favour the inclusivity and historicity of the latter, I have no intention of denigrating the former. Rather, I seek to provide a historical work that accounts for "how" as opposed to "what." The following study, as mentioned, considers many institutions, including residential schools, theological seminaries and colleges, and secular departments of religious studies. I certainly do not want to imply that the movement from seminary to university was an evolutionary process, let alone a teleological one. On the contrary, in telling the story of the study of religion in Canada, it was necessary to tell it in its many contexts. I should note, however, that though my own training has taken place solely in secular departments, in both Canada and the United States, I refuse to focus solely on them in what follows.

Those who are familiar with my other work might expect me to approach some of the debates encountered herein from a sociopolitical perspective in order to demonstrate how many of the social actors in the pages that follow are invested in maintaining a particular economic and political status quo. I opt not to do this here, however, in the interest of fairness and accuracy. My goal, simply stated, is to provide a historical narrative – the data – that can be taken in any number of ways. I do indeed hope that others will do that and theorize the debates encountered here. But before there can be such redescription there needs to be description.

Contents

Chapter 1, "Inauspicious Beginnings," examines the rise of the first institutions devoted to the study of and teaching about religion in the new colony. It shows the deep-rooted connections between theology, perceived religious truth, and politics as various denominations sought to create institutions to promote their interests and, in the process, "civilize" First Nations. Indeed, this was behind the formation of some of the first major institutions of higher learning in Canada, such as Laval, McGill, Queen's, and the University of Toronto.

The second chapter, "The University of Toronto: A Case Study," uses that institution to illumine some of the features outlined in the previous chapter. U of T was established as King's College, an Anglican institution, by a Royal Charter in 1827; later, a series of political battles sought to extricate it from either religious control or religious affiliation. Thanks to the Baldwin Act of 1849 and the Hincks Act of 1853, U of T finally came into existence as a "godless" institution in 1887.

I use this story as way to illumine further some of the sectarian battles that wracked universities and colleges in the early years. It was only through these political battles about the place of religion in higher learning that secular universities came to be in eastern Canada (western Canada was significantly different, as will be shown in chapter 4). Such battles, as will be clear in chapter 8, paradoxically had to be refought when the secular academic study of religion emerged on campuses in the 1960s and '70s.

Chapter 3, "Late Victorian Scholarship and the Rise of Higher Criticism," takes some of these political, legal, and institutional battles and begins to focus on some early scholars of religion in Canada, most of whom were theologians and Christian apologists. However, we do begin to see some individuals engage in a more comparative model, specifically the aforementioned George Monro Grant. The chapter argues that this new model could only emerge after the denominational pulls – witnessed so clearly in the previous chapters – began to be challenged if not actually dismantled. In their stead there slowly emerged a more secular and comparative approach to religion.

The fourth chapter, "Westward Bound," traces the impact of Confederation and the Canadian Pacific Railway (CPR) on the rise of universities in the western provinces (British Columbia, Alberta, Saskatchewan, and Manitoba). With the exception of Manitoba, these provinces looked less to England and more to the United States with its land-grant or state universities, which provided a more practical alternative to the divinity schools of private institutions. Following this, the chapter examines how religion, politics, and the study of religion intersected in relation to two radically different interwar politicians: William Aberhart in Alberta and Tommy Douglas in Saskatchewan.

Chapter 5, "Battle Lines," illumines how the theological study of religion in Canada evolved into a more secular study. It charts some of the material conditions that made this possible. Such conditions included the formation of the United Church of Canada in 1924, which destabilized the denominationalism of previous decades. When such events were coupled with intellectual changes, such as the rise of higher criticism and the creation of Oriental studies departments, a more secular approach to religious texts proved to be inevitable in many secular institutions.

The sixth chapter, "Venues of Dissemination," uses two Canadian journals to shed further light on major changes that took place in the study of religion during the twentieth century. The *Canadian Journal of Religious Thought* (1924–32) and the *Canadian Journal of Theology* (1955–70) were, as should be clear from their names, devoted to theological and largely Christian topics. Both, however, were conscious of being Canadian journals, and both regarded themselves as providing venues for religious and homiletical reflection that would be of relevance to all (Christian) Canadians, whatever their denominational affiliation. By 1970, the *Canadian Journal of Theology*'s final year of publication, secular departments of religious studies – devoted to studying all of the world's religions – were beginning to develop throughout the country. It was perhaps inevitable, then, that in 1970, such a journal seemed increasingly anachronistic and ripe to give way to a more secular and comparative journal, *Studies in Religion / Sciences religieuses* (*SR*).

Chapter 7, "From Seminary to University," examines the beginnings of the secular academic study of religion in Canada. It begins by focusing on the demographic changes in Canadian society that took place during the 1960s, and shows how those changes functioned as a backdrop to the rise of a non-theological study of religion in the same decade. Chapter 8 will examine the rise of these departments; chapter 7 focuses on the material conditions that facilitated this rise. It does so, for example, by paying attention to newly created societies devoted to the study of religion in Canada. These included the secular Canadian Society for the Study of Religion (CSSR), which drove the founding of the umbrella Canadian Corporation for Studies in Religion (CCSR), which was responsible for publishing the new non-theological and academic *SR*. The latter journal, because of its mandate, was now open to receive public funds for its publication. These features successfully carved out space for the academic study of religion in ways that were non-theological and, just as importantly, not reducible to cognate fields or departments, such as philosophy or history.

Chapter 8, "Florescence," charts the rise of the first departments of religious studies beginning in the mid-1960s. Almost every post-secondary institution in Canada made a conscious decision to include religious studies and to do so, moreover, not in affiliated theological colleges but in the centre of their arts curriculum. Of central concern was the need to make such curricula more multicultural and reflective of Canadian society by introducing alternative (read: non-Western) takes on enduring questions of human existence. This movement from periphery to centre mirrored, as mentioned, Canada's demography; it also appealed to a new generation of students who, while interested in issues of spirituality and meaning, were increasingly uninterested in mainline Protestant churches in Canada.

The study of religion in Canada, as should now be clear, is a complex phenomenon that reflects many distinct historical, political, social, legal, and other relevant contexts. It cannot simply be reduced to the rise of religious studies departments in the 1960s and '70s, the same years that witnessed the rise of such departments at state universities in the United States. On my telling, the study of religion in Canada is part of a much larger story that encompasses the growth of a young colony into an independent nation, a transformation that included changes in the place of religion, and its study. It is to the earliest years that I now turn.

Chapter One

Inauspicious Beginnings

On 20 July 1534, Jacques Cartier erected a large 10-metre-tall cross above the harbour at Gaspé.[1] It was emblazoned with a fleur-de-lys and the words "Long Live the King of France" written in large Gothic characters. Striking the perfect, if unfortunate, sixteenth-century triangulation of colonialism, political superiority, and religious bigotry, Cartier and his entourage set about doing what explorers had always done: instructing the "savages" in the error of their ways.[2] Their audience that day was a band of Iroquois located in the village of Stadacona, soon to be renamed Québec, who were informed in no uncertain terms that their redemption would occur solely through the Church.[3] Cartier subsequently wrote in his diary:

> We erected the cross at the point in their presence and they watched it being put together and set up. And when it had been raised in the air, we all knelt down with our hands joined, worshipping it before them; and made signs to them, looking up and pointing toward heaven, that by means of this we had our redemption, at which they showed many marks of admiration, at the same time turning and looking at the cross.[4]

Also present at this symbolic event was the chief of the Iroquois, Donnacona, who worried that the cross signified a claim on his ancestral land and objected that it was improper. Fearing the consequences of his discontent, Cartier lied to the chief, informing him that the cross was but a temporary landmark to help him and his crew find their way back home. Cartier then took two of Donnacona's sons hostage to be used as proof of the New World to those in the Old. Upon his return to "Kanata" the following year, moving farther inland, Cartier encountered the Iroquois of Hochelega, later to be called Montreal, whom he felt were "positively predisposed to Christianity." After much intimidation and haranguing, the priests with Cartier offered a mass baptism.[5] In his diary, Cartier wrote:

> This people has no belief in God that amounts to anything; for they believe in a god they call *Cudouagny*, and maintain that he often holds intercourse with them and tells them what the weather will be like ... After they had explained these things to us, we showed them their error and informed them that their *Cudouagny* was a wicked spirit who deceived them, and that there is but one God, Who is in Heaven, Who gives us everything we need and is the Creator of all things and that in Him alone we should believe. Also that one must receive baptism or perish in hell.[6]

Such was the first recorded instruction of religion in what would eventually become Canada. It was to be sure a decidedly non-academic one, in which intimidation and trickery replaced any pretence to pedagogy. The colonizers imagined themselves as superior and the Indigenous inhabitants as "heathens" in need of the salvation that the "true" religion would bestow.[7] It was an encounter laced with prejudice, Christocentrism, and wanton disregard for the diverse political, social, and religious traditions of Canada's first peoples.[8] These negative features, which would continue to play a major role in the centuries that followed, reveal just what is at stake in the theological teaching of religion, especially when it is associated with prejudice and racialism – with "correct" and "incorrect" worship, perceived superiority, and the need to establish and propagate one religion at the expense of others.[9] Such were the inauspicious origins of religious education in the New World.

This chapter seeks, after a brief historical excursus, to chart the ways in which education in general and religion in particular were conceived and taught in the new colonies. Canada's post-secondary institutions are secular today, but the overwhelming majority of them began as denominational colleges that often found themselves caught up in highly sectarian battles. The Church of England saw itself as *the* Church of the new colony.[10] Many of the other mainline Protestant denominations, however, sought to define themselves against it and, in the process, opened their own seminaries. These sectarian and denominational battles would play a major role in structuring, both institutionally and sociologically, the study of religion in the coming centuries.

Historical Contexts

Allow me to survey, especially for the reader not familiar with the major themes of Canadian history, some of the relevant historical and social contexts that form the larger backdrop against which the events in this chapter and the following one took place.

Despite the initial French presence established by Cartier and those who came after him, New France, as it was then called, was largely eclipsed by British imperialism and encroachment.[11] Mainland Nova Scotia, for example, came under British rule with the 1713 Treaty of Utrecht, and the Treaty of 1763 (also known as the Treaty of Paris, but not to be confused with the other Treaty of Paris mentioned below) ceded Canada and most of New France to Britain after the Seven Years' War.[12] The Royal Proclamation that same year created Quebec out of the former Royal Province of New France; it also annexed Cape Breton Island to Nova Scotia, with St. John's Island (now Prince Edward Island) becoming a separate colony in 1769.To avert conflict in Britain's newly acquired French-speaking territory, the British Parliament passed the Quebec Act of 1774, which expanded Quebec's territory to the Great Lakes and Ohio Valley. To appease the French, it re-established the French language, the Catholic faith, and French civil law in the region. This angered many residents of the thirteen colonies on the eastern seaboard of what would become the United States, and further fuelled anti-British sentiment in the years prior to the American Revolutionary War, which began in 1775.

The 1783 Treaty of Paris recognized American independence and ceded the newly added territories south (but not north) of the Great Lakes to the newly created United States. New Brunswick was now split from Nova Scotia as part of a reorganization of Loyalist settlements in the Maritimes.[13] To accommodate English-speaking Loyalists in Quebec, the Constitutional Act of 1791 divided the province into French-speaking Lower Canada (later Quebec) and English-speaking Upper Canada (later Ontario), granting each its own elected legislative assembly.[14]

John Graves Simcoe, the first Governor of Upper Canada, maintained that the religion of the new province was to be Protestant, just as that of the adjoining province, Lower Canada, was envisaged to be Roman Catholic by virtue of its French character and influence. Simcoe also established "a fund for the education, especially of the more respectable class of people by the erection of free grammar schools, and in course of time of a college or university."[15] Such a university, Simcoe reasoned, "would give a tone of principle and manners that would be of infinite support to government."[16] That university or college would also encourage students not to go to the United States, where, "owing to the cheapness of education ... the gentlemen of Upper Canada will send their children."[17]

The Canadas subsequently became the main front in the War of 1812 between the United States and Britain.[18] This same period witnessed increased immigration to Canada, with close to one million individuals arriving from Britain between 1815 and 1850. Upper Canada at this time was ruled by a tight-knit group of men, known as the Family Compact.[19] They were not related by family; rather, they were a small and powerful group of like-minded friends. They were Conservative in orientation, controlled much of the political, economic, and judicial power, and were opposed to any sort of democratic reform, which was increasingly being demanded by many inhabitants. Lord Durham, in his report to the king (discussed below), referred to this Family Compact as "all powerful in the chartered banks, and, till lately, shared among themselves almost exclusively all offices of trust and profit."[20] For example, the members of this compact often used their government positions to further their financial and speculative interests. On account of their connections to England, from which most of them had come and which had placed them in their positions of authority, they were deeply committed to King and Country and to establishing Anglicanism as the colony's "true religion."

The Family Compact derived its power from loyalist tradition, a hierarchical class structure, and adherence to the Church of England. This triangulation, in their view, provided the ideal form of government, which they contrasted with the popular democracy that had taken root in the United States in the aftermath of the American Revolution. They feared that this American form of government would enter Canada and lead to democratic reform, which, of course, would cost them their power and influence.

One of the most important members of the Family Compact was John Strachan (1778–1867), who will play an important role in the following chapter. The Scottish-born Strachan, though born a Presbyterian, would go on to become the (Anglican) Bishop of Toronto; in that role, he would be a key figure in the founding of McGill College (later University), King's College (later the University of Toronto), and Trinity College.[21] In 1823, Sir Peregrine Maitland, the Lieutenant-Governor of Upper Canada, asked Strachan, by then a member of the non-elected legislative council of Upper Canada, to head a general board of education for the province. Strachan subsequently went to England to seek a Royal Charter from the king for the establishment of a university in Upper Canada. His rationale for seeking that charter was to create a more "civil" alternative to the type of education found in the United States, where "politics pervade the whole system of instruction. The school books ... are stuffed with praises of their own institutions, and breathe hatred to everything English ... Some may become fascinated with that liberty which has degenerated into licentiousness, and imbibe, perhaps unconsciously, sentiments unfriendly to things of which Englishmen are proud."[22]

Strachan's goal in establishing a new university in York (later Toronto) was to train Church of England clergy to act as teachers to educate the Indigenous and newly arriving immigrant populations. As we shall see shortly, he was insistent that only Anglicans be allowed at the university – either as professors or as students – lest other denominations corrupt it. On 25 March 1827, King George IV granted Strachan a charter for the "establishment of a College ... for the education of youth in the principles of the Christian Religion, and for their instruction in the various branches of Science and Literature ... at or near the town of York ... to continue for ever, to be called 'King's College.'"[23]

King's College, as we shall see in the next chapter, would have a relatively short lifespan. In response to the frustrations associated with the Family Compact and its unwillingness to entertain political reform, there arose a series of rebellions in 1837 and 1838 in both Upper and Lower Canada.[24] To ease the tensions and investigate their causes, the British government sent John George Lambton, Lord Durham, to the colony. He noted the conflict between the traditionalistic French and the modernizing English, and he referred to the compact as "a petty corrupt insolent Tory clique." Of the latter, he further remarked:

> For a long time this body of men, receiving at times accessions to its numbers, possessed almost all the highest public offices, by means of which, and of its influence in the Executive Council, it wielded all the powers of government; it maintained influence in the Legislature by means of its predominance in the Legislative Council ... Successive governors, as they came in their turn, are said to have either submitted quietly to its influence, or, after a short and availing struggle, to have yielded to this well-organized party the real conduct of affairs. The bench, the magistracy, the high offices of the Episcopal Church, and a great part of the legal profession, are filled by the adherents of this party.[25]

The *Report on the Affairs of British North America* (1838), often referred to as the Durham Report, recommended that responsible government be established and that Upper and Lower Canada be united into one province, with equal representation despite the fact that English Upper Canada had a smaller population.[26] To rectify this discrepancy, he encouraged immigration to Canada from Britain so as to overwhelm the existing numbers of French Canadians; he hoped they would thereby be assimilated into what he considered to be the superior British culture.[27] He wrote:

> Those who have reflected on the powerful influence of language on thought, will perceive in how different a manner people who speak in different languages are apt to think; and those who are familiar with the literature of France, know that the same opinion will be expressed by an English and French writer of the present day, not merely in different words, but in a style so different as to mark utterly different habits of thought.[28]

This was further exacerbated, he noted in his report, by the different educational systems in the two Canadas, something that, so he argued, heightened the tensions between their peoples.[29] An immediate result of the Durham Report was the Act of Union, which in 1840 merged the two Canadas into a united Province of Canada, with its capital initially in Kingston.[30] Notwithstanding the amalgamation, however, Upper Canada was referred to as Canada West and maintained English common law, whereas Lower Canada was referred to as Canada East and maintained the French Civil Code.[31] This, of course, only further heightened tensions between the anglophone and francophone populations.[32] The same act also established responsible government, through, for example, the creation of an independent judiciary and a court of appeal, and the termination of debtor's prison.

A key figure in the attempts to weaken the Family Compact and its influence on higher education in the province was Robert Baldwin (1804–1858), a political reformer who believed in non-denominational education.[33] As premier of the United Canada, along with Louis-Hippolyte Lafontaine (his francophone colleague),[34] he helped foster the notion of "responsible government," thereby paving the way for independence from Britain.[35] He was also responsible for the bill – the Baldwin Act of 1849 – that freed King's College from denominational strictures, thus transforming it into the secular University of Toronto.[36]

With the relevant historical context in place, I now turn more specifically to the founding of religious colleges and the impact these would have on education, including higher education, in the province.

Precursors to Royal Charters

The earliest colleges and universities in the new colony were established by Royal Charters granted by the British monarch. These charters had been (and indeed still are) used to establish significant organizations, such as towns, universities, and learned societies. For example, the

British East India Company was created by Royal Charter in 1600, and the Hudson's Bay Company in 1670.[37] The first such charter to create a college in Canada was granted, as we shall see in much more detail below, to King's College in Nova Scotia in 1802 (though it was founded as early as 1789) by George III.[38] This made it the oldest chartered university in Canada and, for most of its history, a bastion of High Anglicanism. Prior to that year, however, there did exist several non-chartered institutions responsible for teaching religion.

Among the latter we must certainly include the Séminaire de Québec, a society of diocesan priests, which was founded on 26 March 1663 by Bishop François de Laval, the first Bishop of New France.[39] This seminary was among the earliest such institutions devoted to the inculcation of religion in the New World.[40] By 1674 the diocese of Quebec had been established, with dominion over all of North America.[41] The colony's Reformation-era Catholicism, in the words of Kaell, "was communal, hierarchical, and all encompassing, coloured by a continual round of daily prayers, Sunday masses, and religious holy days."[42] The aim of the seminary was to sustain the mission of the Catholic Church in North America by preparing young men for ordination and ministry in parishes and missions throughout the New World, as far away, for example, as Louisiana. This was known as the "major" seminary. In addition to this, a "minor" seminary was founded that would help impose French language and customs, including religion, on local Indigenous populations.[43] This seminary, known as the Petite Séminaire de Québec,[44] functioned as a boarding school for Indigenous children and the children of settlers who wished to enter the priesthood.[45]

Mention should be made here of the now infamous residential school system. That system – funded by the government and administered by Christian churches – provided a network of boarding schools for Indigenous children. It was created as a means to remove children from their families and thus from the influence of their own cultures and languages, for the purpose of assimilating them into the dominant anglophone or francophone culture.[46] Needless to say, these children were subject to abuse, both corporal and sexual.[47] Though it would pick up steam after Confederation in 1867 and the passage of the Indian Act in 1876, institutions like the Petite Séminaire show how its seeds existed much earlier.[48]

Here, once again, we run up against an issue that plagues the early history of the study of religion in Canada, namely, its investiture in colonialism and the denigration of Aboriginal traditions in the New World. In places like King's and the Séminaire, the teaching of religion was about a self-perceived superior group's need to impose its religious truths on a group imagined as inferior with the intent of erasing the latter's religion, culture, and language. This was far from an academic enterprise. Rather, it was intertwined with the illusion of civilization and connected to the more universal need to place religions on a spectrum between the "highest" (i.e., Christianity) and the "lowest." This is in keeping with the argument of David Chidester, who links the rise of comparative religion to the colonial period and who sees it as taking place at the frontiers of empires, in colonial outposts such as South Africa – and to these we could certainly add places like Canada. On the frontiers, different customs and religions were often constructed as "primitive" compared to those of Europe – indeed, they *had* to be understood as such for the sake of colonial manipulation and governance. This investiture in colonialism and empire maintenance created the trope of "primitives" and "primitive religions" that would go on to play a prominent role in theories of religion being developed in metropoles such as Vienna, Paris, and London.[49] It is certainly no coincidence that many Victorian theories of religion, including discourses of origins, used such "primitives" as their main data.[50]

We must not forget, then, that "secular and religious expansion," as Grant reminds us in his history of the missionary encounter, "were connected by intimate but complex ties of mutual influence."[51] In other words, territorial expansion went hand in hand with perceived religious superiority. One was justified in conquering for one's God and King because of some perceived spiritual destiny. Once one had conquered the land, it was only natural that one would try to impose one's own mores on the newly conquered.[52] This is perhaps best summed up by the final report of the Truth and Reconciliation Commission (TRC), which the federal government established in 2015 to document and address some of the wrongs perpetrated on First Nation communities. Its executive summary reads in part: "Underlying these arguments was the belief that the colonizers were bringing civilization to savage people who could never civilize themselves. The 'civilizing mission' rested on a belief in racial and cultural superiority."[53]

At any rate, after the British Conquest in 1760, the Séminaire was granted a Royal Charter in 1852 by Queen Victoria. This led directly to the founding of Université Laval,[54] the first Catholic French-language university in North America. Laval was meant to provide a francophone and Catholic alternative to the anglophone and largely Protestant McGill College, which, as we shall see below, had received its own Royal Charter in 1821.[55]

In like manner, New Brunswick, which as we saw above came into existence with the division of Nova Scotia in 1784, was home to the earliest non-chartered post-secondary institution in the anglophone colonies. As early as 13 December 1785, William Paine and other Loyalists petitioned the Governor-in-Council for "the establishment in this infant province of an academy for liberal arts and sciences."[56] The result was the founding in 1785 of the Provincial Academy of Arts and Sciences, which in 1800 received a charter from the province to become the College of New Brunswick, and in 1827 received a Royal Charter.[57]

The charter of the college, like that of King's in Nova Scotia, was based on the 1754 Royal Charter that had established King's College, New York (later to become Columbia College and then Columbia University).[58] Despite their geographic differences, all three of these colleges shared a number of features: all were Anglican, loyalist, and largely Tory institutions. When the college in New York ceased in the aftermath of the American Revolution, British loyalists migrated to Nova Scotia and New Brunswick, where they were instrumental in creating Anglican-inspired educational institutions in those provinces.

King's College in Nova Scotia was founded in 1789 and received its Royal Charter in 1802, making it the oldest chartered institution of higher education in English-speaking Canada. Though the Provincial Academy of Arts and Sciences in Fredericton had been founded four years earlier, in 1785, it did not receive its charter until 1827. With that charter, the College of New Brunswick came into existence, and, as at King's in Nova Scotia, it was open only to Anglicans.[59] The president was to be in the Holy Orders of the Church of England, and all professors and students had to be members of the same communion. Needless to say, this drove many non-Anglicans to seek an education in the United States.

In 1827 the College of New Brunswick received a new Royal Charter and changed its name to King's College, Fredericton.[60] It was, however, much more liberal than its predecessor and namesake in Nova Scotia in that it was founded as a non-denominational institution, with no religious tests or oaths required for either faculty members or students.[61] This was the opposite of King's in Nova Scotia, which required all matriculating students to assent to the Church of England's Thirty-Nine Articles of Religion.[62]

As with most other Canadian universities, the "Oxbridge model" seems to have functioned as the paradigm for the College of New Brunswick, which set out to copy that model, which it did with varying degrees of success. Since Fredericton was neither Oxford nor Cambridge, and its students lacked the same preparation as those in the English public (i.e., private) school system, the model could not be replicated in its entirety. Many provincial legislators in New Brunswick complained about the college, arguing that its curriculum was too narrowly focused on the classics and not on more practical matters for a largely rural place. Many wanted the college to be an agricultural school with a model farm attached; they thought this would better meet the needs of the fledgling colony.[63] Others criticized it, even after the shift from denominationalism to non-denominationalism, as a stubborn bastion of Tory privilege. This seems to have been a common charge levelled against Canada's Anglican institutions of higher learning – be it in Toronto, New Brunswick, or Nova Scotia.

The arguments over class prejudices and sectarianism would gradually fade, however.[64] In 1859, the college became the University of New Brunswick.[65] Its new charter, the result of an act of the provincial legislature as opposed to Royal Charter, specifically stated that the president of the university had to be a layman, that the chair of theology was to be abolished, and that no religious tests were to be imposed on any instructor or student.[66] However, so as not to be charged with "godlessness," the university required every student to attend each Sunday a "divine service" conducted by the denomination of their choice.[67]

The Church of England and the Founding of Colonial Universities

As just witnessed, the Church of England played a not insignificant role in the creation of post-secondary education in the provinces of the colony of Canada. The teaching of theology – or, as it was sometimes called, "moral philosophy" – was regarded as instrumental to establishing the moral fortitude of the colony, which was imagined either as white and Christian, or as French-speaking (i.e., Catholic) and Indigenous, with both of the latter groups viewed as in need of "civilizing." Thus theology was included in the curricula of most arts faculties. Young men were to be instructed in divinity, for they would be the clergy, spiritual leaders, and missionaries of the next generation. The three King's Colleges – in Toronto, New Brunswick, and Nova Scotia – all taught such subjects under highly restricted parameters. This is not what we would today recognize as the academic study of religion, but was instead a form of catechesis. This meant that religion was never taught about, especially from a humanities or social scientific perspective – only Christianity was, and this was done, moreover, in a manner that presented it as part of the manifest destiny of the young colony. By and large, Anglican faculty taught Anglican students about the religious truths of Anglicanism. There were no departments or schools, as there are today, but rather single professorships or chairs, often with names like "Moral Philosophy and Divinity" attached to them, and these were exclusively devoted to the dissemination of Anglican theology at the expense of other denominations. The main purpose of such chairs was to inculcate the truth-claims of the denomination into young men, who would then either go on to administer actual congregations or become outstanding citizens, loyal to both God and Crown.

The study of religion in Canada during this period was, to be sure, a heavily apologetical enterprise predicated on nation-building in a young colony. There was no interest in comparison, or if there was, that comparative model was predetermined: whatever denomination of Protestantism was imagined as superior was counterposed with other denominations and religions, which were then found to be wanting.[68]

Different denominations, especially in Toronto, would later develop their own theological colleges (to be discussed shortly); at the time, though, the goal was to create Anglican institutions in the province as a way to protect the political and financial interests of the Family Compact. In Toronto, for example, the newly established King's College was created with the aim of training Anglican clergy to serve as teachers in the province. When John Strachan received the Royal Charter for King's in Toronto he made certain that the president would for "all times" be the Archdeacon of York (which Strachan then was).[69]

King's College in Toronto will be the subject of the following chapter. Allow me here to examine its namesake in Windsor, Nova Scotia, before it moved to Halifax after a fire on 5 February 1920.[70] This will show more clearly the links among Anglicanism, theology, and higher education in anglophone eastern Canada. As we have seen, King's College received its Royal Charter in 1802, which immediately made the Archbishop of Canterbury the Patron of the College, and made the Bishop of Nova Scotia the Visitor (i.e., overseer), and both men members of the board of governors.[71] In a 5 May 1790 letter to Richard Cumberland, an English dramatist and agent for the province residing in London, Charles Inglis, the first Bishop of Nova Scotia, gave his reason for creating a college: "With respect to our seminary, one of my principle motives for pushing it forward was to prevent the importation of American Divines and American policies into the province. Unless we have a seminary here, the youth of Nova Scotia will be sent for their education to the Revolted Colonies – the inevitable consequence would be a corruption of their religious and political principles."[72]

That the new college was only open to Anglicans meant, of course, that any non-Anglican in Nova Scotia would have to go to the United States or, at the least, to another province. Regardless, this was part of Inglis's larger plan to establish the Church of England in Nova Scotia. After the Royal Charter was decreed on 12 May 1802 the governors of the new college met in Halifax and maintained that they would use as their model the Statutes of the University of Oxford, which, of course, was a bastion of Anglicanism and Toryism in England. Alexander Croke, one of its first governors, went so far as to declare that "we have made it a qualification of the President, and Professors or Fellows that they should have been educated at Oxford or Cambridge, or under persons of that description at Windsor."[73]

Such was their attempt to replicate what they perceived to be the best of England in the new colony. Individuals like Croke had no interest in the needs of the new province; instead, they sought to import the elitism and bigotry of the Old World into the New. At a subsequent meeting the governors of King's clarified the above statement: "We think that it is of no small importance to this seminary to teach the genuine use, practice and pronunciation of the English language, which in distant colonies is too apt to degenerate, and that the purity of that language, undebased by local or national accents and solecisms, is undeniably to be found in the Kingdom of England only."[74]

We here see how the early framers of King's attempted to model themselves, their college, and ideally all of Nova Scotia (and Canada) on what they perceived to be the superiority of the Oxbridge model.[75] The first draft of the statutes made it mandatory for every student to sign the Thirty-Nine Articles of the Anglican Church on matriculation. Bishop Inglis, however, objected to this, and, writing to Bishop Mountain of Quebec in a letter dated 19 October 1805, he contended that "on our receiving the Royal Charter a set of Statues were framed, and unfortunately adopted much against my judgment, which were adapted to Cambridge or Oxford, but not to the infant state of our Seminary; thereby a check has been given to its growth."[76]

The statutes of the new college were divided into five "books" – the first three dealing with the college, the fourth with the university; and the fifth, an appendix, with oaths. Book One, Title 7, "Of the Professors and Fellows," reads: "No Professor directly or indirectly shall teach or maintain any atheistical, deistical or democratical principles, or any doctrine contrary to the Christian faith, or to good morals, or subversive of the British constitution, as by law established."[77]

Book Three, Title 2, reads: "No member of the university shall frequent the Romish mass, or the meeting houses of the Presbyterians, Baptists, or Methodists or the Coventicles, or place of worship of any other dissenters from the Church of England, or where Divine Service shall not be performed according to the Liturgy of the Church of England, or shall be present at any seditious or rebellious meetings.[78]

And, finally, Book IX, Title 9, "Of Oaths and Subscriptions," reads, in part: "No degree shall be conferred till the candidate shall have subscribed to the thirty-nine Articles of the Church of England and the three Articles contained in the thirty-sixth Canon of the Synod of London, held in the year of our Lord 1603."[79]

The history of King's in Nova Scotia shows clearly the problems that arise when religion becomes involved in education. It leads toward elitism and, if not checked, to bigotry and exclusion. We see clearly how the study of religion was caught up in these early decades with class, empire, and status. It was believed that religion was the glue that held these three together. Thankfully, other institutions were by then trying to develop less bigoted models of higher education. This would largely involve, as we shall see in the following section, removing the teaching of religion from the centre and marginalizing it to separate schools or colleges, or, as in the western provinces, the avoidance of teaching religion altogether.

McGill

The Church of England was not the only game in town. Indeed, when John Strachan returned in 1826 with the Royal Charter that would set up King's College in Toronto, he was criticized in the local press for greatly exaggerating the number of Anglicans in Upper Canada in a pamphlet he had prepared and circulated in England.[80] It is important to realize that Anglicans were, whatever their claims, a minority in the colony, albeit a sizeable one.

Another large group was the Presbyterians. One of the most influential of its members was James McGill (1744–1813). McGill was born in Glasgow, Scotland, and graduated from the University of Glasgow before moving to Montreal. He had made his fortune in the fur trade and eventually devoted his life to public service.[81] He was keenly aware that the province needed a system of public education.

In England, education was largely the responsibility of parents and various religious and charitable groups, whereas in Canada, it was increasingly viewed as falling to the government. This was intimately connected to the idea that education, particularly a religious-based curriculum, would aid in the assimilation of Indigenous and francophone populations. There were also political reasons: education would stem the tide of anglophones travelling to the United States for training, thus reducing the likelihood that they would absorb the subversive principles of "democratic republicanism."[82]

McGill's will provided the financial means for establishing a college on his Burnside property in Montreal.[83] John Strachan, who had married McGill's brother's widow, later claimed that it was he who had suggested to McGill that he endow a university informed by the tenets of the Anglican Church.[84] Nowhere, however, did McGill, who was not even a member of the Church of England, refer to the potential religious character of his proposed college. Unlike the Anglicans, the Scottish and Presbyterian McGill seems to have had no interest in establishing one denomination of Christianity to the exclusion of others in his new country or in creating religious tests for faculty or students. The only thing that McGill's will stipulated was that the college be built within ten years of his death or the property would revert to his wife's family, the Desrivières.

On 31 March 1821, a Royal Charter was granted to establish McGill College (it became McGill University in 1885) "for the Education of Youth in the principles of true religion and for their instruction in the different branches of science and literature."[85] At no point, however – protestations of those like Strachan to the contrary – was the denomination of the "true religion" defined. Whatever McGill's intentions, his adopted children, francophone Catholics, contested his will, just as Roman Catholic clergy resisted the notion of an English-language liberal arts college, especially in the absence of any similar provision for them.[86] Moreover, though McGill had envisioned a non-denominational institution, four of the initial five professorial appointments were Anglican clergy. In the words of McGill's historian, the ideal "of 'an unprejudiced seminary offering a liberal education' to the general population of Lower Canada had now been reduced to the provision of a liberal arts college serving the needs of the English-speaking minority of the city of Montreal. Moreover, it was a decidedly Anglican affair."[87]

As the case of McGill clearly shows, even institutions that did not start out as Anglican could be co-opted by that denomination. For example, John Bethune, an early principal of McGill College, had drawn up statutes for the college's governance early in 1843 that included the stipulation that "all members of the university should attend the Montreal Parish Church [Anglican] on Sundays and be present at morning and evening prayers in the college each day and with the provision that the B.D. degree would be reserved for clergymen 'in full orders in the United Church of England and Ireland or the Protestant Episcopal Church of Scotland.'"[88]

No religious tests, however, were to be given for faculty or students. Indeed, of the first three students to matriculate, one, Myer Valentine Hayes, was a Jew. In a province with such a heavy Catholic population, and the call on the part of many influential individuals for McGill to be run on "liberal and unsectarian" principles, the college seems to have avoided what happened in both Nova Scotia and New Brunswick, and what Strachan originally envisaged for the new university in Toronto. In terms of the larger British context, it is worth noting that Parliament had passed the Catholic Emancipation Act in 1829, which, as the name suggests, removed restrictions that, among other things, barred Roman Catholics from public office. This law had been preceded a year earlier by the repeal of the Test Act, which had required civil servants to take a religious test, though its repeal excluded the Universities of Oxford and Cambridge, which, as seen, served as the basis for several of the new universities in Canada.

Despite attempts to create an educational system that was bilingual and religiously neutral, one in which francophones and anglophones, Catholics and Protestants, might equally share, the Syndics Act was passed in 1820. This act established that the francophone community would have no part in any educational system or institution that was not dedicated to the preservation of its language and culture. In 1853, as we have seen, the University of Laval in Quebec City received its own Royal Charter to establish a francophone institution.[89] In the words of Frost, "the English-speaking community in general wanted its institution to be as clearly Protestant as its francophone neighbours wanted their institutions to be Catholic, and the only debate within the Anglophone community was as to the style of Protestantism."[90] Unlike at the King's Colleges, Protestantism at McGill came to be defined to include Presbyterians, Methodists, and Baptists.

Most Canadian universities needed a towering figure to help create the infrastructure responsible for subsequent growth. McGill found its man in John William Dawson (1820–1899).[91] Born in Pictou, Nova Scotia, he sought to create a national and non-denominational institution that was not necessarily "godless." He did not like the Oxbridge system of the English – so imitated at other institutions in Canada – which reserved education for elites; he preferred the Scottish tradition of making education available to all. It seems that in these early years, those Canadian universities that stressed the Scottish model tended to be the most ecumenical religiously and the least prone to elitism.[92]

Queen's

Another important early institution is what would eventually emerge as Queen's University in Kingston, Ontario. This institution, even more than McGill, represented a concentrated effort to establish a Presbyterian centre of higher learning. Presbyterians had argued in Upper Canada that their tradition too represented an important denomination in the colony and therefore was, like the Church of England, entitled to some of the millions of acres set aside by the Crown as "Clergy Reserves." But Christopher Hagerman, a former pupil of Strachan, a leading member of the Family Compact, and a member of the Assembly for Kingston, had other ideas. He insisted that the Church of England had been established in all of the British colonies. The Scots, he reasoned, "are too poor to have any colonies ... to which to extend their religion."[93]

On 2 August 1832, the Synod of the Presbyterian Church of Canada, in connection with the Church of Scotland, presented an address to Sir John Colborne, the Lieutenant-Governor of Upper Canada. They prayed "that His Majesty's Government may be pleased to endow a Theological Institution, or Professorships, for the Education of Young Men for the Ministry in connexion with this Synod."[94] Based on another report, the committee of the Presbytery of Toronto believed that "locally educated ministers [would] be more useful in Canada than men trained in Scotland, that Canadians cannot afford to go to Scotland for their education, [and] that the supply of ministers from Scotland is inadequate."[95] The petition was successful, and in 1840 the Upper Canada Act established St. Andrew's College of Canada (which would change its name in 1841, with a Royal Charter, to the Scottish Presbyterian College, and then later the same year to the University of Queen's College at Kingston). Kingston was chosen because it was thought that that city would be the future capital of a united Canada, being equidistant between Toronto and Montreal.

There was some debate over what the function of the new institution was to be. Was it to be a university? Or was it to be a Presbyterian seminary? Some Presbyterian leaders were opposed to the new institution because they thought that the creation of their own college would be perceived as relinquishing a claim to the newly formed King's College in Toronto. Others thought that King's and McGill should be used for general education, with the newly formed Queen's functioning as a theological department for the Presbyterian Church.

The charter of Queen's stipulated that trustees, principal, and professors, before entering upon their duties, were to declare their "belief in the Doctrines of the Westminster Confession of Faith" and that they would subscribe to "a formula to this effect."[96] Though it should be noted that this would be done away with under the leadership of George Monro Grant (1835–1902), who – though an ordained minister and the Primarius Professor of Divinity – fought to secularize the university.[97] On 1 April 1912, two years after Grant's death, Royal Assent was given to separate Queen's University and Queen's Theological College. Clause two read: "The management and discipline of the University shall be in every respect freed from all denominational restrictions."[98] In 1925 (to be discussed in a later chapter), Queen's Theological College left its association with the Presbyterian Church and entered into a similar relation with the newly formed United Church of Canada.

McMaster

A similar story of movement from denominational affiliation to a major research university is that of McMaster University, which began humbly enough as a Baptist seminary.[99] Baptists, like Presbyterians and unlike Anglicans, were interested in creating a non-sectarian university where students would be taught secular subjects without any need to sign creedal statements. Their model was the University of London, which was founded in 1826 as a secular alternative to Oxford and Cambridge, thereby becoming the first university in England to exclude explicitly religious qualification as an entry requirement.

What would eventually become McMaster opened humbly enough as the Canadian Literary Institute in 1860 in Woodstock, Ontario (120 kilometres southwest of Toronto).[100] Though the institute was Baptist, not all of its trustees were of that denomination. When its main principal, Rev. Robert Alexander Fyfe, died in 1878, there were plans to relocate the theology department to Toronto. Fyfe had resisted this for both financial and spiritual reasons, fearing that the big city would offer carnal temptations to the largely rural-born students.[101]

The main driver of the move, however, was the wealthy Irish-born senator, William McMaster (1811–1887). He was the first President of the Bank of Commerce (later to become the Canadian Imperial Bank of Commerce) and was an ally of George Brown and Alexander Mackenzie, two influential Grit leaders, who were opposed to the "pretensions of the Church of England and its political allies and sought a better deal for evangelical non-conformists in the community."[102] The result was the creation of the Toronto Baptist College in 1881. McMaster wanted the new institution to be under strict Baptist control, unlike its predecessor.[103] Whereas Anglicans and Presbyterians looked to Britain for institutional prototypes, McMaster had in mind the great Baptist universities and seminaries in the United States, such as the Rochester Seminary in New York, the oldest Baptist seminary in that country, and the University of Chicago Divinity School.

Notwithstanding McMaster's desire to make the institution Baptist, the new college maintained a fairly general policy when it came to the doctrinal qualifications of prospective faculty in order not to reproduce theological conflicts of the sort that had racked the Baptist community over communion (should it be, for example, open or closed?) or over millennialism (pre- or post-). McMaster asked John Harvard Castle, an American minister, a product of the Rochester Seminary, and leader of the recently built Jarvis Street Church, to be the president of the new college, which opened on 4 October 1881. In his opening remarks,

Castle informed his audience that "nevertheless it is true that the ministry which creates stable, intelligent, enterprising churches – which molds and controls public sentiment for Christianity, which maintains its hold upon our children and keeps them from drifting away from the faith of their fathers to other communions is a ministry trained in secular and sacred learning."[104]

Castle also proposed in 1884 that the new college adopt the Abstract of Doctrine that had recently been developed by the Constitution of the Southern Baptist Theological Seminary, "one of the ablest and most conservative bodies of Baptists, and which has stood the test of criticism and trial."[105] This may well have been a conservative reaction to the rise of the "higher criticism" in education (which I shall discuss in further detail in chapter 3), an intellectual movement that would profoundly influence Protestant, and particularly evangelical, institutions in North America.[106]

Some contended that the Baptist College should affiliate with the newly secularized University of Toronto (see next chapter). Others, however, argued that independence would maintain the school's "spiritual integrity." William McMaster gradually came to support the idea of an independent institution of higher learning. The motion was subsequently carried that the new university "be organized and developed as a permanently independent school of learning, with the Lordship of Christ as the controlling principle."[107] In 1888 the Toronto Baptist College was folded into the new university as its theological department. The new institution was described in its charter as a "Christian school of learning." It would appoint to arts positions only those who were "members in good standing of an Evangelical Christian Church"; however, faculty of theology would have to be Baptists. Moreover, the 1887 act, which gave McMaster its charter, stated that as far as students were concerned, there was to be "no compulsory religious qualification, or examination of a denominational character."[108]

In 1930, the newly named McMaster University moved to Hamilton. Affiliation with Baptists ended in 1957, at which point it became a non-denominational institution. However, its Divinity School (but not the Department of Religious Studies, which came into existence in 1966) retains into the present day an affiliation with that Church.[109]

Conclusions

This chapter has examined the beginnings of post-secondary institutions in Canada prior to Confederation. It was, as we have seen, an era during which the Church of England sought to establish itself as the official religion in the new colony, as it was in England. This is evident in the Royal Charters that created King's Colleges in Toronto, New Brunswick, and Nova Scotia. These were, to be sure, elitist institutions that sought to administer a theologically infused education to Anglicans at the expense of other denominations. Needless to say, these other denominations, most notably Presbyterian and Baptist, resisted such overtures. In response, they established their own institutions to train future ministers in their own orders.

This period, in other words, was marked by sectarianism, elitism, and exclusion. These universities/seminaries conceived the study of religion exclusively as propagating truth-claims to believers. Religion was viewed not as part of a humanistic endeavour but rather as providing the moral fabric of the colony. The following chapter will explore many of these themes in greater detail, using the University of Toronto as a case study.

Chapter Two

The University of Toronto: A Case Study

Some of the themes encountered in the previous chapter – sectarianism, bigotry, religious tests, the struggle to create a secular university – were particularly visible at what would eventually become the University of Toronto. That institution provides an important case study for the rise of the modern university in Canada and, just as importantly, for the role that religion in general and religious education in particular played in that rise. The present chapter accordingly looks in detail at some of the struggles that went into the creation of Canada's most important centre of higher learning. It seeks to show that, while today we might take the end product for granted, we must also consider the religious tumult that went on behind the scenes and that was ultimately responsible for the creation of the modern Canadian university.[1] The University of Toronto played a prominent role in this transformation, being an important stage on which the early secular study of religion – be it as higher biblical criticism or Oriental studies – would emerge.

The study of religion today plays an important role in the humanities curriculum associated with most arts faculties across the country, but this was not always the case. As seen in the previous chapter, until roughly the mid-1960s the study of religion tended to denote almost exclusively theology and was associated with the concomitant explication of a particular denomination's truth-claims. There was nothing comparative or secular about this endeavour, unless of course comparison was used nefariously to highlight the superiority of one religion (i.e., one's own) over others. It was only fitting, then, that as theology became increasingly regarded as denominational, its place at the centre of university life increasingly shifted from the centre to the margins. By the mid-twentieth century, no secular university could afford to devote its resources to affiliation with a particular denomination.

Establishing an Imperial College

In 1796, John Graves Simcoe – the first Governor of Upper Canada – wrote to the Anglican Bishop of Quebec arguing for the creation of an institution of higher learning in his province. Such an institution would, so he reasoned, "strengthen the union with Great Britain and preserve a lasting obedience to His Majesty's authority." It would also, he maintained, "have a great influence in civilising the Indians ... and what is of more importance, those who corrupt them."[2] Once again, we see the intersection of religion, colonialism, and the desire on the part of colonial elites to "civilize" those who were non-Anglican, non-white, and non-British. We also clearly see how the study of religion, here imagined as theology, contributed to this process. Universities and colleges were meant to teach religious truths, which were thought to be a civilizing force. Such colleges would also teach religious truths to future clergy and (just as important) help preserve English tradition in the heart of the New World. French-language universities in Lower Canada saw themselves as *citadelles nationales* against English-speaking Protestantism; similarly, those of Upper Canada and the Maritimes sought to stem the tide of American republicanism.[3] Indeed, many of the colleges in New Brunswick and Nova Scotia were Loyalist, and their founders were acutely aware of the need for such Loyalist institutions. Five clergymen – including Charles Inglis, the future first Bishop of Nova Scotia in 1787 – wrote on 8 March 1783 a letter to Sir Guy Carleton, the governor-in-chief of British North America, encouraging him to found

> a College or Seminary of learning on a liberal plan in that province where youth may receive a virtuous education and can be qualified for the learned professions. [This] is, we humbly conceive, a measure of the greatest consequence, as it would diffuse religious literature, loyalty and good morals among His Majesty's subjects there. If such a seminary is not established the inhabitants will have no means of educating their sons at home, but will under the necessity of sending them, for that purpose either to great Britain or Ireland, which will be attended with an expense that few can bear, or else to some of the states of this continent, where they will soon imbibe principles that are unfavourable to the British nation.[4]

A Christian nation thus needed a Christian populace.[5] In the words of John Beverly Robinson, the Chief Justice of Canada, writing in 1840, religion was "the only secure basis on which civil service can rest."[6] Schools thus became the primary means to inculcate people into the "good" religion of the "true" Church, that Church, of course, being the one that one happened to belong to. Schools were where morality was taught and where Christianity's principles were instilled through religious exercises. In the words of Egerton Ryerson (1803–1882), the Superintendent of Schools in Canada West and a Methodist minister, religious instruction "should be the basis of the Provincial system of education."[7] Ryerson, the first Principal of Victoria College (a Methodist institution that would eventually affiliate with the newly created University of Toronto), would subsequently state that "if one branch of education must be omitted, surely the laws of the universe, and the works of God, is of more practical advantage socially and morally, than a knowledge of Greek and Latin."[8]

Seminaries and colleges came to serve as the epicentre of the Christianization and anglicization of the new colony. They were the instrumental institutions where teachers and clergy – the erstwhile vehicles of dissemination – could be taught. Thus seminaries became the central focus of the colony, and that is why, as we shall see in this chapter, there arose such anxieties around them. They were the places where young men entered the clergy, where they were taught, and from which they would emerge to become teachers and clerics who would be responsible for teaching the like-minded and civilizing the rest.

For this to happen, however, funds and lands had to be secured from the metropole. We see this, for example, in a statement issued on 4 November 1797 by King George III, who declared his support for the creation in Canada of "seminaries of a larger and more comprehensive nature for the promotion of religious and moral learning and the study of the arts and sciences."[9] This meant that the Crown would set aside land for the Church and for the institutions it would create to attain this goal of "religious and moral learning."[10] It also reveals to just what extent the creation of colleges of higher learning in Canada in these early years was invested in the promotion of morality in general and of religion in particular. Georgian and Victorian universities, unlike their modern counterparts, were not meant to be bastions of specialized and technical knowledge, but rather catalysts for nationhood and founts of all of the general and religious knowledge that the citizenry would need for nation-building.

In 1826, as we saw in the previous chapter, Simcoe appointed John Strachan, the future Bishop of Toronto, to travel to England to arrange a Royal Charter to found a university that would be closely connected to the Church of England. On 25 March 1827 that charter was granted – it is worth repeating here – for the "establishment of a College ... for the education of youth in the principles of the Christian Religion, and for their instruction in the various branches of Science and Literature ... at or near the town of York ... to continue for ever, to be called 'King's

College.'"[11] That college would teach the virtues of God and Crown and inculcate in youth both the principles and the virtues of the "British Constitution" so that they would be equipped to govern themselves.[12]

Despite the diverse Christian population of Upper Canada, Strachan – a key figure in the Family Compact – was determined at all costs to make the new institution an Anglican one that would follow strictly the teachings associated with the Church of England, in which he was an influential figure.[13] The college was to be run by members of that Church, with the president being for "all times" the Archdeacon of York, a position that not coincidentally Strachan then held. It was expected that the governing council would have to "sign" and "subscribe" to the Thirty-Nine Articles of Religion of the Church of England.[14] Students, however – and here the new college would be more liberal that its namesake in Nova Scotia – could be of any faith, though many of the early ones were, perhaps not surprisingly, Anglican. The desire, then, was to create an *Anglican* institution with the aim of establishing that religion in the new province of Upper Canada.[15] As with the other King's Colleges discussed in the previous chapter, it was also a means by which the Church of England's values could be disseminated throughout the colonies. This was increasingly viewed as a protection against the unchecked democracy ushered in by the American Revolution and the concomitant development of republicanism there.

Many, however, seem to have been uncomfortable with this turn of events. Efforts to establish or even privilege Anglicanism in the new colony, given that denomination's links to the Family Compact and its anti-democratic whims, generated considerable opposition among reformers. A committee created by the House of Assembly reported back that should such a university come into existence, it "should not be a school of politics, or of sectarian views. It should have about it no appearance of partiality or exclusions. Its portals should be thrown open to all, and upon none who enter should any influence be exerted to attach them to any particular creed or church ... Most deeply, therefore, is it to be lamented that the principles of the charter are calculated to defeat its usefulness and to confine to a favored few all of its advantages."[16] The report concluded with the bold recommendation that the king cancel the recently received charter and, in its place, grant one "free from these objections." Needless to say, Strachan and his Church of England supporters were opposed to any such initiative.[17]

In 1828, a little over a year after the issuance of the original charter, the British House of Commons created a committee to look into it and related matters. That committee recommended that the charter of the university be changed so that two theological professors would be employed – one from the Church of England and the other from the Church of Scotland – and that neither professors nor students be required to sign a religious oath or pass a religious test. It also recommended that, except for professors of theology, faculty should sign a declaration that, while recognizing the truth of the Christian Revelation, they would abstain altogether from inculcating the doctrines of a particular denomination.

But even while attempting to create some sort of ecumenical framework, the committee also decided that

1 the Anglican bishop of the diocese should have "supreme judicial control of the University";
2 the president had "to be a clergyman in holy orders in the United Church of England and Ireland, and made the Archdeacon of York the *ex-officio* president";
3 the entire executive of the university be "in the hands of a council, consisting of the chancellor, the president and seven members, who were required to be members of the Church of England, and to subscribe to her articles"; and
4 degrees in divinity could only go to persons in holy orders in the Church of England (thus excluding clergymen from the Church of Scotland and other denominations).[18]

Around the same time, in 1829, Major-General Sir John Colborne (later Lord Seaton), the Lieutenant-Governor of Upper Canada, created Upper Canada College in the hope that it would serve as a "feeder school" for the newly established King's College in Toronto.[19] England's great public schools, such as Eton and Rugby, had long been sending elite (Anglican) students to the Anglican-affiliated Oxford and Cambridge; Upper Canada College was created to play a similar role, and thus it was to be associated exclusively with the Church of England. Again we see Britain's elite educational model functioning as the paradigm for educational institutions in Upper Canada.

In response to this, and to the concomitant fear that the Church of England was being promoted to the exclusion of other denominations, other churches opened their own seminaries. Wesleyan Methodists, under the leadership of Egerton Ryerson, received a Royal Charter in 1836 to create Upper Canada Academy in Cobourg (95 km east of Toronto), which became incorporated as Victoria College in 1841 before relocating to Toronto in 1892. As seen in the previous chapter, the Presbyterians created their own seminary as Queen's College in 1841, and the Baptists founded theirs as the Canadian Literary Institute in 1860 in Woodstock. Again, the founding of these institutions was a practical matter, in the sense that these denominations needed to train young men for their respective clergies, but also a political and ideological one, that is, a means to prevent the establishment of Anglicanism in the new colony.

In February 1831 a report of a select committee of the Upper Canada House of Assembly reported back on the fate of King's:

> That while this House appreciates His majesty's gracious intention in granting a royal charter for the establishment of a University in this Province, we must humbly beg leave to represent that: As the great majority of the inhabitants of this Province are not members of the Church of England, we regret that the University charter contains provisions which are calculated to exclude from its principal offices and honours all who do not belong to that Church."[20]

Despite such pleas for tolerance, however, the council of King's College refused to surrender either the charter or the endowment, arguing that it had received express orders from the King of England to promote higher education on certain well-defined religious principles, and that it was not at liberty to abandon those principles or to forgo the financial endowments that accompanied them.[21]

Since neither John Strachan nor the council of King's College was willing to relinquish the charter or disestablish Anglicanism at the institution, over the next few years the government of Upper Canada proposed a number of bills to amend the charter. In 1836, for example, a bill was passed by the House of Assembly stating that the president of the college did not have to be an "incumbent of any ecclesiastical office" and that members of the College Council or any other professors did not have to be members of the Church of England. All they had to believe in was the authenticity and divine inspiration of the Old and New Testaments, and the doctrine of the Trinity.[22]

King's College (Toronto) Opens Its Doors

There was a fifteen-year delay between Strachan's receipt of the Royal Charter and the laying of the cornerstone of the first building. Much of that delay seems to have been on account of concerns among numerous constituencies about the dominance of the Church of England in the new college, as well as the creation of a post-secondary institution that would be so closely connected to the Family Compact. There were also some financial irregularities, including loans to Strachan, which bothered some in the Assembly.[23] At any rate, on 8 June 1843 King's

College officially opened. There were twenty-six matriculating students enrolled, and in his opening speech, the president of the college, Strachan, greeted those assembled:

> Here among our youth we may confidently look for generous emulation, a noble desire for highest fame, an ardent love for truth, and a determination to surpass in knowledge and virtue the most sanguine hopes of their parents and friends. In this institution many holy aspirations will doubtless arise in minds yet untainted, and which by Divine grace shall become a panoply to protect them through life against all the temptations which can assail them. And the time will come when we, too, can look back to our line of celebrated men brought up at this seminary, and whose character and attainments will cause a glory around it, and become, as it were, the genius of the institution."[24]

It is worth noting that Strachan, all members of council, all professors, and twenty-two of the twenty-six students were associated with the Church of England. In response, the Board of Trustees of Queen's College in Kingston issued a statement that it,

> in common with the Presbyterian population of the Province, always entertained the conviction that it was most expedient that King's College, with its ample public endowment, should be in the proper sense a university for the whole population without respect to the religious creed of the students, and that they were led to take measures for founding and establishing a separate college only when the prospect of the actual commencement of King's College and the attainment of the Presbyterian population of their due influence in the administration of that college seemed to be indefinitely postponed.[25]

It seems that this was in reference to Queen's desire, at least at this date, to unite with King's College. Strachan, not surprisingly, opposed such a union with the Presbyterians.[26] Instead of an inclusive institution for all of the province's inhabitants, he desired an exclusive institution that would try to limit access to one particular denomination, namely, his own.

Theological Colleges

In responding to the Church of England's attempt to make King's a bastion of Anglicanism, other denominations in the province saw at least two options. One was to lobby for other churches to be granted the same privilege, namely, that they be allowed to establish their own theological chairs *within* King's. Strachan and others, of course, would have refused such a suggestion. The other option, the one ultimately taken, was for each mainline denomination to create its own seminary where it would be able to train its own clergy. While this was seen by many as an attempt to create rival institutions to King's, it should be noted that the latter had a much larger endowment than the other theological schools by virtue of its Royal Charter from the king, which set aside land for it as well as the money generated therefrom.

The Presbyterian Church, for example, pushed forward the idea of having a theologian of a different denomination within King's, something that the Royal Committee in England had suggested. A commission on education appointed by the Upper Canada House of Assembly wrote in 1839, however, that it was their "conviction that it would be wholly subversive of the order of an University, to have within it, chairs for the Professors of different Denominations of Religion." It therefore recommended that "Theological Seminaries should be established, one for each Denomination that might appear to require such an establishment for the education of their clergy."[27] In 1837 a select committee of the Legislative Council approved a proposal made by the British House of Commons that a theological professorship of the Church of Scotland be established at King's. This never came to pass, however, and the money was instead given, as noted in the previous chapter, to establish St. Andrew's College of Canada (later given the name of Queen's University) in 1841 in Kingston.[28]

Meanwhile, the Basilian Fathers from Annonay, France, founded St. Michael's College in 1852 at the request of the Most Rev. Dr. de Carbonnel, then the Catholic Bishop of Toronto. Wycliffe College was founded in 1877 as the Protestant Episcopal Divinity School. And the (Free) Presbyterian Church of Canada founded Knox College in 1884, a year after the disruption in the Church of Scotland.[29]

The Baldwin Act (1849)

Robert Baldwin (1804–1858) was Canadian-born, the scion of a prominent Reform-minded family, an Anglican, and a former student of Strachan. Alongside his political partner, Louis-Hippolyte Lafontaine, another moderate reformer, he would lead the first responsible government in the newly created province of Canada. The two leaders of Lower and Upper Canada, respectively, worked together after the 1841 Union to lead a reformist movement for responsible government that would be run by elected citizens as opposed to a colonial governor appointed by the king. Their government, referred to as the "Great Ministry," was elected on 11 March 1848 and is generally regarded as marking the colony's democratic independence. John Ralston Saul regards the partnership of Baldwin and Lafontaine as responsible, just as much as Confederation in 1867, for the creation of a set of equitable principles and programs that would lead to the founding of modern Canada.[30] One of these principles was the importance of public education, free from denominational interference and theological entanglements. Both men believed this would sustain democracy and egalitarianism in the colony.[31]

As early as 1830, Baldwin had chaired a large public meeting, sponsored by the Friends of Religious Liberty – a group opposed to the control of education by one denomination – to address what was slowly becoming known as "the university problem." This problem, as we have seen time and again, revolved around the clear denominational affiliation of what many saw as the key post-secondary institution in the province. It had been an important issue in the election of 1847–8 that had brought the reformers to power. Many, Baldwin chief among them, wanted King's to have no religious affiliation whatsoever. They maintained that a public university should be open to all citizens regardless of religion. The Friends of Religious Liberty petitioned the monarch to exclude sectarian tests and preferences for faculty and students.[32] Though they collected more than a thousand signatures, the Upper Canada Assembly did not want to give up the Royal Charter for King's.

It was the Baldwin Act of 1849, passed a year into the new Reform government, that essentially created the University of Toronto. That bill was precipitated by complaints on the part of some faculty at King's about undue clerical influence at the college. Critics like Strachan and William Boulton – Strachan's spokesperson in the Assembly – criticized the bill, not unsurprisingly, as an attempt to make the university "entirely infidel."[33] For them, a university without a religious character was unthinkable. Again, their model seems to have been the one provided by Oxford and Cambridge. Many of the reformers instead looked to non-denominational universities in Scotland or to the recently created University of London as their model for what an institution of higher learning should look like.

The so-called Baldwin Act passed by a vote of forty-four to fourteen and became law on 30 May 1849.[34] It effectively created the University of Toronto, to which was transferred all the university powers and functions that King's College had previously enjoyed. The bill also gave the state control of the university and led to its complete secularization, making the university separate from the denominational colleges. Strachan, needless to say, opposed such a transformation. His main objection was that "religion in some form is an essential element of education and should not be excluded from the university."[35]

The University of Toronto came into existence on 1 January 1850, at which time King's College ceased to exist. The same bill abolished public funds to support a Professor of Divinity, any Faculty of Divinity, and the right to confer degrees in Divinity. Within days of the bill taking effect, Strachan began to organize a campaign to fund his proposed new Church of England institution, Trinity College. "On the first day of January [1850]," he wrote, "the destruction of King's College as a Christian Institution was accomplished ... To see it destroyed by stolid ignorance and presumption, and the voice of prayer and praise banished from its halls, is a calamity not easy to bear."[36] He returned to England to petition the king, Members of Parliament, and all those "members of the Church in our Fatherland," whom he believed "would feel the same indignation at so flagrant an outrage on our Holy Religion and the honour and dignity of the Crown, as had been felt here, and in the hope that they would not only feel, but act, and enable us by their offerings in addition to our own, to found a new College under a holier and better form."[37] He tried to get another Royal Charter, but neither the government of the colony nor the University of Toronto wanted another university in Toronto. Students at his new institution, Trinity College – what he called a "Church university" – had to declare allegiance to the Church of England, and clergymen from Oxbridge were hired as professors. George Whitaker, its first provost, declared that "the foundation of this College is a solemn protest against the separation of religion from education: we have joined together what others had put asunder."[38]

The Hincks Act (1853)

In 1851, Baldwin resigned as co-premier, and Francis Hincks (1807–1885) was asked to form the government with a Lower Canadian colleague, Augustin-Norbert Morin. Though Hinks, an Irishman, had been educated at Trinity University in Dublin, he was familiar with both Queen's University in Belfast and the University of London. Those two universities, not unlike the Scottish ones, provided a different paradigm from the one supplied by the Anglican institutions of Oxford and Cambridge that people like Strachan and others in places like Nova Scotia privileged. The former two universities functioned as administrative units and examining bodies, with some topics taught in affiliated denominational colleges and other topics taught at a non-denominational University College. Hincks used these universities as his model when, in

1852, he proposed a bill that would turn the newly created University College into a separate teaching institution, with the University of Toronto as the examining body. In 1853 the Hincks Act essentially created University College – "the vital center of the university" – in which instruction would be provided. However, it also included Church-related colleges that were to become affiliated with the university.

Yet many of the denominational colleges continued to attack the university for its perceived privileged position. Their attacks were not motivated simply by financial concerns, including how resources were divvied up; they also related to the proper purpose of a university education. Many of these critics believed in a model of university education that included the study of religious truths, which would aid in the intellectual and moral formation of young men (women were not yet allowed to enrol), who would thereby become upstanding citizens. Samuel Nelles, the President of Victoria College (then located in Cobourg), wrote in a letter to the *Globe* that at a university "there is no father to counsel, no mother to instill, from the lips of love, the lessons of Sacred Truth. A stranger has taken the place of both father and mother ... Christian fathers and mothers will want to know who that stranger is."[39]

The Federation Act (1887)

After Confederation in 1867, which united the provinces as the Dominion of Canada, education was transferred to provincial jurisdiction and the new government of Ontario, led by Premier John Sandfield Macdonald, abolished all grants to denominational colleges. One opponent of this, Egerton Ryerson – the founder of Victoria College and, from 1845 to 1876, the Superintendent of Education for Ontario (then called Canada West) – argued that there is a "necessity for advocates of Christianity ... to buckle on their armour and by prayer and faith and courage to challenge and meet the enemy in open combat."[40] Ryerson seems to have had in mind the forces of secularism that were taking over higher education in Ontario – forces that at this time, as we shall in the following chapter, functioned as handmaidens for Darwinism and Darwinian ideas, in the sciences as well as in the humanities, where it took the form of so-called higher criticism.

In 1883, William Mulock, the Vice-Chancellor of the University of Toronto, gave a commencement address that again opened up the question of the relationship between the university and the denominational colleges. Several of the colleges supported the idea of some form of federation. Nelles, at Victoria College, for example, supported the idea and wrote that a university cannot function with "a single professor for all the natural sciences and with a laboratory something similar to an ordinary blacksmith shop ... Every sect cannot have a genuine university."[41]

In 1884, George Ross, the Minister of Education, convened a series of meetings to discuss the issue with representatives of the university and all relevant colleges. This led to an agreement according to which University College and the theological colleges would teach a range of subjects in the humanities, and the university would be responsible for instruction in the sciences. Ethics, for example, would be a topic for the colleges, whereas philosophy would be one for the university. This, of course, had the potential to cause problems. It still tended, for example, to conceive of ethics as a function of the churches. Moreover, it implied that religiously affiliated colleges had something to offer secular education. As we shall see in subsequent chapters, critics vehemently disagreed with this.[42]

Some colleges chose not to affiliate. Queen's, for example, decided to remain in Kingston, where it would serve the needs of eastern Ontarians. The Toronto Baptist College, which wanted "scientific knowledge to be put under a theological censorship fully and as admirable as that of the Dominicans in Florence under Galileo's time," eventually moved to Hamilton, changed its name to McMaster, and lost its theological orientation.[43] Knox and Wycliffe formally affiliated in 1885; St. Michael's in 1889; and Victoria in 1890.

Trinity, which had been founded in 1851 by Bishop Strachan after the disestablishment of King's, initially refused affiliation because the province would not compensate it for the move from Queen Street. It did eventually affiliate, however, in 1904.

Conclusions

This chapter has revealed just what was at stake in the creation of the modern university in Canada. Many at the time felt that post-secondary education ought to be tightly linked to religious concerns and the inculcation in young men of religious truths. Secular subjects ought only to be taught, in other words, when mitigated by a proper understanding of spiritual truths provided by religious teaching and instruction. Unfortunately, this sentiment quickly turned to one of denominational sectarianism and the desire, especially on the part of the Church of England, to become the official religion of the young colony. Denominational affiliation came to determine who could or could not administer, teach, or study at many of these institutions.

The transformation of King's College into the University of Toronto is emblematic of these tensions and fractures. It shows clearly how the study of religion – defined, at least initially, as the study of theological truth-claims – generated a series of sectarian battles so vociferous and even medieval that the only way to avoid them was to create a paradigm of secular education. Indeed, the overwhelming majority of post-secondary institutions in Ontario emerged under the shadow of precisely this religious sectarianism. While some of them were certainly less exclusive than others, religion (whether we call it divinity, theology, or moral ethics) in these early years was imagined to be central to education.

As we see in the case of the University of Toronto, the subsequent struggle to remove theology or the study and teaching of religious truths was no easy task. On the contrary, it was intimately connected to the political reforms brought about by the "Great Ministry" of Baldwin and Lafontaine. It was, in other words, a process that echoed political debates concerning democratic reform. In this new climate of political equality, it was gradually determined that a country could not afford to have university agendas dictated by theological proclivities.

Chapter Three

Late Victorian Scholarship and the Rise of Higher Criticism

The previous two chapters examined some of the major trends, scuffles, and entanglements inherent to the study of religion in Canada prior to and at the time of Confederation in 1867; the present chapter switches focus and begins to examine some of the scholars involved in these early conversations. My goal is to provide an account of what topics were of interest to scholars of religion in these early years and to show how they conceptualized and thought about religion "on the ground." These were not the administrators responsible for the formation and governance of seminaries, but the actual individuals procuring and producing scholarship on religion. While most, to be sure, were theologians, and while many were, as seen in previous chapters, engaged in the project of showing the superiority of their own denominational perspectives, there are certainly surprises – in particular, some individuals were able to look beyond their own tradition and take an interest in a more "comparative" perspective on the study of religion.

Neither time nor space permits me to survey the writings, op-eds, or sermons of every professor of Divinity employed at a Canadian seminary or university during the nineteenth century. My goal, indeed, is much more modest in scope. I have opted to look closely at the writings of a few select individuals who were working between the years 1850 and 1900, using their writings as a window through which to examine the discourses on religion in Canada during these early years. What, for example, were some of the critical or key issues? Did the study of religion have to be merely a theological or philosophical enterprise, or were there outliers to this more regnant model? In the latter respect one of the more interesting voices is that of George Monro Grant (1835–1902), who, though an ordained Presbyterian minister, wrote some of the earliest comparative work in North America, and who was among the first to do so in Canada. Though still informed by the assumption that Christianity was the superior expression of the religious life, he nonetheless treated other traditions sympathetically, and he worked on the assumption – one of the leitmotifs for the non-theological study of religion in Canada – that one can truly appreciate one's own religion only if one has also appreciated those of others.

Another strong influence on the study of religion, especially religious texts, in Victorian times was the development and subsequent rise of "higher criticism" in European and American universities. Such criticism was at the time revolutionary and undermined what previous generations had taken for granted. The goal of such criticism was to investigate the social and historical origins of ancient texts in order to understand them in their immediate contexts.[1] This would have major repercussions. Higher criticism assumed that the biblical text was, like all texts, the product of human creativity. Unlike religious believers, those who practised "higher criticism" regarded the Bible not as the inerrant word of God but instead as a fallible human document. As we shall see, higher criticism of the Bible often coincided with the new science associated with Darwin, which radically transformed the way many thought about the human species and the natural world. This union of higher criticism and Darwinism would make major inroads in Canadian universities and set off a chain of often vitriolic accusations and counter-accusations. Such intellectual skirmishes would, in turn, create the epistemic space for the secular study of religion in subsequent decades.

The Recruitment of Faculty

As we saw in previous chapters, many of the new universities and colleges in Canada were obsessed with the Oxbridge model of elite education. Recall the statement by Alexander Croke, an early governor of King's in Nova Scotia, that the only pure language, "undebased by local or national accents and solecisms," was to be found among the educated of England. As a consequence, many administrators, themselves trained in the United Kingdom, turned to that country when recruiting faculty for the new colleges and universities.

Bishop Strachan, for example, tried to hire only Oxbridge-educated Englishmen (who, by definition, were Anglican) to staff the newly created King's College in Toronto. However, very few talented individuals wanted to relocate to the colonies, and many turned him down. In other cases, suitable candidates were overlooked because they were not Anglicans. For example, James Sylvester, an English Jew, had applied for the job of mathematics tutor but was rejected because he could not subscribe to the doctrine of the Trinity. He would go on to become the

Savilian Professor of Mathematics at Oxford[2] and a renowned mathematician.[3] A Hebrew tutor, Jacob Maier Hirschfelder, was hired instead, but only because he had converted to Christianity.

The first professor of Divinity at King's in Toronto was the Reverend James Beaven (1801–1875), whom Martin Friedland describes as "at least their third choice."[4] When the secular University of Toronto formed out of the ashes of King's, and there was to be no more professor of Divinity, Beaven's position was transformed into that of a professor of metaphysics and ethics.[5] It is perhaps telling that Strachan did not bother to offer him a position in Divinity at his newly created Trinity College.

Beaven's *Elements of Natural Theology* (1850) is generally regarded as the first work of philosophy written in English Canada. An anonymous review of it in *The English Review* describes it as follows:

> Dr. Beaven, in this work, furnishes his readers with a clear and well-arranged digest of all the principal proofs of the existence, the moral attributes, and the Providence of God. The especial interest in the volume is, the frequent reference to the arguments and inferences of heathen philosophy, approximating so closely as they sometimes did to the truth. The argument from design which Paley has so ably drawn out, is here very well exhibited and illustrated; and on the whole we may remark, that Dr. Beaven's reasoning is throughout cautious and accurate.[6]

Beaven was a natural theologian who sought to outline a rational basis for Christian belief. As this review says, his goal was also to show how Christian philosophy (= theology) was superior to "heathen" philosophies or, at the very least, to show how the latter never made it to the towering and sublime heights of Christian philosophy. He was making an attempt, however feeble, to proffer some model of comparison. His was not, however, an objective or value-neutral comparison, but rather one in which the conclusions were foreordained. Another anonymous review of his book, this one in *The Gentleman's Magazine and Historical Review*, noted that the volume was "a very able exposition of the utility of the study of Natural Theology, the history of the study, and the best modes (apart from the authority of revelation) of providing the being and unity of a Spiritual Creator, his continual government of the world, the existence of a future state, the immortality of the soul, and the other leading doctrines of natural theology."[7]

It seems that Beaven's work was an extension of the philosophy of religion that played such an important role in the development of religious studies in England.[8] This subfield set out to ascertain the rationality of belief, show the spiritual importance of an active creator of the universe, and establish truth-claims for believers.

Another individual who provides some insight into the manner in which individuals imagined and conceived of religion in these early years was John William Dawson (1820–1899), who was mentioned in chapter 1 of this volume in the context of the early years of McGill. Born in Pictou, Nova Scotia, and trained at the University of Edinburgh, Dawson had a deep concern with religion, even though he had been trained as a geologist rather than a theologian. He also had an abiding interest in education and educational reform.[9] He was appointed Nova Scotia's first Superintendent of Education, a position he held from 1850 to 1853, and was mentored by Egerton Ryerson, president of Victoria College, when he went to Upper Canada to study the school system there.

Dawson desired, in his own words, "a national and non-denominational institution [that would not necessarily be] godless."[10] With this principle in mind, he set about reforming the educational systems in Nova Scotia and New Brunswick. His model was not the English system, which reserved "the best in education for the best of the people," but the Scottish and American tradition "of making whatever education could be provided available to all."[11] Such a model, he maintained, would prevent the elitism of the English model, one that was already embedded in King's College in his own province.

Dawson was appointed principal of McGill College in 1855 and oversaw much of its growth after the initial years of familial and sectarian bickering. His goal was to create a practical institution and not, as other Canadian administrators had promoted, a pseudo-medieval Oxbridge-type college that focused solely on classical literature and that sought to conform to eighteenth-century notions of what a gentleman's education ought to involve. During these same years he founded the Royal Society of Canada (RSC), meant for distinguished Canadian scholars and scientists, which was established by an Act of Parliament in 1883.[12]

Dawson was writing at a transformative moment in the history of science – a time when the "natural sciences" were about to fracture into a host of specialized subfields focused on research. In the latter context, Dawson, a devout Christian, became a leading anti-Darwinist of the late Victorian period.[13] In the Preface to his *The Origin of the World, According to Revelation and Science* (1877), for example, he wrote:

> The intention of this new publication is to throw as much light as possible on the present condition of the much-agitated question respecting the origin of the world and its inhabitants. To students of the Bible it will afford

> the means of determining the precise import of the biblical references to creation and of their relation to what is known from other sources. To geologists and biologists it is intended to give some intelligible explanation of the connection of the doctrines of revealed religion with the results of their respective sciences.[14]

Dawson was a harsh critic of Darwin's theory of evolution, for it threw into doubt everything the believer thought to be true about the natural (and, by extension, supernatural) world, which included creation, revelation, and ultimate redemption. Again, in his *The Origin of the World*, we read:

> Christians have been accustomed to rest on the cosmogony and prophecy of the Bible; but we are now frankly told on all hands that these are valueless, and that even ministers of religion more or less "sacrifice their sincerity" in making them the basis of their teachings. On the other hand, we are informed that nothing can be discerned in the universe beyond matter and force, and that it is by a purely material and spontaneous evolution that all things exist. But when we ask as to the origin of matter and force, and the laws which regulate them – as to the end to which their movement is tending, as to the manner in which they have evolved the myriad forms of life and the human intelligence itself – the only answer is that these are "insoluble mysteries."[15]

To tackle these "insoluble mysteries," Dawson made it his agenda to provide a "foothold of assurance" in the "revelations and traditions of the past" as opposed to waiting "further [for] progress in science."[16] Near the end of his book, he wrote:

> Twenty years ago nearly all geologists were believers in creation, though, it must be admitted without precisely understanding what they meant by the term. Now, the great impression produced by Darwin's speculations and the prevalence of the evolutionist philosophy have produced a leaning in the other direction. More recently, however, the absurdities into which the extreme revolutionists find themselves driven have produced a reaction; and we hope that views consistent with revelation, or at least with Theism, will again be in the ascendant, and that present controversies will serve to give more precise and definite views than heretofore of the relation of nature to God.[17]

Dawson here was using scripture to legitimate a pre-Darwinian scientific view of the world, while simultaneously using that view to legitimate Scripture. "Scripture and science both testify," he argued, "to the great fact that there was a beginning – a time when none of all the parts of the fabric of the universe existed."[18] As for evolution, he concluded that the "introduction of new species of animals and of plants, while indicating advances in the perfection of nature, does not prove spontaneous development, but rather a definite plan and law of creation."[19]

Thus in his scientific works Dawson maintained a distinctly theological attitude, rejecting the theory of human evolution from brute ancestors and holding that the human species made its appearance on this earth in quite recent times. He would maintain this stance in his *Facts and Fancies in Modern Science: Studies of the Relations of Science to Prevalent Speculations and Religious Belief* (1882), which he based on a series of lectures he delivered at the Crozer Theological Seminary in Upland, Pennsylvania, which was associated with the American Baptist movement. In that volume he declared that his goal was to "show the necessary relation and parallelism of all truths, physical and spiritual."[20] Without such parallelism, Dawson warned his readers, the repercussions of scientific understanding unfettered by spiritual concerns would be pernicious:

> The attempt to make science, or speculations based on science, supersede religion is one of the prevalent fancies of our time, and pervades much of the popular literature of the day. That such attempts can succeed the author does not believe. They have hitherto given birth only to such abortions as Positivism, Nihilism, and Pessimism.[21]

In the conclusion to the lectures, Dawson wrote that

> when Science has led us into the presence of the Creator, she has brought us to the threshold of religion, and there she suggests the possibility that the spirit of man may have other relations with God beyond those established by merely physical law. Science may venture to say: "If all nature expresses the will of the Creator as carried out in his laws, if the instinct of lower animals is an inspiration of God, should we not expect that there will be laws of a higher order regulating the free moral nature of man, and that there will be possibilities of man communicating with, or receiving aid from, the Supreme Intelligence."[22]

It is surprising that, for all their differences, there was not a huge discrepancy in intellectual proclivities between Beaven, the professor of Divinity at King's, and the geologist Dawson. Both were trying to rationalize religious faith and show how it was in accord with the teachings of modern science, at least when the latter was properly understood. Both men, in other words, were seeking to justify faith in the face of contemporaneous scepticism. This was a far cry from what we today recognize as the academic study of religion; rather, it was an endeavour based on and subsequently focused on apologetics, on establishing truth-claims, and on the ultimate reconciliation of religion and science.[23] It was moreover decidedly Eurocentric and Christocentric, and rarely, if ever, interested in other religious traditions or, indeed, in even examining religion from a non-religious perspective.

The Comparative Study of Religion

Such overt theologizing in the guise of science, rationalism, and Christian apologetics was not, however, the only path one could take in the second half of the nineteenth century. Others were more interested in comparing the world religions – though, of course, Christianity tended to serve as the lodestar to which other religions were compared and comparable. Still others began to be influenced by the emerging fields of anthropology and sociology, which, like Darwinism, were beginning to pay increased attention to human origins, in addition to political and social development. Such new fields – inspired by the likes of Sigmund Freud, Émile Durkheim, and James George Frazer – promised many more new insights into religious behaviour and organization than did the study of theology alone. We thus begin to see a gradual chipping away at the theological paradigm for the study of religion.

This was hardly a uniquely Canadian phenomenon. Indeed, my interest is less in the intellectual originality of Canadian scholars than in the institutional, political, social, and legal contexts that created an academy and that provided these Canadian scholars with an intellectual forum for articulating their ideas. There was, to repeat, no singular Canadian "take" on the academic study of religion. There were, however, distinct features that permitted said study to occur. The theories and methods applied in Canada by Canadian scholars were ultimately derived from elsewhere – from England, from Europe, from the United States – an inevitable result of the free exchange of ideas and the movement of faculty. Yet how such theories and methods played out in a Canadian context was ultimately structured by broader forces, which this study seeks to uncover.

One exceptional example was George Monro Grant (1835–1902).[24] Born in Albion Mines, in Pictou County, Nova Scotia, to Scottish parents, he was trained at Glasgow University, where he was ordained as a

Presbyterian minister in December 1860.[25] He returned to the Maritimes and had small parishes in Prince Edward Island and Nova Scotia before taking up the pulpit at St. Matthew's Church in Halifax – the oldest, largest, and most influential Presbyterian congregation in Nova Scotia.

Grant was an eloquent orator and often spoke on political topics. On the eve of Confederation in 1867, Nova Scotia was the province most strongly opposed to federal union. Taking the opposite point of view, Grant argued for national unity, and his oratory is credited with helping secure the acceptance of Confederation in the province. When the consolidation of the Dominion by means of railway construction began to be discussed in 1872, Grant travelled across Canada, from the Atlantic to the Pacific, with the engineers who were surveying the route on behalf of the Canadian Pacific Railway.[26] He would recount his adventures in *Ocean to Ocean* (1873), his book about the expedition of its chief engineer, Sir Sandford Fleming:

> Travel a thousand miles up the St. Lawrence; another thousand on great lakes and a wilderness of lakelets and streams; a thousand miles across prairies and up the valley of the Saskatchewan; and nearly a thousand miles through woods and over great ranges of mountains, and you have travelled from Ocean to Ocean through Canada. All this country is a single Colony of the British Empire; and this Colony is dreaming magnificent dreams of a future when it shall be the Greater Britain, and the highway across which the fabrics and products of Asia shall be carried to the Eastern as well as to the Western sides of the Atlantic.[27]

Thus opens Grant's memoir. He then makes the case for Confederation:

> By uniting together, the British Provinces had declared that their destiny was – not to ripen and drop, one by one, into the arms of the Republic [i.e., the United States] – but to work out their own future as an integral and important part of the grandest Empire in the World. They had reason for making such an election. They believed that it was better for themselves and for their neighbours; better for the cause of human liberty and true progress that it should be so.[28]

Here Grant juxtaposes the Canadian situation with the American one. In this book, he consistently argues that Canada's best hope lies in unity with the rest of the British Empire rather than in forging an American-style republic. We see this further in his *Advantages of Imperial Federation* (1891), which was based on a series of lectures he gave at the Imperial Federation League. That league was founded in London in 1884, with branches in Canada, Australia, and New Zealand, among other places, and its goal was to promote federation across the British Empire. The league used as its model the Dominion of Canada, a one-time colony now managed through a central representative authority (e.g., the Queen or Governor General). In this book, Grant argued that Canada would be better off economically in such a federation: "This, then, is our definition of national advantage – material prosperity in strict subordination to duty and honour, the independent development of our political life, the safety, unity, dignity and well-being of the Commonwealth. These secured, our advantage will be the world's advantage as well as Canada's."[29]

Besides working tirelessly on behalf of Confederation and expressing his desire for the former colony to remain part of the British Empire, Grant showed himself to be a very able administrator. In 1877 the Third General Assembly of the Presbyterian Church in Canada appointed Grant the Primarius Professor of Divinity and the Principal of Queen's College in Kingston. Note that such positions were decided at the church level, not the faculty level. Grant had always stressed the importance of the humanities and philosophy as opposed to solely scientific or more practical studies. Notwithstanding his religious bona fides, he spent much of his time at Queen's trying to secularize the institution and resisting federation with the University of Toronto, which proponents had hoped would create one degree-granting institution in the province.[30] For him, Queen's was not a "denomination college," but was doing the exact same work in the arts and sciences that was being done at University College at the University of Toronto.[31]

Through Grant's efforts and influence, Queen's eventually transformed itself into a large and influential institution of higher learning. He was able to attract important faculty members, with the aforementioned Sir Sandford Fleming – who, among other things, designed Canada's first postage stamp, helped found the Royal Society of Canada, and served as chief engineer of the CPR – serving as chancellor for most of Grant's tenure. It was Grant, more than anyone, who succeeded in making Queen's non-denominational. In April 1889, for example, he proposed amending the charter so that new trustees, elected by the University Council as their representatives on the board, would not need to be Presbyterian, and so that trustees would no longer be required to sign a religious declaration.[32] At the Board of Trustees' annual meeting of 2 May 1900, Grant proposed that the corporation end its membership in the Presbyterian Church of Canada.[33]

What concerns me most in the present context, however, is Grant's writings that relate to the academic study of religion. Germane here is his *Religions of the World in Relation to Christianity* (1894), published as part of the Fleming H. Revell Company's Guild Text Book series. That book, as Grant made clear in his Preface, was intended as a textbook "for the use of Guilds and Bible Classes, of the great extant non-Christian religions."[34] Though he did note, in perhaps typical Victorian fashion. that he would not be dealing with "Talmudism, Jainism, Shintoism, and Parsîism" because they were "accepted only by small sections of the race. Besides they have evidently finished their work and have entered upon a long euthanasia."[35] Instead, he was most interested in "Mohammedanism, Hinduism or Brahmanism, Buddhism, and the native religions of China."[36] Grant also informed the reader that the book was written "from the point of view of one who believes Christianity to be the perfect religion, and therefore the standard by which all others may be tested."[37] Notwithstanding the supersessionist exclusions and the fact that Christianity served as the ground for comparison, there were several new features here. Primary was that Grant was showing interest in other religions. Notwithstanding the tone he set in the Preface, he would go on to acknowledge that Christianity was but one species in the broader genus of religion.[38] This was a major advance from the likes of Beavan and Dawson.

In his introduction to the volume, Grant writes not as a theologian but as a scholar of religion. Religion is, for him, a universal, that which "indicates what is the highest in man."[39] He subsequently divides the religions of the world into the "systematised" and the "unsystematised": "The latter include all those crude and incoherent notions by which savage tribes explain to themselves the mystery of existence. Strange and horrible as these religions are, they indicate man's nobleness, for they express his gropings after God."[40] Grant is certainly familiar with the major theorists of religion of his day. He invokes, for example, the likes of F. Max Müller and C.P. Tiele, who were the most prominent comparative religionists of the time. Grant's more academic approach to comparative religion comes to the fore when he writes that the scholar of religion cannot be an apologist for his own creed. Thus, his approach will be

> very different from that which prevailed in Britain more than a century ago. Then, a shallow deism considered all religions alike as having originated in the policy of statesmen or the craft of priests, operating on the ignorance and credulity of the masses, with the object of securing an effective moral police or of gaining wealth and power. When all religions were thus considered equally worthy of contempt, the sole object of the apologist was to defend Christianity.[41]

Grant is particularly critical of the theological tendency to "believe that other religions were from the devil as to believe that ours was from God."[42] This disparaging view of other religions, according to Grant, has no place in the academic study of religion. Rather, for him, "all religions are considered legitimate products of that faith in the unseen which is recognised as an essential part of man's constitution."[43] He then sets outs his own methodology: "The true way, however, to meet criticism of this kind is not by taking up a pharisaic attitude towards other religions, but by instituting a thorough and impartial examination and comparison of all. We believe in the superiority of Christianity to other religions, but we cannot entertain this belief intelligently until after such comparison."[44] Grant makes clear that, though he considers his own religion to be the superior one, it is nevertheless necessary to study the other major religions of the world impartially. And this is the novelty of George Monro Grant regarding the academic study of religion in Canada: for all intents and purposes, he was Canada's first non-theological scholar of religion.

Others would pick up his approach. Here it is worth mentioning Louis H. Jordan (1855–1923). Jordan, from Halifax, Nova Scotia, was a Presbyterian minister who had studied at Dalhousie before moving on to further his education in Edinburgh and Oxford and then in Germany.[45] After serving in pulpits in Halifax, Montreal, and Toronto, he retired and devoted his life to travel and writing. In Montreal, he had also served as a lecturer on Church Polity at the Presbyterian College.[46] As Remus notes, he also served as a special lecturer in comparative religions at the University of Chicago.[47]

His *Comparative Religion: Its Genesis and Growth* (1905) provides another early example of a Canadian contribution to the comparative study of religion. Like Grant, Jordan was critical of the old theological approach to such study. He was particularly critical of Christian apologetics, which he characterized in the following terms: "That branch of instruction, as formerly understood, was practically limited to a defense and vindication of the tenets of Christianity; but it is now widely recognised that no one can expound the real significance of that Faith until he has made himself acquainted with its relationships to the various non-Christian faiths."[48] This was quite a common motif in late Victorian comparison of religions: in order to truly know one's own tradition, one must know others. "To know one," in F. Max Müller's famous locution, "is to know none." Even if the author's aim is to show the superiority of his or her own tradition, one must nevertheless examine other religions of the world in order to appreciate fully one's own.[49]

Unlike Grant, however, Jordan reflects on the very nature of comparison. His goal is to "give the reader a condensed yet comprehensive view of the origin, progress, and aim of the science of Comparative Religion."[50] To that end, he informs the reader that he had to travel the world in order to examine religious actors in their native environments. According to him, "pursuing this method, I have been privileged to watch the worship and to converse with the adherents, of almost all the great Religions of the world; and it may be remarked, in passing, that *in no other way* can one secure so prompt and radical a corrective of opinions which – however honest – are often much too hastily arrived at."[51] Once again, this is new. Not content to consult the sacred scriptures of the world's religions and then to juxtapose them with the Old and New Testaments, Jordan now stresses the importance of anthropological observation. The only way to understand other religions, for Jordan and for those who would follow him, is to observe their adherents in their natural habitats *in addition* to studying their scriptures.

Perhaps most interesting for the present context is an appendix Jordan includes in the book. In a chart devoted to "the Present Position of Comparative Religion in the World's Universities, Colleges, etc.," he lists all of the Canadian (and other) institutions where "comparative religion" is taught.[52] The first part of the chart is devoted to the topic "If a chair for imparting Instruction in Comparative Religion Exists." He then duly notes that not one single Canadian institution has one. Then in the second part of the table, we have the topic "If no such Chair exists," subdivided into "Is Such a Foundation Possible?" All the Canadian institutions have either "no," "doubtful," or "not at present."

Jordan, a Canadian, thus laments that in Canada there is no place to study comparative religion. The only option for a Canadian is to do what he himself did: to go abroad to the United Kingdom, to Europe, or increasingly to the United States to seek out one's own education. Indeed, when one compares the paucity of resources at Canadian universities and colleges in Jordan's appendix with those found in these other places, the results are astounding. Despite the path-breaking work of those like Grant and Jordan, it would be some time before the academic, as opposed to the theological, study of religion was taught in Canadian institutions of higher learning.

Biblical and Oriental Studies: Maintaining the Equilibrium

Biblical and Oriental studies, two cognates to the study of religion, offer us a somewhat different picture. Like comparative religion, biblical studies in Canada dates roughly to the 1880s. It was, however, much more popular than the latter field on account of the importance of the Bible for theology and the training of clergy. Until the arrival of higher criticism, though, biblical studies tended to focus almost exclusively on homiletics and catechesis. As with comparative religion, the rise of more critical biblical studies informed by higher criticism can be traced to the impact of German scholarship in Canadian universities and seminaries and even in churches.[53] Prior to this introduction, the Bible was studied uncritically and as part of the university curriculum (where it was allowed) as a preparation for virtuous Christian living. When the Bible was taught in such a manner, learning biblical languages and investigating its ancient Near Eastern sources or how the biblical text was redacted tended to be avoided. This too, however, was about to change in the second half of the nineteenth century and the beginning of the twentieth with what Masters calls the gradual liberalism witnessed in Canadian Protestant churches during this period.[54]

One exception to this rule was Jacob Maier Hirschfelder, whom we encountered briefly in the previous chapter.[55] A convert to Christianity, Hirschfelder was born in Baden-Baden in 1819. He studied at Heidelberg and Esslingen before immigrating to Canada in the late 1830s. In Montreal he taught Hebrew, Aramaic, Syriac, and Arabic before being hired in 1842 to teach these same languages at a preparatory school in Toronto. Two years later, in 1844, he was appointed lecturer in Oriental languages at King's College in Toronto, where he taught these classes solely to Anglican divinity students. When the Baldwin Act passed, Hirschfelder was appointed lecturer in Oriental literature at University College. The rationale of teaching these languages at King's and then the University of Toronto, in the words of John S. Moir, was "that such studies promoted appreciation of the Bible as long as they were governed by common sense and obvious personal piety."[56] Since Darwinism and historical criticism had yet to make much of an impact on the young colony, this equilibrium was fairly easy to maintain, but only briefly.

It might also be worth mentioning in the present context the career of Alexander Abraham de Sola (1825–1882). De Sola, born in London, England, was appointed rabbi of Shearith Israel, the Spanish and Portuguese Synagogue of Montreal, in 1848.[57] In 1853 he became Professor of Hebrew and Oriental literature at McGill. In 1858, McGill conferred the degree of LL.D. upon him, making him the first Jew to attain that honour in an English-speaking country. On account of his pulpit addresses and publications, de Sola was recognized in the United States as one of the most powerful leaders of Orthodoxy, at a time when there was a bitter struggle between the Orthodox and Reform movements over which denomination best represented Judaism in the modern world. In 1873 the administration of Ulysses S. Grant invited de Sola to open the United States Congress with a prayer.[58] The event was significant not so much because de Sola was a Jew, but because he was a British subject.[59]

Higher Criticism: The Floodgates Open

Only in the 1880s do we begin to see the emergence of departments of "Orientals." This occurred at Victoria College in 1881 and at University College in Toronto in 1886. The equilibrium that had been maintained by the likes of Hirschfelder and de Sola would become increasingly difficult to maintain. A case in point is the career of Frederick Julius Steen (1867–1903), who, after training in Orientals at the University of Toronto, was appointed Chair of Apologetics and Ecclesiastical History at the Montreal Diocesan Theological College in 1896. The following year he became Special Preacher at Christ Church Cathedral in the same city.[60] Adams writes that Steen was influenced by higher criticism, which was still relatively new in the Canadian context: "His sermons were simple in character but in them he frequently touched upon the results of recent investigations and modern discoveries which had thrown new light on certain biblical statements and he explained in simple language, in what way and how far, these new discoveries had confirmed, illuminated or modified conceptions or beliefs which had been formerly held."[61]

This, of course, did not bode well for the young Steen, and in 1900 the troubles began. In class one day a student accused him of denying the uniqueness of the Bible and the divine inspiration behind it. Steen was subsequently interrogated at a meeting of a committee appointed by the board on 17 January 1901. His views on the nature of religion and the Bible apparently satisfied the committee charged with looking into his case. However, that committee also examined the notebook of the student who had complained about Steen's views. Steen maintained that the notes were substantially correct, but this did not satisfy the committee members. On the basis of these notes and his sermons at Christ Church Cathedral, they demanded Steen's resignation.[62]

In this brief portrait we witness just what was at stake for the first generation of Canadian scholars who tried to introduce higher criticism into the classroom and the pulpit. Since many such courses in Canadian institutions were taught in denominational settings, it was perhaps only natural that this type of resistance would exist. In this respect, it was not unique to the Montreal Diocesan Theological College. Similar events unfolded at the Toronto Baptist College, which, as noted in chapter 1, tended to privilege spiritual truths over scientific investigation. In 1904, its Chair of Systematic Theology, Dr. Calvin Goodspeed, retired. He had long held out against new scholarship on the Bible and was an ardent critic of higher criticism. His successors, however, were George Cross and the Reverend Isaac George Matthews, both of whom were accused by their detractors of "lacking in spirituality."[63] Their main accuser initially was the Reverend Elmore Harris, a Toronto Baptist College graduate, a pastor of Walmer Road Baptist Church in Toronto, and a respected member of the University Senate.

At issue was the strengthening connection between Toronto Baptist College and the University of Chicago, another institution of higher learning that had been founded under Baptist auspices. During the 1880s the latter institution, newly revitalized with Rockefeller money, quickly became the epicentre in North America of subjecting scripture to exhaustive analysis based on form and redaction criticism with the aim of adapting the church to modernity. Under the leadership of its president, William Rainey Harper, the University of Chicago's Divinity School attracted many famous biblical scholars such as Shailer Mathews, Ernest de Witt Burton, Shirley Jackson Case, Gerald Birney Smith, and George Burman Foster.

In *The Function of Religion in Man's Struggle for Existence* (1909), for example, Foster (1858–1918) could write: "Psychology assimilated itself to biological sciences, and now, in due time, theology is beginning to think of religion and of God after the analogy of the thought of consciousness and of the soul as cherished by the psychologist."[64] Needless to say, such views were thought by his contemporaries to support scientific, naturalistic, and humanistic views that contradicted the teachings of the Baptist Church. Yet given the university's Baptist heritage and its swift emergence as a leading institution in the United States, not to mention the presence there of people like Foster, the University of Chicago naturally became one of TBC's favourite graduate schools to which to send its students.

Not surprisingly, the Reverend Harris described the University of Chicago as "a menace to Church and Society."[65] It was a period, to quote Johnston, "of muckraking, of progressivism, of the social gospel, and of reform at nearly every level of political activity."[66] George Cross (1862–1929) had been hired by TBC in 1901, but asked for a deferment so that he could spend a year and a half studying at the University of Chicago before accepting his position. Cross was interested, in his own words, in the "problem for the theologian [of] how to conserve the true Christianity while at the same time admitting that there were elements of truth in other religions."[67] We can read such an interest as protecting

Christianity, but clearly, scholars like Cross were willing to submit the tradition to examination in ways hitherto unheard of in a Canadian context.

Once again, then, we see how the likes of Darwin, Freud, and Frazer were all chipping away at the dominant theological paradigm for studying religion. This development was advancing in the United States and gradually seeping into Canada. The assumption was that emerging fields and disciplines such as anthropology and sociology would provide deeper insights into human religious behaviour. As seminaries began transforming themselves into universities, curricula were changing from general homiletics to ones with more distinct departments with specific focuses. This would generate new methodologies for understanding religion. Even Baptist institutions were being impacted by this intersection of the study of religion with new disciplines. It is in this context that we must situate individuals, like Cross, who brought this approach to Canada with them from places like the University of Chicago.

However, the fact that he was in a Baptist college would inevitably cause him problems. Harris, leading the charge, argued that, to use the words of Johnston, "those who endorsed the scientific treatment of the Scriptures were prone to elevate the past in terms of the present's moods and attitudes ... Out of this, the complaint went, had come an excessive concern with the problems of the 'here' and 'now' to the distinct disadvantage of the 'hereafter.'"[68] Rationalism and unaided human reason, in other words, undermined revelation.

Cross however returned to the University of Chicago shortly after arriving in Toronto. The result was that Harris and other detractors singled out the Reverend Isaac George Matthews, Cross's colleague, as the main instigator. On 11 May 1909 Harris formally accused Matthews of unorthodoxy, claiming to have in his possession a stenographic record of a series of courses that Matthews had delivered in which he stated that the early chapters of Genesis were folklore "exactly in line with the folklore of every people under the sun."[69] The committee tasked with investigating Matthews's heresy submitted its report on 29 May 1909, in which it was stated that the charges were not proved. The same report stated that, while Matthews accepted the results of much modern scholarship, he "held firmly to the inspiration and supernatural character of the Old and New Testaments."[70] Finally, the report concluded by stating that the College

> must welcome truth from whatever quarter, and never be guilty of binding the spirit of free enquiry. As a Christian school of learning under

> Baptist auspices, it stands for the fullest and freest investigations, *not only in the scientific realm but also in the realm of Biblical scholarship*. Holding fast to their historic position on the personal freedom and responsibility of the individual, refusing to be bound by any human creed, rejecting the authority of tradition and taking their stand on the word of God alone as the supreme and all-sufficient rule of faith and practice, the Baptists have even been ready to accord to all students of the Sacred Scriptures the largest possible measure of freedom consisted with loyalty to the fundamentals of the Christian faith.[71]

At issue, based on this concluding statement, was the idea of intellectual freedom in higher education. The case of Matthews, however, brings to the foreground the tensions inherent to just what a scholar of religion or a biblical scholar could or could not say or teach at a theological college. The charge against Matthews, while certainly bringing a better result than the one against Sheen, thus reveals some of the struggles that the study of religion faced in the late Victorian period in a predominantly Christian country. It is worth noting that in 1919 Matthews resigned and took up a pulpit in New Haven, Connecticut, with part-time teaching duties at Yale Divinity School.

James F. McCurdy: Higher Criticism Enters the Mainstream

This tension would presumably take a different direction when biblical and/or Oriental studies entered more secular institutions, such as the recently formed University of Toronto. Here it is worth examining the career of James F. McCurdy (1847–1935), who is generally regarded as father of biblical studies in Canada. Born in Chatham, New Brunswick, he received his BA from the University of New Brunswick in 1866 and his PhD from Princeton in 1878.[72] He seems to have been fond of the newly emerging higher criticism, and for this, he found few sympathizers at conservative Princeton. He subsequently travelled to Germany to continue his studies, at Göttingen and then Leipzig, where he studied with some of the leading German higher critics of the day.[73]

He returned to Canada in 1885 and took up an appointment in 1886 as tutor in Oriental languages at University College at the University of Toronto, where he would serve as an understudy to and subsequent replacement for the aging Hirschfelder.[74] McCurdy, writes historian Moir, "was certainly central to the development of biblical studies in Canada. McCurdy represented the best in contemporary scholarship and was a dedicated, thorough, and inspiring teacher who trained a brilliant collection of young Canadians in rigorous methodology."[75] We get a sense of this new methodology in his *Aryo-Semitic Speech: A Study in Linguistic Archaeology* (1881), in which he writes that the new science of language "has been rescued from the confusion of uncertainty which marked its superstitious and mythical treatment in pre-scientific times."[76] This "new science" is one that seeks to compare the morphology of various languages, and their dialects, with actual, historical correspondences and not just hunches. He continues:

> What the investigator has to do is to make the comparison of Aryan and Semitic roots after the forms chosen for the purpose that have been reduced to their simplest expression. That is, they must be proved to be actual roots in their respective idioms, and they must be treated as expressing the root-idea. This, however, involves a careful study of the principles of root formation and development in the two systems in their primitive individual history.[77]

I have chosen this rather dry passage to show how far we have come since the publication of the Rev. James Beaven's *Elements of Natural Theology* in 1850. If the latter was interested in establishing truth-claims for the Church of England and shows clearly the British influence on the study of religion in Canada, McCurdy's is much less apologetical and is based on the new science of comparative linguistics pioneered in Germany and the United States. This difference clearly reveals the clash of paradigms felt in the young nation of Canada, just as it also mirrors the struggle for scientific respectability and secularism that had recently occurred to create the University of Toronto.

McCurdy's method, however, is in many respects more similar to that found in the likes of Grant and Jordan. Like the latter two, McCurdy is interested in the clear articulation of a method that will guide his comparative analysis. Unlike theirs, however, his actual comparison is much more small-scale and rigorous. Grant and Jordan, as is not untypical of the comparative project more generally, tend instead to work with essentialized notions of what each religion is or should be.

We are able to witness the impact McCurdy's work had on other Canadian scholars. W.G. Jordan, a biblical scholar at Queen's in Kingston, reviewed the final volume of McCurdy's *History, Prophecy, and the Monuments* (1901). In that review, he wrote that "the significant thing about this volume is that the author, one of Dr. Green's [McCurdy's mentor at Princeton] most distinguished pupils, accepts cordially and unreservedly 'the documentary theory' of the Pentateuch against which the great Princeton scholar fought so valiantly to the very last."[78]

With this we see just how far higher criticism has come and how it has, for all intents and purposes, entered the Canadian academic mainstream. Certainly there would be hold-outs, but with McCurdy, who was responsible for training the next generation of biblical scholars in Canada, the path had been forged. The following years would see the rise of biblical and Oriental studies in numerous universities and colleges and even in some of the affiliated theological colleges within the University of Toronto. Canadian scholars were also beginning to enter the world stage of Near Eastern studies and Egyptology. Samuel Alfred Brown Mercer (1880–1969), for example, born in England but raised in Newfoundland, received his PhD in biblical studies from Harvard before going on to become one of the world's leading Egyptologists. He was the only Canadian present when Tutankhamun's tomb was opened in 1922.[79]

Conclusions

In the writings of the individuals discussed in this chapter we see three clear examples of what the study of religion looked like in Canada in the late Victorian period. The first model, which I think is safe to say is that of the overwhelming majority of scholars, is decidedly theological in scope and Christocentric in terms of conclusions reached. One such scholar examined in this chapter is James Beaven, who was engaged in religious apologetics. Another is John Dawson, who fought hard against the emergence of the new sciences, be they natural or biblical. The second model witnesses scholars of religion beginning to recognize the liabilities of such approaches and, in their stead, offering correctives that acknowledge that other religions exist in the world which, while inferior to Christianity, are nevertheless worthy of study. We now begin to see the emergence of reflection on the very category of "religion." Examples of such scholars include Grant and Jordan. The third model, presented by the likes of McCurdy, seeks to historicize the biblical text by situating it in the larger context of the Ancient Near East.

It is important to be aware, however, that none of this was unique to Canada. All of the methods mentioned in the previous paragraph, and examined at length in this chapter, were ultimately imported from abroad, be it England, Germany, or the United States. What *is* significant is the reception these methods received in Canadian institutions and how they contributed to what would become the academic study of religion in the country.

We must, however, also remember the fallout from this reception. As higher criticism entered universities, seminaries, and even local churches, there was considerable turmoil. Many resisted higher criticism because, for them, the Bible was the inspired word of God and thus immune from the types of interrogation and criticism reserved for more mundane texts. The late Victorian period, in sum, was a tumultuous one for the study of religion in Canada. Yet it was also a period that would have a profound impact on the future. Without the more "secular" approaches taken by scholars like Grant and Jordan on the one hand, and McCurdy on the other, the academic and largely secular study of religion would have looked considerably different, and more apologetic, in the following decades.

Chapter Four

Westward Bound

As should be clear from even the quickest glance at a globe or a map, Canada is a huge country, extending from the Atlantic to the Pacific and north up to the Arctic Ocean, covering a land mass of roughly 10 million square kilometres. On account of its northern climate, it has a relatively sparse population of roughly 36 million people, most of whom live quite close to the 49th parallel. Today, the country is divided into ten provinces and three northern territories, with the provinces frequently charting their own courses in many different jurisdictions, including social policy and higher education.[1] Indeed, as Donald J. Savoie has noted, a pressing Canadian question is how the country can continue to function as a national union in light of the fact that it has become increasingly factionalized along regional lines.[2] This regionalism has increasingly defined Canada, with each region – western Canada, central Canada, Quebec, and Atlantic Canada – in possession of a distinct history. This is no less true for the academic study of religion. Each region or province frequently had its own set of unique concerns, and these concerns would, in turn, influence how religion was configured both institutionally and socially. As we saw in previous chapters, most of the provincial universities in Ontario (e.g., the University of Toronto, McMaster, Queen's), had their origins in denominational seminaries. By contrast, what would become the provincial universities west of Manitoba – in Saskatchewan, Alberta, and British Columbia – did not. If anything, they set out to avoid the types of problems that had developed in eastern Canada. These differences reveal the great diversity among the provinces regarding the role and function of religion in higher education, as well as the sheer difficulty of drawing superficial comparisons.

In this larger context, and perhaps paradoxically, Canada possesses both an "old" world and a "new" one. The earliest provinces – Nova

Scotia, New Brunswick, Quebec, and Ontario – quite early on developed their own institutions and organizations, many of which were modelled on those found in the United Kingdom or, in the case of Quebec, in France. These were the provinces, perhaps not surprisingly, that witnessed the greatest denominational battles and the most vitriolic struggles against attempts to establish one religious tradition, Anglicanism, at the expense of others. Western Canada – from Manitoba to British Columbia – had a different set of concerns and tended to look less toward Britain (with its supposedly superior Oxbridge model of education) and more toward the United States, and the land grant and state universities developed there. This meant that religion, at least initially, was frowned upon, especially given the problems that divinity and theological seminaries had created at eastern universities. Many of the earliest administrators of western Canadian universities came from eastern Canada, and they sought to avoid the denominational battles in higher education they had witnessed there. There was not nearly the same desire to establish one religion in the West; however, religion played a central role in the political sphere, particularly in Alberta and Saskatchewan, in the first half of the twentieth century.

This certainly does not mean there were no connections between eastern Canada and the newly developing West. This connection is perhaps best exemplified by the building of the Canadian Pacific Railway (CPR), one of the longest railway lines ever built up to that time. It was what joined the Atlantic to the Pacific, and some provinces only agreed to join Confederation because it was promised. Not infrequently, educators associated with eastern universities – most notably McGill and the University of Toronto – journeyed west on the CPR with the aim of establishing new institutions of higher education. It was these individuals, perhaps the most famous being the indefatigable Henry Marshall Tory (1864–1947), who sought to avoid the sectarian problems that had plagued the creation of centres of higher learning in the four founding provinces. He and others envisioned colleges and universities for the "new century" that would include women and avoid religion tests or affiliations.

While this mistrust of religion would have repercussions for the secular and humanistic study of religion, it is important to be aware that such studies would not appear until several decades later. There was no history of teaching religion in these new institutions; however, it is also worth noting that they also lacked a tradition of Oriental studies – a tradition that, as seen in the previous chapter, functioned as an important prerequisite for the secular study of religion in some eastern universities. Thus as late as the 1960s and '70s, these western universities would still have to draw on models imported from eastern Canada. However, in keeping with the tenor of my study, it is also worth noting that the institutional structures set in place in these early years would have repercussions for how that study would later be imagined and configured.

Before I examine these institutional structures, it is necessary to trace, however briefly, some of the broader historical, social, and economic contexts that made the West possible.

Confederation

On 19 March 1867, the British North America Act (since 1982, referred to as the Constitution Act) established the new Dominion of Canada:

> It shall be lawful for the Queen, by and with the Advice of Her Majesty's Most Honourable Privy Council, to declare by Proclamation that, on and after a Day therein appointed, not being more than Six Months after the passing of this Act, the Provinces of Canada, Nova Scotia, and New Brunswick shall form and be One Dominion under the Name of Canada; and on and after that Day those Three Provinces shall form and be One Dominion under that Name accordingly.[3]

Confederation thus represents the process whereby the original British colonies – Canada (the combined Upper and Lower, and then West and East), Nova Scotia, and New Brunswick – were united into a semi-independent Dominion on 1 July 1867. Upon Confederation, the old province of Canada was divided into Ontario and Quebec, with the result that, along with Nova Scotia and New Brunswick, the new country consisted of four provinces.[4] Those provinces and territories that subsequently became part of Canada after 1867 are also said to have joined, or entered into, confederation (but technically not *the* Confederation).

After the initial Act of Union in 1867, the Province of Manitoba was subsequently established by an act of the Canadian Parliament on 15 July 1870, over the objections of the Métis,[5] who rebelled under their leader, Louis Riel.[6] British Columbia joined Confederation on 20 July 1871, with the proviso that the federal government agree to build a railway connecting the new province with the rest of Canada within ten years of union. Prince Edward Island joined Confederation on 1 July 1873, also contingent upon the federal government operating a ferry link to the mainland.[7] Acts of the Canadian Parliament subsequently established Alberta and Saskatchewan on 1 September 1905. And Newfoundland joined on 31 March 1949, again contingent upon the establishment of a ferry link.

Confederation, while certainly influenced by the same forces of liberalism that had created American republicanism, was nevertheless a conscious attempt to avoid the latter's perceived excesses and violence.[8] Canadian politicians – indeed, many Canadians – were horrified by the bloodshed of the American Civil War. Canadians tended to favour a monarchical form of government, one that would maintain close links to Great Britain, over a republican one. John A. Macdonald, the first prime minister of Canada, speaking in 1865, had the following to say about the proposed Confederation and the need to differentiate the new country from the United States:

> It is the fashion now to enlarge on the defects of the Constitution of the United States, but I am not one of those who look upon it as a failure. I think and believe that it is one of the most skillful works which human intelligence ever created; is one of the most perfect organizations that ever governed a free people. To say that it has some defects is but to say that it is not the work of omniscience, but of human intellects. We are happily situated in having had the opportunity of watching its operation, seeing its working from its infancy till now. It was in the main formed on the model of the Constitution of Great Britain, adapted to the circumstances of a new country, and was perhaps the only practicable system that could have been adopted under the circumstances existing at the time of its formation. We can now take advantage of the experience of the last seventy-eight years during which that Constitution has existed, and I am strongly in the belief that we have in a great measure avoided in this system which we propose for the adoption of the people of Canada the defects which time and events have shown to exist in the American Constitution.[9]

Confederation sought to preserve ties with Great Britain by, among other things, having the monarchy function as the foundation of all branches of the federal and provincial governments: the executive (Queen-in-Council), the legislative (Queen-in-Parliament), and the judicial (Queen-on-the-Bench). This means that the monarch of Britain is, by definition, the monarch of Canada, who is represented in the country by the Governor General, a political appointment made by the Queen on the advice of the prime minister.

It was only in 1982, through the Canada Act passed by the British Parliament at the request of the Canadian government, that the constitution was repatriated to Canada. While Canada's political history began with the British North America Act of 1867, which established Confederation, for all intents and purposes Canada only received its own constitution in 1982, which, as we shall see in chapter 7, would have major repercussions for the study of religion in the country.

The CPR

As we have seen, George Monro Grant, an early Canadian scholar of religion and a key institution builder at Queen's, in 1873 wrote a book titled *Ocean to Ocean* that recounted the surveying and building of the railway that would bind the new country together. According to him,

> by uniting together, the British Provinces had declared that their destiny was – not to ripen and drop, one by one, into the arms of the Republic – but to work out their own future as an integral and important part of the grandest Empire in the world ... But, to be united politically and disunited physically, as the different parts of Prussia were for many a long year, is an anomaly only to be endured so long as it cannot be helped; and when, as in our case, the remedy is in our own hands, it is wise to secure the material union as soon as possible.[10]

Here Grant echoes John A. Macdonald's words, cited above. If Confederation is one half of the story of the emergence of Canada, the building of a national railway to link the diverse regions of the new Dominion, so that it would not be "disunited physically," is the other half. In 1881, some fifteen years after Confederation, the Canadian Pacific Railway began laying track west from Ontario in an effort to link together the newly expanding country.[11] It was completed in 1885 and, though troubled by delays and scandal, was ultimately considered an impressive feat of engineering and political will for a country with such a small population and with such vast and difficult terrain.[12]

Nineteenth-century Canada was largely wilderness. The CPR received from the federal government more than 25 million acres (100,000 km^2) on the prairies as part of its payment for building the railway. To make money from that land, it launched a campaign to attract immigrants to Canada. To that end, Canadian Pacific agents operated in many overseas locations, where they sold prospective immigrants packages that included passage on a CP ship (to Canada), and travel on a CP train (across Canada), as well as CP land for $2.50 an acre.[13]

Thus the CPR was instrumental in populating western Canada. To transport immigrants, it developed a fleet of more than a thousand "colonist cars," low-budget sleeper cars designed to transport families to the West from eastern Canadian seaports. These helped populate the prairies – Alberta and Saskatchewan – which grew at a rapid rate during the early years of the twentieth century.[14]

Universities were subsequently established in these western provinces to train the new populations. Unlike in the eastern provinces, however, these universities were not – not even initially – run along denominational lines. The new provinces did have seminaries, but these did not form the nucleus for new universities as they had in the East. Again, the model was American state universities, often referred to as land grant institutions. These were based on the Morrill Acts of 1862 and 1890, which allowed states to use the proceeds of federal land sales to establish and endow "land grant" colleges.[15] Based on the mandate of the 1862 Act, these institutions tended to focus more on practical subjects such as agriculture, science, and engineering. Though this did not necessarily mean the exclusion of more traditional classical and literary topics, state lawmakers recognized that the mandate of these universities was to educate the citizens of their states in ways that would benefit the state rather than train elite men for divinity. Moreover, religion was forbidden from being taught at such institutions owing to the legal separation of Church and State in the United States. As we will see in a later chapter, this would not change until the US Supreme Court ruling in *School District of Abington Township, PA v. Schempp*.

Western Canada: Four Paradigms of Universities

The four major universities in western Canada – the University of Saskatchewan, the University of Alberta, the University of Manitoba, and the University of British Columbia – all emerged in rather specific local and political contexts. If their model was American land grant institutions, all, with the possible exception of UBC, still had to deal with – whether by repudiation or absorption – pre-existing theological colleges. The result was four paradigms, which, while distinct, shared the desire not to reproduce the denominationalism and sectarianism that had plagued so many educational institutions in eastern Canada.

University of Saskatchewan

The first university in what would become the Province of Saskatchewan was Emmanuel College, founded in 1879 in Prince Albert.[16] It was later incorporated by a Dominion statute, which gave to it degree-granting powers, and at which point, in 1883, it became known as "the University of Emmanuel College." It was, however, an Anglican and not a secular institution, and in 1907, two years after the province joined

Confederation, Rev. George Exton Lloyd, its principal, welcomed sixty catechists from England with the intention of establishing a three-year course in theology.[17] As was so often the case with these institutions that imagined themselves to be universities or centres of higher learning, the goal was simultaneously to train clergy, establish churches and schools, and help "civilize" Indigenous populations.[18]

After Confederation, however, in 1907, the new provincial legislature created a non-sectarian University of Saskatchewan, which was to be located in Saskatoon.[19] Walter Charles Murray of Dalhousie University in Halifax was appointed its first president. Emmanuel College,[20] which saw itself as the original University of Saskatchewan, initially resisted but was eventually persuaded that the new institution in Saskatoon would be *the* University of Saskatchewan.[21] Emmanuel subsequently relocated to Saskatoon and affiliated itself with the new provincial university.[22]

In September 1909, classes began, with seventy students, about half of whom were supplied by Emmanuel.[23] The goal of the Faculty of Arts and Sciences was to prepare students – again, the model being American land grant universities – for one of the professional schools such as medicine, education, or divinity. Since the University of Saskatchewan was not chartered for theological education, the latter had to occur in the context of the Anglican-affiliated Emmanuel College.[24] Nevertheless, the BA degree at the University of Saskatchewan allowed students who were interested in proceeding into divinity to specialize in Greek and Hebrew with "three theological options" (i.e., Anglican, Presbyterian, Lutheran).[25]

Saskatchewan being a farming province, it is no surprise that the new university's administrators focused their attention on agriculture. Many did not want the agriculture school, which required a farm, to be in a different location. A three-man team visited a number of state universities in the American Midwest to see what they did.[26] On 15 November 1908, they handed their report to the university's Board of Governors, its Senate, and the provincial government:

> We believe that union will prevent both the waste due to separate institutions and the demoralizing rivalry which too frequently appears between them. Union will also secure for the teachers trained in the University the advantages of courses in Agriculture and Domestic Science, and will in this way greatly facilitate the introduction of the teaching of Agriculture into our Public and High Schools. While union will place at the disposal of the students of Agriculture the literary, social, and scientific advantages of the University, it will also bring the University students into close touch

> with Agriculture and quicken their interest in the great industry of the Province.[27]

In other words, the agricultural college should not be separate from the university. If the two were amalgamated, young men and women would receive both practical and theoretical wisdom.

Murray, the first president, sought good relations with the various religious denominations, many of which had developed their own theological seminaries. He welcomed university affiliation with them – with none of the debates that had coincided with affiliation at the University of Toronto – and he offered space on campus to those that wished to affiliate.[28] St. Thomas More College, for example, founded in 1936 by the Catholic Basilian Fathers (Order of St. Basil) of Toronto, was located on the university's Saskatoon campus. It functions to this day as an arts college in federation with the university and offers courses that lead to a BA in the latter. The college provided recreational and devotional activities to Catholic students at the university, which, however, refused to be financially responsible for its maintenance.

In like manner, two Anglican institutions – St. Chad's, formed in Regina in 1907, and the aforementioned Emmanuel College – both relocated to Saskatoon to affiliate with the University of Saskatchewan in 1910. In 1964 they amalgamated to form the College of Emmanuel and St. Chad, which remains to this day the Anglican college on campus.[29] St. Andrew's, a Presbyterian college before that denomination joined the United Church, affiliated with the university in 1913. And in 1925, Lutheran College and Seminary (German Lutheran Synod), originally located in Edmonton, affiliated with the University of Saskatchewan. Finally, in 1949, Luther Theological Seminary (Evangelical Lutheran Church) affiliated, with the two Lutheran schools merging as the Luther Theological Seminary in 1958. All of these affiliated colleges were to be "self-dependent, self-supporting, and self-governing" and "able to secure for their students, at minimum cost, a Bachelor of Arts course of high standard and yet of specialized value to divinity students."[30] The University of Saskatchewan, then, had no problem configuring its BA degree to the needs of these various theological denominations.

By the 1920s some religious denominations had established small "colleges" in Saskatchewan, which functioned as residential schools (though not in the sense as described in chapter 1), where students could enrol in a secondary school program in order to prepare for university matriculation. In 1924 the university's senate empowered the university's council to recognize such denominational colleges as junior colleges of the university and to allow them, under certain conditions, to offer classes equivalent to the first year BA course.[31] Like the affiliated theological colleges, they had to demonstrate that their courses would be of equal quality to those of the university. In 1926, four such colleges arose, and many of these had a religious affiliation: Regina College (originally Methodist and then United); Campion College and Sacred Heart Academy (Catholic, both in Regina); and St. Peter's College (Catholic, in Muenster).

Regina College, which had been founded as one of these residential high schools in 1911, was in dire financial difficulty in the 1930s. Thanks to a grant from the Carnegie Corporation in New York City, the college became the Regina branch of the University of Saskatchewan in 1934, before becoming the University of Regina in 1974.[32] Campion College federated with the latter university in 1966, and Luther did the same in 1971.[33]

Campion College had been founded in 1917 as the "Catholic College of Regina." The Archbishop of Regina, O.E. Mathieu, the former rector of Laval, had hoped that the college would become an independent Roman Catholic university.[34] Under the control of the Jesuits, in 1925 it had, as just noted, junior college status with University of Saskatchewan. The college also ran a joint degree program with University of Manitoba (to be discussed shortly) on the topic of scholastic philosophy. This degree, however, was terminated in 1936 after the Manitoba government passed legislation that forbade out-of-province coursework. On 25 July 1960, Campion formally applied for federation with the newly formed University of Regina. Under the statutes of the latter's senate, a federated college had to satisfy three requirements: it "must be authorized by the University to give classes recognized for credit towards a Bachelor of Arts degree in the subjects of at least four departments of the College of Arts and Sciences"; "the members of the College staff teaching the above University courses must be recognized as members of the Faculty of Arts and Science"; and "the College must be situated on or adjacent to the main University campus."[35]

In 1963, Father Peter W. Nash became the rector of the college. Nash, who had a PhD in philosophy from the University of Toronto, arranged that Campion would be able to appoint its own faculty and give them promotion, though both decisions would require final approval from the president of the University of Regina. Through these negotiations, it was also established that courses offered at Campion College had to be "equivalent in extent and standards to [those] given in the University."[36] The agreement, however, did not specify whether Campion faculty were to be members of university departments or could attend departmental meetings. Nash was acutely aware of the tension between religious faith and secular learning, especially among faculty who were also clergy. In a lecture delivered to the Newman Convention in Edmonton in September 1968, he said:

> The Christian community wants to be inserted into that human reality, the University, in order to be enriched by it and to bring to it a new dimension. It has to be in the University in order to learn from the University if it is going to speak to contemporary society in language it understands. It has to be in the University, which, *par excellence*, is the frontier of new truth and the testing ground of old truths, if it is to live up to its declared devotion to truth. The Church must at its peril be genuinely involved in scholarship at the University level. Hence, it must seek to attract its members, cleric and lay, into serious scholarship and research and encourage them to become genuine scholars and teachers, dedicated to truth wherever it may be found, freely pursuing truth and proclaiming it responsibly. The Church cannot adequately witness to the Word of God without some of its members committed to scholarship not only in theological investigations but in secular subjects.[37]

Nash's statement here gets to the heart of the matter on the place of theology and theological studies in the secular university. If it is to be a part of the university, then it must open itself up to secular matters, including those of what will eventually appear as the academic and non-sectarian study of religion. This, of course, called the entire theological study of religion into question. Nevertheless, such statements show clearly how the University of Saskatchewan largely avoided the types of debates witnessed in the eastern part of the country.

University of Alberta

The population of Alberta expanded rapidly from some 73,000 people in 1901 to more than 375,000 by 1911.[38] Since Calgary was tied to the Conservative Party in national politics, and Edmonton to the Liberals, it was perhaps only natural that Wilfrid Laurier, the Liberal prime minister at the time, chose the latter as the provincial capital in 1905.[39] At its first session in 1906, Alberta's newly formed government passed an act, sponsored by Alexander Cameron Rutherford (premier and Minister of Education) for the establishment of a provincial university,[40] for which the proposed institution would be granted 258 acres on river lot #5.[41] Rutherford, an alumnus of McGill, recruited the formidable Henry Marshall Tory,[42] a professor of physics there, to be the new president "of a university without staff, students, or buildings."[43]

Tory's initial journey out west was to Vancouver to examine the feasibility of establishing a college there that would affiliate with McGill.[44] On his return journey, he also toured Alberta and Saskatchewan to ascertain the feasibility of establishing affiliated colleges there.[45] Tory, like Rutherford, was a devout Christian; he was also an ordained Methodist minister (though he resigned from the ministry in 1906).[46] Despite this, both he and Rutherford were determined to avoid any religious affiliation with the new province's university. Tory was a Nova Scotian and was acutely aware of his home province's pattern of small denominational colleges that were primarily focused on the training of clergy and that subsequently divided available resources to such a degree that no institution could advance beyond what he considered to be mediocrity. Also, as a scientist, Tory was wary of the constraints that religious orthodoxy might impose on scholars and researchers.[47] In like manner, Rutherford – himself a Baptist, and vice-president of the national Lord's Day Alliance – wanted to avoid the University of Toronto's model, which was being replicated, as we shall see shortly, both in Manitoba and British Columbia. That model, it will be recalled, created universities as examining bodies that were subsequently dependent on poorly funded denominational colleges to do their teaching. Both men desired to create a new university for the new century.[48] As such, there would be no religious affiliation, no religious tests, and women would be admitted.

In his first meeting with his new senate on 30 March 1908, Tory, aware of what had happened in places like the University of Toronto and Queen's remarked that

> the establishment and organization of a university is a great work in which only few can participate. We are not called upon, fortunately, to reorganize some old, disrupted institution, but we are laying the foundations of a university as a whole. We can congratulate ourselves on the fact that we are not called upon to deal with religious strifes of any nature, but are starting the work as a united body. We ought to realize too that we cannot cut loose from tradition. We must use tradition as a guide, and take from it the best that it contains as a lead for us in our work.[49]

Thereupon he set about recruiting professors of classics, English, and modern languages: William Hardy Alexander in classics (recruited from the University of Western Ontario); Luther Herbert Alexander in modern languages (recruited from Columbia in New York City, and who returned there after one year); Edmund Kemper Broadus in English (recruited from Harvard); and William Muir Edwards in mathematics and civil engineering.[50] None, of course, were in Divinity. Broadus subsequently wrote about his meeting with Tory:

> On a day in June, 1908, the president of a university not yet in being, in a province which I have never heard of, in a country which I have never visited, came to Harvard and offered me the professorship of English. The offer sounded like midsummer madness. I think that what I accepted was, not the position or the salary, but the man. There was something about him that made me feel that to whatever no-man's land he went, there – somehow – the kind of university I should like to have a hand in would get to be.[51]

As many as one quarter of the original matriculates were candidates for the ministry from Alberta College, a Methodist institution that had been in operation since 1903, which eventually became affiliated with the United Church and became, in 1927, St. Stephen's College.[52] Rutherford and Tory worked out a model that would allow denominational colleges a presence on campus, but their teaching would have to be confined strictly to theological topics. In return, they would be allowed one representative on the university senate.[53]

Faculty saw it as their goal to "impart appropriate social values along with academic training."[54] To inculcate this across the young province, Tory set up "extension lectures" that involved faculty travelling to rural areas to give lectures. Tory was also instrumental in forming the so-called Khaki University, an educational institution set up and managed by the Canadian army in Britain at the end of the First World War.[55] Its purpose was to boost morale during the war and to provide personnel with an opportunity to continue their education in preparation for re-entering civilian life after the war. The first classes were taught by university-educated chaplains and officers, who served as instructors and spiritual counsellors. Tory now sought to make the program more mainstream. He wrote: "I would strongly recommend that plans be put on foot to plant an educational institution into one central camp, a University in Khaki – say the Khaki University of Canada – where practically all branches of study that could possibly be offered and with the Extension Department going out to every other camp in the country."[56]

Once the Canadian government formally recognized Khaki University, Canadian universities began sending professors to Europe to augment the skeleton force of teachers from military headquarters. Khaki University credits were recognized as equivalent to those of Canadian institutions.[57] It was Tory who, in his typical whirlwind fashion, contacted all Canadian universities and provincial departments of education to arrange acceptance of Khaki University courses.

University of Manitoba

The Red River Settlement was founded by Lord Selkirk in 1812 at the confluence of the Red and Assiniboine Rivers. It subsequently became the largest community of "mixed blood" people in western North America (the term Métis would only be employed later).[58] In 1869 the Hudson Bay watershed (also known as Rupert's Land) was ceded to Canada by the Hudson's Bay Company and incorporated into the Northwest Territories.[59] The federal government's unwillingness to address Métis concerns about their religion, culture, and political voice spurred Louis Riel, their leader, to establish a local provisional government as part of the Red River Rebellion, which became the first crisis of the young, post-Confederation Canada. Prime Minister John A. Macdonald responded by introducing the Manitoba Act in the House of Commons, as a result of which Manitoba was brought into Canada as a province in 1870. Its principal city, Winnipeg, was incorporated in 1873.

Even before the Red River Rebellion, it was thought that without religion and education, there would be no way to "civilize" (read "anglicize") the Métis. In 1818 the first Protestant clergyman arrived in what is now Manitoba – Rev. John West, the chaplain to the Hudson's Bay Company, who soon opened a Bible school.[60] That same year the first Catholic priests arrived and set up a school to administer to the area's French-speaking Catholics, many of whom were Métis.

In 1833 the Hudson's Bay Company established the Red River Academy at Upper Church. At that time it was the only source of secondary education for Protestant children.[61] The academy would become St. John's Collegiate School in 1850, making it the oldest anglophone educational institution in western Canada.[62] The new institution was meant, as Bishop Machray commented in 1865, to "establish a College for the training of those who wish a better education, in the fear of God, in useful learning, and in conscientious attachment to our Church."[63] Its main goal was to engage in missionary work among Métis and Indigenous peoples.[64]

On 3 May 1871, St. John's College was incorporated by an act of the provincial legislature. According to its constitution, its purpose was "to prepare fit persons for the sacred ministry, to provide instruction in the higher branches of education usually taught in universities, and to provide a collegiate school."[65] Bishop Machray had wanted a charter for the college so that it would be able to offer theological degrees;

however, unlike Strachan, the Bishop of Toronto, he did not want Anglican control of general education. Instead, he hoped that a provincial university would minister secular education for the province.

Two other denominational colleges were later founded: St. Boniface College, a French-language Catholic institution, was established in 1818 and incorporated in 1871; Manitoba College, a Presbyterian seminary, was created in 1869 in Kildonan but moved to Winnipeg in 1874. These two colleges, along with St. John's, would be the founding colleges of the University of Manitoba, which was established by a provincial act on 28 February 1877.[66] It was created so that bright young men would not have to go elsewhere to receive an education (and, most likely, never return to the province). The three theological colleges, then, would have the newly created university function as an abstract degree-granting body.[67]

Bishop Machray's hope was for a secular provincial university that would have affiliated denominational colleges to teach theology, not unlike what would be the case in Alberta and Saskatchewan. What he got instead was the University of London model: federated colleges in which the university would function as nothing more than an administrative unit that examined candidates for degrees and subsequently granted them. This meant that St. John's College, along with the other two institutions, had to create a secular faculty of arts and sciences in order to share the burden of the teaching now imposed on them by the enabling legislation.[68]

In 1901 the Legislative Assembly of Manitoba amended the University Act so that the university could do its own teaching. This led, in the words of J.M. Bumstead, to three models for colleges:

> One strategy was to continue as if the university had not come into existence. This was the choice adopted by St. Boniface College and Wesley College. Another was to give up non-theological teaching to the university. This was the strategy of Manitoba College, which then merged what was left of its operation with Wesley as United College. The third strategy was to attempt to fit a curriculum within the university structure. This would be the choice of Saint John's College.[69]

The model for teaching in both the university and the colleges remained the British model. This might seem strange in a province in desperate need of skilled professionals. However, it is important to note that colleges were intended, in the first place, to be the training ground for clergymen, and in the second place, to serve their denominations as undergraduate liberal arts institutions. In such institutions, the emphasis had always been on building character and leadership rather than on specific professional skills.

University of British Columbia

British Columbia joined the Dominion of Canada in 1871.[70] Early debates on higher education involved whether or not the new province should establish a practical curriculum or develop a more liberal arts curriculum. As with the University of Alberta, the early framers of the proposed provincial university wanted it to be non-denominational and secular.[71] Although a University Act was passed as early as 26 April 1890, the university would take years to materialize on account of political upheavals.[72] In 1892 the Methodist Church established Columbian Methodist College and affiliated with Victoria College in Ontario,[73] which itself had recently affiliated with the University of Toronto.[74] Soon thereafter, Columbian College began offering theology degrees and, to a very small number of students, a year of an arts curriculum. Indeed, the hope – and this was a recurring pattern in the early years of post-secondary instruction in British Columbia – was that a student could complete another province's arts degree, be it at the University of Toronto or McGill, without having to leave the province.

In 1894 the Vancouver School Board approached the University of Toronto and McGill to sponsor university-level instruction in the local high school. The University of Toronto was legally unable to spend funds outside of Ontario, but McGill could, since it was a private institution with a royal as opposed to a provincial charter.[75] Thus McGill had already set matriculation exams for students across Canada. In addition, McGill's chancellor, Donald Smith, was a principal shareholder in the CPR, which was a powerful force in BC's economy. In 1896 the Vancouver High School curriculum was brought into line with McGill's arts and sciences program. By 1902 it was able to offer the second year of the McGill arts program (which included sciences and mathematics).[76]

The new school, called Vancouver High School and College, registered its first university-level students in 1899. It officially affiliated with McGill in 1903, and in 1905 Henry Marshall Tory came to BC with the aim of expanding the affiliation between Vancouver College and McGill. In 1906 a bill was drafted that permitted McGill "to establish a college in [BC] with the functions and privileges set out in the McGill charter."[77] This effectively created a new University College, which would offer the first years of the McGill curriculum to residents of the new province. This, despite the objections of local graduates from U of

T, who thought this unduly favoured McGill. People in Victoria, the provincial capital, also objected, fearing they might be left behind.

Notwithstanding such objections, on 20 February 1906, McGill University College of BC (often just called McGill BC) came into existence.[78] For the first few years all exams were set at and marked in Montreal. Initially it was in the same space as Vancouver College, but in 1907 it moved into its own building. That same year, Richard McBride's Conservatives were re-elected with a big majority – marking the first time a government had been re-elected in BC – and with the mandate to get things done. It had been an embarrassment to many in BC, which prized itself as western Canada's leading province, that Alberta and Saskatchewan, the other two western provinces, had already established their own universities. To correct this, the new government created a land endowment that would support a provincial university.[79] On 7 March 1908, UBC was born by a provincial act, with women to be admitted and with a practical rather than an Oxbridge mandate. However, the actual university did not open up until 1915.[80]

This section has surveyed the founding of the four main universities in western Canada in the years immediately following Confederation. There would certainly be other universities in each province – the University of Winnipeg in Manitoba, the University of Regina in Saskatchewan, the University of Calgary and University of Lethbridge in Alberta, and the University of Victoria in British Columbia, some of which will make appearances in chapter 8 below – yet it was these four institutions that established the paradigm for how higher education would be structured in each province.

As far as the academic study of religion is concerned, while these four institutions had much less tortured relationships with the various denominations, they were all quite clear that religion would play no role in higher education in their provinces. While most of these universities had no problems with denominational colleges affiliating with them, many sought to avoid the University of Toronto model, which gave the colleges more power and which made the university little more than a degree-granting administrative unit. Most of the theological colleges and seminaries that affiliated with universities in western Canada had to abide by clearly defined rules about what they could and could not do and what topics they could and could not teach. This reflected a conscious decision to avoid the types of problems experienced in eastern Canada.

It is also worth noting that in order for the secular study of religion to develop, many of these early issues over secularism and the role of religion in a public university would have to be revisited. In this context, many secular universities in the 1960s and early 1970s were worried, as we shall see in chapter 8, that newly configured departments of religious studies would once again threaten the line that had earlier been drawn between the secular and the religious.

Two Models of Religion and Politics on the Prairies: William Aberhart and Tommy Douglas

Religion, of course, was hardly confined to universities. It is a paradox that the two provinces that had done the most to create secular universities that were not encroached upon by theological seminaries, produced two governments during the interwar years that were among the most religious the young country had hitherto seen. As in eastern Canada, the turn of the century and the rise of the Great Depression would see many people turn to religion for solace and social change. In the latter regard, the prairie provinces of Alberta and Saskatchewan became hotbeds of political change whose governments were heavily infused with religious sentiment and were themselves connected to some of the religious institutions surveyed above. Yet at the same time, as we shall see, these two provinces had radically different ideas about the place and role of religion in the public square. This section puts in counterpoint the idiosyncratic fundamentalism of William Aberhart's Social Credit government in Alberta and the Social Gospel of Tommy Douglas's Co-operative Commonwealth Federation (CCF) in Saskatchewan.

William Aberhart was born in Egmondville, Ontario, and grew up Presbyterian in a not particularly religious family. At some point during his high school years, he experienced a religious conversion.[81] He subsequently trained to be a teacher, and during one of his first positions in Brantford he became attracted to dispensationalism, a form of Christianity that maintained that God had divided history into distinct periods, each of which was to be administered in a certain way, and with humanity held up as the responsible steward during that time. This form of Christianity was especially popular in southern Ontario at the time and was articulated at the Niagara Bible Conferences, which attracted dispensationalists from the region and throughout the United States. Aberhart credited Cyrus Ingerson Scofield (1843–1921) as an important influence.[82] Scofield, a denominationalist, taught that between creation and the Final Judgment there were seven distinct eras that would delineate God's relationship with humanity and through which the Bible could be explained.[83] Perhaps most importantly, Scofield developed a correspondence Bible course that formed the basis for his *Reference Bible*, an annotated and widely circulated study Bible that would be published by Oxford University Press in 1909.[84] Scofield's correspondence courses helped spread dispensational premillennialism among fundamentalist Christians in the United States and Canada.[85] Aberhart would claim that "it was Dr. Scofield who started me on my Bible study. He advertised a Correspondence Course of some fourteen lectures for $5.00. I sent for it and his first four lessons started me on a path that has proved more bright as the days go by."[86]

Aberhart began to develop a fundamentalist outlook, one wherein he disapproved of the theatre, card playing, drinking, and smoking. In the early 1900s he began preaching as a layman. He would take his bike to semi-rural schools and preach to locals. He struck up many friendships with individuals associated with the Moody Bible Institute in Chicago, founded by Dwight L. Moody (1837–1899), a non-conformist Evangelical preacher.[87] It was around this time that he decided to study for the ministry. He enrolled in a correspondence program at Queen's University in Kingston. He took his entire degree by correspondence without interacting with his teachers or fellow students. His marks were very poor: he failed Greek twice and Hebrew once and received a grade of 35 per cent in political science.[88]

While studying for the ministry (he graduated with a BA in 1911), he began to teach throughout southern Ontario. His main interest was in the Rapture as espoused, for example, by the Plymouth Brethren, who rejected the Social Gospel and instead preached about how the Bible prophesied social turmoil at the end of days.[89] In 1910 he moved to Calgary to take up a position at a new school. Calgary was at that time a place where the denominational lines between Presbyterians, Methodists, and Baptists were rather fluid – and Aberhart would function as a supply preacher for all. Previously he had toyed with the idea of becoming a Presbyterian minister, but it was now becoming quite clear to him, and to others, that his own ideas were moving theologically beyond that denomination.[90] At Wesley Methodist Church, he met Nellie McClung, the famous Canadian suffragette, who would become a frequent guest speaker at Aberhart's schools and who worked closely with him when he became chairman of the Prohibition campaign sponsored by all of Calgary's Sunday schools. He subsequently moved to Westbourne Baptist Church, where he continued to preach and essentially became the leader of the church, though he was neither an ordained minister nor even a Baptist. He had the largest Bible study class in the city, and it became so popular that he had to hold it in the public library. According to Elliot and Miller, Aberhart "came to be recognized by the Baptist Union as Westbourne's lay minister; but his powerful personality, his obsessive desire to preach, his refusal to become ordained and submit to ecclesiastical authority, and the unusual beliefs he had been teaching were of continued concern to Baptist officials. He had developed a theology peculiar to himself."[91]

His rallying cry was "The Bible, the whole Bible, and nothing but the Bible!" He held the 1611 King James Version to embody the literal, unabridged, and undiluted Word of God, and he was extremely critical of all developments in textual criticism, archaeology, and the study of cognate Near Eastern languages that had shed new light on biblical studies.[92] He excoriated biblical scholars who knew Greek and Hebrew, whom he accused of forming a guild that functioned as a type of modern priesthood. This may well have been based on his own failure in those languages at Queen's. Aberhart increasingly defined his own fundamentalist outlook in contrast to the higher criticism he had witnessed at Queen's.

He continued to preach of the Rapture, which, for him, signalled the "divine evacuation" of Christians from this world. It was, he believed, an event that was imminent and could happen at any moment. He connected it, as others did, to the current political situation: the Rapture would occur after unprecedented chaos and a war in which China and Japan attacked the West. From this would emerge a charismatic Antichrist, who would be born to a Jewess living in Turkey and who would pretend to be a diplomat.[93] There were clear anti-Semitic overtones in his message:

> As a result of the league of the Antichrist, the Jews would be allowed to build their temple in Jerusalem and resume the daily sacrificial system. However, after several years, Great Britain would perceive that the Jews were being used by the Antichrist and would launch an attack on Russia – but it would fail. The Antichrist would then stop the daily sacrifices in Jerusalem and desecrate the temple – whereupon 144,000 loyal Jews, 12,000 from each of the twelve tribes, would oppose him and be killed in battle.[94]

As can be seen from this description, Aberhart – not unlike other dispensationalists – filtered world events associated with the First World War and its aftermath through a strange theological prism. His ideas were gradually becoming closer to Pentecostalism, and he decided to be baptized into that tradition in 1920. Around this time, he also founded the Calgary Prophetic Bible Conference, which evolved into one of several evangelical post-secondary schools in southern Alberta. In 1922, Aberhart became one of the most vocal leaders in a dispute at Brandon College (Baptist) – which mirrored the one that had occurred at McMaster a few years earlier: Baptist ministers from BC had accused the faculty there of being modernists and undermining the faith of their students, and Aberhart, not surprisingly, took the side of those ministers.

Aberhart is most famous for his "Back-to-the-Bible" radio broadcasts, which began in 1925. The broadcasts enabled him to reach thousands. And in 1926 he began his Radio Sunday School. The Calgary School Board grew uncomfortable with his principalship at a secular school on the one hand and his fundamentalist radio preaching on the other. Then came the stock market crash of 29 October 1929 and the subsequent Great Depression. It was in response to this that Major C.H. Douglas – a Scot who was obsessed with Jews taking over the world – developed his notion of Social Credit.[95] This political teaching, which was popular in the interwar years, stressed the need for radical monetary reform, so as to provide all citizens with a dividend as capital. In his "Yellow Pamphlet," a quasi-manifesto, Aberhart suggested that dividends be given "every month to every bona fide citizen in the form of credit."[96] This was not money; rather, it came in the form of non-negotiable certificates that would provide for necessities such as food and clothing.

Aberhart now began to link the current political situation explicitly to biblical prophecy. He became fascinated with Benito Mussolini, the Italian dictator, and claimed that the Antichrist was already alive and living incognito.[97] At one point he exclaimed that "one of the finest and greatest exponents of Social Credit was Jesus Christ Himself, His one mission in life was to feed and clothe His people."[98] Along with his friend and future political colleague, Ernest Manning, Aberhart produced a play in 1931 called *The Branding Irons of the Antichrist*, based on Sydney Watson's *Mark of the Beast*.

Aberhart began to talk more and more about economics on his radio shows. His "Yellow Pamphlet" shows clearly how his thought interweaved Social Credit economic theory with the Bible:

> The appeal of God today is for the individual to understand that God's policy is to provide man with a salvation full and free, without money and without price, and then to offer him future reward for his individual enterprise in the service of God. I am convinced that this is the basic principle of a practical economic system. Government credit, such as advocated by Major Douglas, gives to the individual, who is a bona fide citizen of the Province, the essentials of physical life, such as food, clothing, and shelter, and then offers him additional reward for his individual enterprise.[99]

As we see from this passage, Aberhart's preaching was becoming more secular and concerned with his own idiosyncratic understanding of social justice.[100] He now mobilized Social Credit into a political party. In the 1935 provincial election, it took fifty-six of the province's sixty-three seats. Social Credit would rule the province for the next thirty-five years.

Aberhart's government brought in needed reforms in education, labour relations, social welfare, and debt legislation. However, in terms of its ideology, "his administration was the most radical of any Canadian provincial government before or since."[101] As many of his biographers have noted, while he and his government sought to provide necessary social and economic reforms to address the ravages of the Depression, much of his ideology bordered on fascism, and his legislation was frequently overturned by the federal government on account of its illegality.

While his idiosyncratic theology brought him opposition from Pentecostals, Baptists, and other more "fundamentalist" denominational movements, paradoxically much of his political support came from people who belonged to mainline churches and who had only a marginal religious commitment.

In 1935, at the same time that Aberhart was taking the reins of political leadership in Alberta, another experiment in the admixture of religion and politics was taking place just to the east, in Saskatchewan. That same year, Tommy Douglas was elected as a federal MP for Saskatoon under the aegis of a new socialist party.

Tommy Douglas was born in 1904 in Falkirk, Scotland, and moved with his family to Winnipeg, Manitoba, in 1912.[102] His mother was a Baptist, his father a Presbyterian; as a young boy he was exposed to the Social Gospel movement through the All People's Mission in Winnipeg. The family moved back to Glasgow but returned to Canada in 1919, at the peak of the civil unrest brought on by the high inflation at the end of the First World War. Many farmers on the prairies were in debt to world markets, and the civil unrest and strife this created led to the Winnipeg General Strike, one of the most famous strikes in Canadian history, in May 1919, and to "Bloody Saturday" the following month.[103]

During these turbulent years, Douglas became a printer's apprentice and participated in local theatre productions. Like Aberhart, the young Douglas was a masterful rhetorician, and he was soon in demand as a speaker. He saw himself as a young radical who "wanted to work for social change as an expression of God's will for men on earth."[104] To further this goal, he decided to train for the ministry, and in 1924, he enrolled at Brandon College, the same Baptist seminary that Aberhart and other BC Baptist leaders had accused of liberalism a few years earlier. While attending Brandon College, the young Douglas realized that a literal interpretation of the Bible was naive.[105] Here we see the influence of such seminaries on the political landscape: higher biblical criticism had a lasting impact on both Aberhart and Douglas, negative in the case of the former and positive in the latter.[106]

As a seminary student he took charge of Knox Church (Presbyterian) in Carberry, Manitoba, and he preached vociferously against anti-Semitism in this rural region. When the stock market crashed in October 1929, he became a social activist and the leader of the Calvary Baptist Church in Weyburn, Saskatchewan, where the federal government began to monitor his activities.[107] In 1930 he took a leave from his church and went to the University of Chicago to begin (but never finish) a PhD in sociology.[108] In the summer of 1931 he did fieldwork in the slums of Chicago and began to realize just how dire things were, with different levels of government refusing to take responsibility for eradicating poverty. He also disliked the academics there, who were aware of the social pain and suffering and were willing to talk about it theoretically, but who refused to engage in the requisite activism to alleviate it.

When he returned to Saskatchewan, he began to preach sermons with political implications, including those dealing with "Jesus the Revolutionist." During this time, he was often asked by the United Farmers of Saskatchewan to speak at their meetings and then to lead their delegations to talk with the provincial government about the economic hard times.[109]

Meanwhile in July 1932, the Co-operative Commonwealth Federation (CCF) was founded in Calgary. This was a coalition of the Labour Party, the United Farmers of Alberta, and the railway union. The following year the CCF released its "Regina Manifesto," which outlined a socialist vision to improve society.[110] It called for, among other things, the creation of a central bank, the upholding of the rights of religious and ethnic minorities, and a Canadian constitution and charter of rights. It also advocated for standardized workplace conditions across the nation, publicly funded health care, unemployment insurance, and adequate pensions. These are things that all Canadians take for granted today, and it is worth noting that the CCF proposed them all in the name of Christianity.

In the 1935 federal election, Douglas ran as a CCF candidate in Saskatoon. He won, which made him one of seven CCF members elected. In 1942 he was elected the leader of the Saskatchewan CCF and led the party through a harshly negative campaign, in which his enemies, which included the banks, said that a CCF victory would take away farms, ban opposition, and so on. Douglas responded by telling voters they had a choice between "as [things] were before the war: a period of free enterprise and all the poverty it caused, or a change to a commonwealth of social justice."[111] The party won forty-seven of fifty-two seats, making it North America's first socialist government.

Douglas, who would go on to found the national left-of-centre New Democratic Party (NDP) in 1961, is widely recognized as the father of universal public health care in Canada. It should be clear that Douglas was not a communist, but a preacher of the Social Gospel, which argued for the equality of all people regardless of religion, race, or gender. Douglas, the Baptist minister, contended that "the religion of tomorrow will be less concerned with dogmas of theology and more concerned with the social welfare of humanity. When one sees the church spending its energies on the assertion of antiquated dogmas but dumb as an oyster to the poverty and misery all around, we can't help but recognize the need for a new interpretation of Christianity."[112]

Conclusions

Aberhart and Douglas represent two fascinating, albeit diametrically opposed, examples of the ways in which religion was used in the political sphere in Canada at the beginning of the twentieth century. Aberhart's idiosyncratic vision has now been largely discredited; Douglas is often heralded as a great Canadian.[113] Both were products of theological institutions, and both, in their radically different ways, incorporated the teachings they had learned at those institutions into their political messages. While neither engaged the academic study of religion, which was largely confined to biblical studies at a few select institutions, both were students of these theological institutions, and the two would leave their mark not just on their home provinces but on all of Canada.

Aberhart graduated from Queen's without ever having interacted with a professor, whereas Douglas graduated from Brandon College, a Baptist institution that Aberhart had criticized for its liberal attitude toward the Bible. Both men show how political ideas both developed in and reacted to what was going on in these religiously informed centres of higher learning. Their ideas, though certainly also related to their personalities, show clearly how these religious institutions played a role far beyond the halls of academe.

More generally, this chapter has focused on the westward movement of centres of higher learning and how the post-secondary institutions of the new provinces, especially their provincial universities, dealt with religion. If the eastern provinces tended to look to Britain for their intellectual models for setting up universities, those in the West looked to the land grant institutions of the United States. The universities established in the western provinces tended to be more accommodating in allowing theological seminaries and colleges to affiliate; nevertheless, they proscribed what these seminaries and colleges could and could not teach, presumably having learned their lesson from what had occurred in universities in the East.

Chapter Five

Battle Lines

Previous chapters have focused on the theological entanglements of colleges and universities, particularly the manifold ways in which the study of religion was embroiled in and co-opted by and for a host of sectarian and political issues. This impeded a certain propensity for freethinking when it came to religion. Indeed, I think it is safe to say that much of the scholarship produced in these early years tended to be on the conservative side. Those Canadian scholars interested in religion had to be trained abroad, in the United Kingdom, Germany, and increasingly the United States. Only after University College at Toronto developed a graduate program in Oriental studies could young Canadian scholars study in Canada for advanced degrees at the highest level.

Prior to this, the study of religion – and it certainly was the study *of* religion and not *about* religion – only occurred within seminaries associated with denominations imported from the Old World. So long as religion was taught within such strict theological parameters and so long as faculty and even students had to sign declarations of religious faith, the formation of anything resembling a non-sectarian and secular study of religion was impossible. Epistemic space would have to be carved out in order to make such a study not only possible but also respectable in terms of the larger and increasingly secular university curriculum. For this to happen, however, real intellectual battles would have to take place to force the structural changes required for the secular study of religion. It was not the case, in other words, that theological studies simply mutated overnight during the 1960s and '70s into non-theological studies associated with a humanities curriculum that reflected national and international events (regarding the former, changing demographics and multiculturalism; and the latter, the *Abington School District v. Schempp* US Supreme Court case of 1963).

This chapter seeks to chart some of these events – the debates, the entanglements, the contestations – that at least in hindsight drew lines between the theological and the secular study of religion. Those lines were only made possible, of course, by a number of much larger contextual forces. Moreover, it was not a simple teleological or evolutionary process: theology did not simply morph into secular studies, and the places where change did occur were not all the same. Rather, the academic study of religion arose on account of certain material conditions relevant to each region and indeed often to each institution. Let us, then, examine how, when, where, and why the more secular and academic study of religion began to emerge.

Driving this metamorphosis was the rise and increasing dissemination of higher criticism in biblical studies. While the academic study of religion was either non-existent or stuck in a "religious knowledge" paradigm in the years leading up to the Second World War and even beyond, biblical studies in Canada – heavily influenced by intellectual trajectories in both Germany and the United States, the two main places where young Canadians went to train in the late nineteenth and early twentieth centuries – was increasingly invested in historical and largely sceptical methodologies.

Forming part of the larger social and religious context against which these intellectual transformations took place was a uniquely Canadian experiment in denominational union. In 1924, three large mainline Protestant denominations – Presbyterian, Methodist, and Congregationalist – joined forces to found the United Church of Canada with the goal of establishing *the* national Church of the young country. Though it could never of course fulfil that role, it is worth noting – as this chapter also argues – that the United Church succeeded in destabilizing the denominationalism described in previous chapters and, in so doing, further cleared the necessary intellectual space for a less sectarian and potentially more ecumenical approach to the study *about* religion. It is with these experiments in church union that I begin this chapter before moving on to a larger discussion of biblical studies and higher criticism, with an emphasis on how this combination facilitated a more academically rigorous study of religion.

Canadian Denominationalism

Canada, unlike the United States, was never seen as a religious haven or refuge for Christians escaping persecution in the Old World. Canada has no myth of origins, nor is there an emphasis here on religious tolerance as reflected, for example, in the American story of the landing of the Puritans. On the contrary, as historian John W. Grant notes, "practically none of the early colonists came to Canada for religious reasons."[1] They instead came to the new colony to get rich through the fur trade and related commercial activities. The Industrial Revolution had led to strong population growth in Britain and the rest of Europe, but it was also associated with a falling number of jobs owing to the transition from a manual-labour–based economy to one that was increasingly driven by and largely focused on machine-based manufacturing. The mechanization of the textile industry, advances in iron-making techniques, and the increased use of refined coal led to a decrease in the number of jobs available for populations that were expanding at a rapid pace.[2] This forced many to look to the New World, especially Canada, for jobs and the hope of economic success. One direct result of this was the Great Migration (1815–1850), which saw more than 800,000 immigrants arrive in Canada from Britain and other parts of Europe.[3]

Many of these immigrants, perhaps not surprisingly, brought with them religious denominations long established in the Old World. These included, as seen in previous chapters, Anglicanism, Presbyterianism, other Protestant denominations, as well as Roman Catholicism. The relative isolation of Canada, especially when compounded by the dearth of pastoral care, created a situation in which traditional denominations were no longer regarded to be as paramount as they had been in Britain and, indeed, as they still were in the United States. While there may have been "no thought of comity," again in the words of historian John W. Grant, "in a vast country there was little surplus energy for deliberate overlapping."[4]

Denominational differences, then, were much less pronounced in Canada than in other countries. This, along with the subsequent indigenization of churches in a more rural and isolated Canadian environment, led to various unions that might not have been possible in other places. For example, as early as 1770, Presbyterians and Congregationalists joined forces, and in 1797, Congregationalists and Baptists united to create the United Baptist Convention of the Maritime Provinces.[5] A Presbyterian union in 1817, moreover, led James MacGregor, a missionary of the General Associate Synod of Scotland to Pictou, Nova Scotia, to remark that traditional theological differences between the denominations had "no practical relevance" in Canada.[6]

Isolation, large-scale immigration, and the need for theological creativity thus triangulated to produce a situation that was well-disposed toward new forms of, or at least experiments with, traditional Christian denominations that had not been entertained in the Old World. One of the most prominent of these forms was ecumenicism, which achieved its quintessence in the formation of the United Church of Canada in 1925.

Denominationalism and Its Limitations on the Study of Religion

As seen in previous chapters, the institutional study of religion in Canada began with, was intimately connected to, and developed structurally through the various Christian denominations. These well-established denominations, as we saw in chapter 1, had their truth-claims articulated in and defended by their own seminaries, which were often linked to specific colleges or universities, largely in eastern Canada. These included, for example, an Anglican seminary at Trinity College in Toronto, a Baptist seminary at McMaster, and a Presbyterian (later United) seminary at Queen's.

This meant that the study of religion initially took place in the intellectual context of seminaries whose raison d'être was the establishment of "true religion." One could not study, say, non-Western or non–Judeo-Christian religious forms in such seminaries. If and when Judaism was taught, for example, it was in a supersessionary manner. Moreover, the emphasis in such institutions tended to be on religious literature and liturgy and not on anything that even remotely approximated what would come to be known later as "theory and/or method." Indeed, as this chapter will argue, the main impulse for a more critically engaged study of religion emerged not from these seminaries but from what was slowly emerging in more secular settings. The most important of these settings for our story were provided by departments of Oriental studies in places such as University College at the University of Toronto. The seminaries would eventually begin to engage – be it by embrace or denial – the types of methods developed in more secular contexts.

At the other end of the spectrum, at least at the dawn of the twentieth century, was what we witnessed earlier in the western provinces, where universities largely eschewed religion in order to avoid the sectarian battles that had arisen in the East. At universities in Saskatchewan, Alberta, and British Columbia – local biblical colleges and seminaries notwithstanding – the overwhelming emphasis was on more technical and practical training for students to meet the educational and other needs of the growing populations of these relatively new provinces. Though the major universities in the western provinces were largely free of the denominational teaching of religion, it is worth noting that – given their emphasis on practical and relevant subjects – they also lacked the tradition of Oriental and related studies. Not until the 1960s did they develop a secular and non-denominational approach to the study of religion, and they did so without any of the turf wars with theological seminaries that had defined higher education in the East.

In the Maritimes, the situation for Oriental and biblical studies was, in the words of John S. Moir, "disheartening": "Oriental languages were taught at Acadia and Mount Allison (Dalhousie and the University of New Brunswick [the two largest universities in the region] apparently offered nothing in the field), but none of the instructors earned reputations as scholars and it is uncertain how far, if at all, their courses reflected the current trends in biblical studies."[7]

The one exception to all of these trends was the University of Toronto, to be discussed in greater detail below. There, though future clergy still needed to be trained in homiletics and catechesis, higher criticism was certainly engaged, if not actually on the verge of being systematically taught. Such engagement, however, was largely contingent on faculty remaining or appearing to remain reverent in their posture and orthodox in their beliefs. While some individuals at the more secular universities may well have been interested in higher criticism, seminaries were at least initially uninterested in it, if not outright hostile, on account of how it interrogated traditionally held beliefs about scripture and the nature of religion more generally. But notwithstanding some of the high-profile accounts examined in previous chapters, as the twentieth century progressed a growing comfort developed with higher criticism in both universities and seminaries, which I wish to argue was a direct result of the easing, at least in some quarters, of more traditional denominational lines engendered by the rise of the United Church.

The United Church of Canada: A Brief History

The United Church is a uniquely Canadian institution that sought to dismantle historically conditioned denominational lines with the aim of establishing a new national church.[8] This process was not entirely unprecedented in Canada, which had previously witnessed the blurring of doctrinal profession on account of scarce pastoral resources, a blurring that only increased as the West was settled. The impetus for a large-scale union, however, was certainly connected to Confederation in 1867, which established a sense of national autonomy and a growing awareness that the country could exist independently of Britain and its religious denominations.[9] There was, then, a growing awareness on the part of some denominational leaders that the fledgling country needed its own church, one that could shape the moral and religious ethos through the values of largely English-inspired Protestantism.

As a reporter for the *Presbyterian*, an official publication of that denomination, put it, the goal of union – articulated as early as 1865 – was to "revive and animate the people, to make our Presbyterianism not a Scotch exotic, but as an element in Canadian society – an institution of the land."[10] Even before the union that culminated in 1925, Canada's Presbyterian and Methodist Churches had achieved an internal union based on the fact that their respective churches were compelled to adapt to the new country. Between 1902 and 1925, the leaders of these two denominations, along with Congregationalists, began proceedings to create what they hoped would be a unified "national" Protestant church.[11] Note, however, that other major denominations, including the Anglicans and Baptists, refused on principle to join the movement toward union.[12] The three churches that united were close in their forms of worship and ecclesiastical policy; for the Baptists and Anglicans to join, considerably different mediation would have had to occur over theological issues – for example, regarding the nature of baptism and messianism.

The United Church, then, represented the union of the Methodist Church of Canada, the Congregational Union of Canada, and roughly 70 per cent of the Presbyterian Church of Canada.[13] Also joining was the small General Council of Union Churches, centred largely in western Canada. Union, reflecting the desire of the young country, as stipulated in the new church's Basis of Union, was "to foster the spirit of unity in the hope that this sentiment of unity may in due time, so far as Canada is concerned, take shape in a Church which may fittingly be described as national."[14]

The goal of church union was to establish one Protestant church in Canada. That the Anglicans and the Baptists refused to join meant, of course, that this would be impossible. The new church was also an attempt to create, insofar as possible, the equivalent of a national church, not unlike what the Anglicans had tried to accomplish decades earlier. However, as historian C.J. McIntire remarks, "the United Church had certainly assembled important churches into one church, but the task remained very incomplete. It became, in effect, one more denomination added to the long list of denominations in Canada."[15]

The union was among the first to cross historical denominational lines, and it attracted international acclaim. The movement for church union began with the desire to coordinate ministries in the vast Canadian northwest and to foster collaboration in overseas missions. In particular, union was driven by the desire to support churches in the western provinces while maintaining those of the East. In the words of John W. Grant,

> how could a divided church hope to weld into one people the polyglot horde that descended on the prairies? And how could the denominations make Canadians of such a variegated lot when they still defined their own identity in relation to a French theologian or an English evangelist? There was also a distinct fear, seldom openly expressed but often hinted at, that a divided Protestantism might not be able to maintain its place in a nation no longer overwhelmingly British in background.[16]

The desire, then, was to create a national church that would be larger, more ecumenical, and thus more national than any other church currently in existence. Indeed, the Basis of Union, issued by the United Church of Canada in 1925, stated this desire on the part of all three previous denominations in clear terms: "It shall be the policy of The United Church to foster the spirit of unity in the hope that this sentiment of unity may in due time, so far as Canada is concerned, take shape in a Church which may fittingly be described as national."[17]

The union was a complex one involving, among other things, property considerations, as well as how to address those churches within each denomination that did not want to join. The Presbyterian Church was the most divided, with 3,728 of its 4,512 congregations becoming part of the United Church and the remainder labelled as "non-concurring congregations" and continuing as Presbyterian.[18] The Presbyterian hold-outs were primarily in southern Ontario and urban Quebec.

There had been talk of union as early as the late nineteenth century, but these initial deliberations were impeded by the outbreak of the First World War. After the war, legislation was introduced at the federal and provincial levels to usher in the merger. In 1924, the federal parliament passed the United Church of Canada Act, which formally recognized and legally incorporated the union. At this point the leaders of the relevant churches all signed the Basis of Union in the name of their respective denominations. The new church – known simply as the "United Church" – quickly became the largest Protestant denomination in Canada, almost double the size of the Anglican Church; only the Catholic Church was larger.[19]

In terms of higher education, fifteen pre-existing theological colleges were now downsized to eight, each attached to a university and each based in a particular region.[20] These were Union College (Vancouver), St. Stephen's College (Edmonton), St. Andrew's College (Saskatoon), Manitoba College (Winnipeg), Emmanuel College (Toronto), Queen's Theological College (Kingston), United Theological College (Montreal), and Pine Hill Divinity Hall (Halifax). Although provincial legislation in Ontario had granted Knox College to the Presbyterian Church, the entire faculty and roughly three-quarters of the student body joined the newly formed United Church. In response, the Presbyterian Church appointed new faculty to teach the remaining Presbyterian students. It is important to note that whereas the United Church claimed to be the continuation of each of the denominations that it unified, for the remaining Presbyterians it represented a "dictation"; they saw themselves as the true church that upheld traditional Presbyterian doctrine. For two years, the two groups of faculty and students were housed in Knox College, at which point the United Church established Union Theological College, which merged with the theological faculty at Victoria College (formerly Methodist) in 1928 to become Emmanuel College.[21]

The United Church of Canada was inaugurated on 10 June 1925 in a ceremony held, perhaps fittingly enough, in the Mutual Street Arena,[22] the main hockey arena in Toronto prior to the opening of Maple Leaf Gardens in 1931. The merger was also, as mentioned, an attempt to create an autochthonous Canadian church, one that would, in the words of one early document, reflect "the common experiences of this new land."[23] As historian McIntire notes, the lead prayer at the First General Council linked Confederation in 1867 with church union in 1925 and gave thanks that God "hast drawn our fathers into a closer fellowship," both at the time of Dominion and in the present time.[24]

The emergence and development of the United Church was, much like the academic study of religion in Canada, linked to the expansion of the country and the fate of the Canadian Pacific Railway. McIntire writes: "The Canadian national church mimicked the Canadian National Railways, achieving transcontinental reach within one corporate system. The new church rode the railways into the Prairies to establish congregations for migrant[s] moving westward and immigrants arriving from overseas."[25]

As the country spread out, and as more and more immigrants – from Europe and beyond – arrived in Canada, new ways to account for diversity developed. This was decades before the peak of international immigration and the rise of multiculturalism as official governmental policy – two phenomena that ushered in the heyday of religious studies in this country in the 1960s and '70s – but still, attempts were made to overcome religious differences. In the first half of the twentieth century those differences were largely Christological; in the second half they would encompass other religions as well. In this respect, the formation of the United Church was an important initial step in ecumenicism, which would become an important prerequisite for the study of religion in Canada. It was also part of a growing trend in both academic and theological studies to appreciate religious alterity so as to better understand one's own religious tradition.

Now that there was a new church, there needed to be a place and a method for the training of clergy to administer pulpits. Training for the ministry, as outlined in the Basis of Union, was predicated on the attainment of a BA that included Greek; this was to be followed by three years in the study of theology, as "strongly recommended by the Church."[26] Theological study, as the document goes on to recount in its listing of "suggested subjects," could be fulfilled by courses such as the following:

> Old Testament Language and Literature, including Textual Criticism. Exegesis, Biblical Theology Introduction, Old Testament History and Old Testament Canon; New Testament Language and Literature, including Textual Criticism, Exegesis, Biblical Theology, Introduction, New Testament History and New Testament Canon; English Bible; Church History, including Symbolics; Systematic Theology; Apologetics, including Philosophy of Religion, History of Religion, and Comparative Religion; Christian Ethics and Sociology; Christian Missions; Practical Training, including preparation and delivery of sermons ...[27]

We see from this list that the newly formed United Church of Canada was not averse to the teachings of modern biblical criticism and so-called comparative religion. Indeed, the church was highly ecumenical from the start, and its policies, perhaps not surprisingly, were, at least relatively speaking, inclusive and liberal. It tended, in other words, to feel less threatened than the more traditional denominations by higher criticism.

Even so, as churches and seminaries encountered higher criticism, their initial reaction was to recoil from it. Such criticism, for example, undermined the entire foundation of biblical inerrancy upon which so many Christian denominations were founded. What changed? I suggest that the catalyst was the United Church's dismantling of traditional denominations coupled with the rise and eventual broad-based dissemination of higher criticism associated with secular institutions such as the University of Toronto. The clash between the secular university and the theological seminary regarding the place and function of biblical criticism was inevitable, and as it turned out, higher criticism would carry the day. And this would clear space for the non-theological analysis of religion and religious forms.

Oriental Studies and the University of Toronto

Oriental studies, much like higher biblical criticism, to which it was related, introduced a more historical methodology that was sceptical of traditional categories such as revelation and prophecy. These fields of study – the questions asked and the methodologies developed – helped nudge the Bible and the Ancient Near East further from the domain of theology. Moreover, the creation and development of an Oriental studies department at the University of Toronto in 1886 meant that one could now specialize in a particular field, along the German model, instead of simply receiving a well-balanced and gentlemanly education revolving around religious and ethical reflection. A doctoral program in Orientals was added in 1897.

As noted in chapter 3, James Frederick McCurdy (1847–1935) is generally credited with being the first Canadian-born critical scholar of the Bible. He had been appointed in 1885 at University College in Toronto to teach Oriental languages. In the words of Moir, he "represented the best in contemporary scholarship and was a dedicated thorough, and inspiring teacher who trained a brilliant collection of young Canadians in rigorous methodology and liberal principles while imparting a reverence for scholarship."[28] Since University College had no theological affiliation, McCurdy was free to develop the program as a part of the university curriculum and not just as a service to future ministers.

Before the University of Toronto was established as a centre of biblical and Oriental studies, young Canadians had to go to the United States or to Europe, specifically Germany, for their graduate training.[29] Toronto was now able to offer Canadians the opportunity to study religious texts in a secular setting at the undergraduate and graduate levels. Moreover, and again in the words of Moir, "Canadians had also developed such confidence in their national educational institutions that postgraduate work at a Canadian university was accepted as a learning experience equal or at least not markedly inferior to that available at older European institutions."[30]

McCurdy's Department of Oriental Studies was now the only one in Canada where a critical and largely historical approach to biblical and related texts could be carried out. Indeed, three of the fourteen PhDs awarded at the University of Toronto in 1902 were in biblical studies, and Oriental studies became the first department in the humanities at that institution to have graduates of the program.[31] Despite the importance of the department at Toronto, it is perhaps worth noting that McCurdy was a Presbyterian and that all his colleagues and most of his students in the department were his co-religionists.[32]

Given the rise in higher criticism, it was only a matter of time before its methodologies and conclusions came under fire.[33] Several high-profile cases brought this tension to the fore. In 1892, Wesleyan Theological College in Montreal hired George Workman to teach Hebrew and the Old Testament. Thirteen years earlier, Workman had been dismissed from Victoria College in Toronto amid a controversy over his liberal attitude toward the biblical text, which had spilled over into the national press.[34] Despite the controversy, Wesleyan Theological College hired him, but in April of 1907 he was charged by his superiors with "having denied inner depravity, the virgin birth, and the historicity of the Fourth Gospel."[35] Workman, in turn, accused them of libel. He was eventually dismissed and subsequently took the college to civil court, which found in his favour and ordered that costs and damages be paid to him.[36] On appeal, however, the verdict was overturned "on the grounds that secular courts had no authority over church courts in matters of belief and discipline."[37]

The second high-profile case also involved the Methodist Church. In 1909, George Jackson, a professor of English Bible at Victoria College, gave a public lecture during which he talked about the Book of Genesis and higher criticism.[38] After a strong outcry, Jackson's teaching was brought before the Methodist Church's quadrennial conference in 1910. There, one of his critics informed the conference that "as the higher critics teach about Him He is no Saviour at all. These higher critics base their arguments on baseless assumptions. Their teachings are shipwrecking the faith of hundreds."[39] The Methodist Church, at the conference, maintained its belief in the Bible as the inerrant word of God, yet Victoria College took no action against Jackson, and he continued teaching there until 1913. This unwillingness on the part of the college to act shows the inroads that higher criticism was making in seminaries and how denominations were increasingly willing to allow for a certain amount of freethinking on their campuses.

When McCurdy left the University of Toronto in 1911 to take up a position at the American School of Oriental Research in Jerusalem, a successor was sought. Robert Alexander Falconer[40] – a native of Prince Edward Island, a scholar of the New Testament, and now President of the University of Toronto – suggested Herbert Loewe, a Cambridge-educated scholar and "a very devout Jew," to succeed McCurdy. The latter objected, contending that Loewe was too specialized in his research and that the affiliated colleges might object to the hiring of a Jew. Falconer agreed that McCurdy had built the department single-handedly at Toronto and thus should play a major role in naming his successor.[41]

McCurdy chose William Robert Taylor, an Ontario native and his own student, to succeed him. Taylor received his MA and PhD from the University of Toronto before accepting a position at Westminster Hall, a newly formed Presbyterian seminary in Vancouver. Falconer had been worried about hiring another Presbyterian for the department and about poaching Taylor from BC, "where at this time of our country's growth, there is need of the strongest type of man for the upbuilding of a young country."[42]

The trends in higher criticism continued at the University of Toronto and elsewhere. In the spring of 1928, William Irwin, a professor of Oriental studies, delivered a paper in the United States in which he accused biblical authors of lying in the service of a message. Local papers in Toronto picked up the story.[43] The following year, Irwin gave his students a final exam with questions such as "To what extent may the stories [of the Bible] be accepted as dependable history?" and "Is the book of Jonah history, allegory, or what is it?"[44] Again, though, his academic freedom was protected.

Religious Knowledge: A Precursor to Religious Studies

On 13 December 1906, S.H. Blake, a prominent Toronto lawyer, governor of the University of Toronto, and proponent of aggressive evangelism, published a letter in the *Mail and Empire* arguing for a non-religious curriculum at the university:

> The university was established and is maintained for the purpose of teaching secular subjects only the classics, Oriental and modern languages, mathematics, science, literature, history, etc. It is to teach these subjects and to teach them in such a way that the very varied religious convictions of its supporters shall suffer no hurt, that the University is maintained, and no professor has a right to teach anything else, he may be an Anglican, or he may be an infidel, a Methodist or a Roman Catholic, but he must keep his convictions to himself.[45]

Blake was worried that religion was being taught in University College in contravention of the Baldwin Act of 1849 and the Hincks Act of 1853.[46] In 1906 the new provincial government had crafted a new University Act to shield the university from political interference and precisely the types of issues that had threatened it in the past. According to Moir, however, trouble arose from the ambiguous language of one of its sections, 129(10), which read: "The curriculum in Arts of the University shall include the subjects of Biblical Greek, Biblical Literature, Christian

Ethics, Apologetics, the Evidence of Natural and Revealed Religion and Church History, but any provision for examination and instruction in the same shall be left to the voluntary action of the federated universities and colleges."[47]

Blake exploited this ambiguity. He seems to have been worried that, whatever the spirit of such acts, the university was actually encouraging the study of religion. In a subsequent letter to John Hoskin, the chairman of the university's Board of Governors, he wrote: "The first objection I heard made was from a Student who ceased to attend [classes] because of the heterodox teaching he found in the class [on Religious Knowledge]."[48] Blake thought that such teaching belonged, not in "godless" University College, but in the affiliated colleges, where such topics could be taught from a more theologically orthodox perspective.[49] He continued in his letter to Hoskin:

> There is a very wide difference between taking "some cognizance of the literature" and the using this liberty as an opportunity to assail the authenticity of the Bible, to introduce and advocate the views of the higher critics, to instill a disbelief in the Messianic character of Old Testament prophecy, and to introduce the idea among Students that large portions of the Bible, accepted by many as God's Word, are mere myths or allegories and to be rejected as "old wives" fables.[50]

What Blake seems to have been opposed to was the recently formed Department of Religious Knowledge, which had been created by several of the church-related colleges federated with the university.[51] This department, according to Luther H. Martin and Donald Wiebe, had been "created by bringing together the teachers of 'religious knowledge' courses from the three religiously-founded undergraduate colleges that [were] federated with the University of Toronto."[52] Martin and Wiebe go on to lament that this Department of Religious Knowledge would be folded into a generically named "Combined Departments of Religious Studies" in 1969 – before being renamed simply the Department of Religious Studies in 1975 – and would remain "predominantly involved in Christian studies and with the quasi-religious formation of student[s] – that is, with providing students with pastoral care and the wherewithal better to appreciate religions and religion."[53] Without challenging their overall assessment, however, I think it important to note that, as Blake's remarks make clear, even in Departments of Religious Knowledge real intellectual battles were being fought as to what the *future* of an academic study of religion might look like.

The Canadian Society of Biblical Studies (CSBS)

On 3 March 1933, nine biblical scholars at the University of Toronto and its affiliated theological colleges founded the Canadian Society of Biblical Studies (CSBS). Its first president was the aforementioned Robert Falconer, who had recently retired as President of the University of Toronto.[54] The individuals represented the Semitics department from University College (T.J. Meek, W.S. McCullough, and Frederick Winnett), Emmanuel College (its principal Davidson, J.H. Michael, and John Dow), Wycliffe College (Charles V. Pilcher), Trinity College (John Lowe), and United Theological College in Montreal (R.B.Y. Scott).[55] Writing about the meeting some thirty years later, Scott reminisced:

> When the Society was organized in 1933, the then senior Biblical scholars in Canada readily responded to the suggestion that a society be formed to encourage Canadian Biblical scholarship, and they generously supported the younger group whose idea this was. We felt that too few were able to enjoy the stimulus of the meetings in the United States of the long-established Society for Biblical Literature and Exegesis, and that Canadian scholarship would be encouraged if there were in existence also an organization of our own. The long-term results have certainly justified this hope.[56]

Four of the charter members were rabbis (Julius Berger, Harry Stern, and H. Abramowits, all from Montreal, and Maurice Eisendrath from Toronto). The overwhelming majority, however, were Protestant clergy who were either professors or pastors.[57] There was also one woman, Gertrude Rutherford.[58]

As Macpherson notes, most of the senior members had been trained outside of Canada – in Europe or the United States. However, many of the younger members had been trained in Canada (obviously, by the now senior scholars).[59] This was part of what Remus calls the gradual "indigenization" of both biblical studies and graduate studies in Canada. Of the early members, twenty-six came from Toronto, six from Montreal, four from Hamilton, seven from western Canada (three each from Winnipeg and Vancouver, and one from Saskatoon), and only one from the Maritimes (Halifax).

This organization was the first academic society in the humanities in Canada. In 1935 it began publishing its annual *Bulletin*, which would play an important role in disseminating biblical scholarship in Canada, publishing presidential addresses and select papers delivered at the annual meeting. In this respect it served, in the words of Harold

Remus, as "a kind of Canadian journal of biblical studies."[60] It is still published today, but only online, and its contents are less formal papers than AGM minutes and member notes.[61] The *Bulletin*, as we shall see in a later chapter, was gradually replaced by other Canadian venues for publication such as the *Canadian Journal of Religious Thought* (founded in 1924) and the *Canadian Journal of Theology* (1955), both of which were superseded by *Studies in Religion / Science religieuses* in 1971.

Conclusions

Prior to the Second World War, the academic study of religion had in many ways grown, but it had done so in fits and starts. There were still no departments of religious studies, at least as that term would come to be defined in the late 1960s and early 1970s, but critical biblical studies and Oriental studies were both in place. By "critical," I refer to a methodology primarily governed by the methods and findings of higher criticism, which put the historicity of the text into question and which chipped away at traditional theological categories such as inerrancy and prophetic inspiration. Though begun in this country with McCurdy and his Orientals department, it gradually was disseminated throughout the country, especially in places such as Queen's, McMaster, McGill, and the University of Manitoba. This approach, once again, would serve as a precursor to the development of an academic study of religion.

This chapter has tried to highlight some of the intellectual debates that, if they did not actually facilitate, then at least helped throw into relief, what was at stake in these early years. Here I have examined some of the institutional and structural changes; in the next chapter I turn to the ideas and texts carried out in those contexts.

Chapter Six

Venues of Dissemination

Earlier chapters examined the diverse institutional settings in which knowledge about religion was produced; this one switches focus to investigate how that knowledge was then disseminated to a larger reading public. The existence of periodicals devoted to religion and religious topics implies not only the presence of intellectual networks among scholars, including scholarly organizations and honour societies, but also a more general reading public interested in theological and related subjects. An analysis of these scholarly and semi-scholarly journals will open yet another window onto a much larger set of social, economic, and intellectual contexts that played a not insignificant role in the development of the study of religion in Canada.

Virtually all publication on religion in Canadian periodicals prior to 1971 – the year that *Studies in Religion / Sciences religieuses* (*SR*) was founded – was theological and Christocentric. These journals did occasionally publish articles about other parts of the world and other religious traditions, but these tended to be written from a thoroughly Christocentric position and by Canadian missionaries in the field. While attentive to their geographical context, they tended to focus either on Christianity in those areas or, more rarely, on comparisons in which other religions were placed in negative counterpoint with the author's own form of Protestant Christianity. They tended to take particular interest in Buddhism, but with the understanding that Buddhism's "life-denying" aspects stood in sharp contradiction to the "life-affirming" ones of Jesus, whose dynamic presence stands at the heart of Christianity. When a non-Christian author appeared in the pages of these journals – even after religious studies as a field began to emerge in Canada – that person tended to write on subjects relevant to a Christian audience and was introduced by the editor as someone who, though not Christian, was nevertheless a "devout" person.

Here it is worth mentioning that Canada was far behind other countries in the theological/religious studies journal market, and especially far behind Germany and the United States, two countries with fairly long traditions of theology, besides being the epicentres of higher biblical criticism. Journals in Canada devoted to the study of religion focused exclusively on non-technical Christian theological topics; meanwhile, various scholarly institutions in the United States, by the beginning of the twentieth century, had begun to develop more technical academic journals such as *Journal of the American Oriental Society* (founded in 1843), the official journal of the American Oriental Society; *Journal of Religion* (1882), associated with the University of Chicago; and *Hebrew Union College Annual* (1924), associated with the seminary of the Reform movement in Judaism at Hebrew Union College in Cincinnati. Even in those journals that tended to devote themselves to biblical topics, higher criticism was on much greater display than in anything witnessed in cognate Canadian journals of the same period. Even *Harvard Theological Review* (1908), which seems to have functioned as a quasi-model for Canadian theological journals, had, by 1924, the first year in which a theological journal appeared in Canada, begun to include non-judgmental or non-secessionist materials on post-biblical Judaism.[1]

As late as 1970, there was no Canadian journal devoted to the academic study of religion. By then, the Faculty of Theology at McGill had developed a comparative religions program, in large part thanks to the founding of the Institute of Islamic Studies there in 1952. In the United States, though, new journals with a distinctly non-Eurocentric and comparative focus were beginning to come into existence, perhaps most notably *History of Religions* (1961), which had been created under the influence of Mircea Eliade at the Divinity School at the University of Chicago. Even journals that had once been overwhelmingly theological, such as the aforementioned *Journal of Religion*, also published under the auspices of the University of Chicago's Divinity School, were beginning to expand their purview so as to include other religious traditions and more critical methodologies.

This is not to imply that Canadians were neither eligible nor able to publish in these American and other journals. Far from it, and some certainly did. My interest in this chapter, however, is not in how Canadian scholars contributed to these journals, but rather in how Canadian scholars created and subsequently contributed to autochthonous Canadian journals devoted to the study of religion. An immediate question we might ask is, why did Canadians not produce journals of the same quality as American and European ones? It seems most likely that

Canadians scholars did not feel they had the resources to create their own venues for non-national publications, especially given that such venues already existed in both Europe and the United States. Indeed, in the opening editorial of *Canadian Journal of Theology* the editors remark that "the Churches in Canada cannot take their place in the Church Catholic by being pallid reflections of the life and theology of denominations elsewhere."[2] There is an explicit acknowledgment, then, that a Canadian journal has to meet the needs of Canadians not only for their spiritual health, but also, as implied, in order to contribute a particularist element to help better illumine the universal Church. This statement also clearly shows that the journal's mandate was less about scholarship than it was about creating a venue in which theological, ethical, and spiritual issues could be addressed for the good of the country.

However, this does not help explain why, for the most part, Canadian theological journals were not specifically devoted to Canadian theology (if such a phenomenon even existed) or to theological issues relevant to Canada. These Canadian theological journals certainly saw themselves as specifically "Canadian" venues intended exclusively for a Canadian reading public, yet their contents were often anything but Canadian in focus and were instead largely devoted to homiletical and exegetical expositions. It is in the editorials that we often see reflection on matters specific to Canada.

This parochialism reveals how the study of religion in Canada, unlike in some European and American contexts, lacked a more secular model. The reason for this should be obvious from previous chapters, namely, with one or two exceptions, the study of religion in Canada was largely confined up until the 1960s to seminary settings, where its main function seems to have been the education and the training of clergy. Even at a place like McGill, comparative religion tended to be more ecumenical than critical or even theoretical.

The *Canadian Journal of Religious Thought* (1924–32)

In 1924, one year before the union that created the United Church of Canada, theologians sought to create a distinctive Canadian periodical devoted to the topic of religion. They felt they had something to contribute to the project of theology; also, a growing sense of Canadian identity and a new nationalism had emerged in the years since the First World War.[3] The periodical was to be called the *Canadian Journal of Religious Thought* (henceforth *CJRT*); note, however, that the terms "religion" and "religious thought" referred solely to Christianity in general and to Protestantism in particular. Though the word "theology" was not used in the title, it was certainly omnipresent in the contents, running throughout all of the volumes, from the first to the last. Though biblical Judaism was often mentioned, on account of the Old Testament, this was always in a supersessionist manner so as to make clear that Christianity was the obvious continuation of the spiritual themes of ancient Israel. The goal of the journal was to create an academic forum that would be of interest to Canadian scholars working in biblical studies, theology, church history, and other related fields. Indeed, the journal noted in its first volume that its policy would be "to publish in each issue an article from outside Canadian ranks."[4] The editors were determined that the journal be solely for Canadian theologians, albeit with one exception in every issue.

The editor of the new journal was George B. King, a professor of New Testament and church history at United College in Winnipeg. King was an early representative of what Flatt calls "modernism" in the field of biblical studies in Canada.[5] Though not subversive in his scholarship, King was aware that the historicity of the Old Testament posed certain historiographic and chronological problems. It is worth noting that while these problems were not infrequently pointed out with respect to the Old Testament, the New Testament was often left alone. King argued, for example, that Abraham was not a real person, but a metaphor for the ancient Israelites. Yet in other places, he had no problems writing as if Abraham were a real person.[6] *CJRT* thus reveals the still rather ambiguous place of higher biblical criticism in the Canadian context.

In the inaugural editorial, we are afforded insights into its rationale. There, we read that

> frankly, and in the most outspoken way, the central interest of this magazine is to be religious ... By every ambition that is in us we are hoping that it will make *vital* religious thought its chief and great concern ... And every age has its task of keeping religion living by keeping it a real and central part of life. And no age ever had a harder task in that direction than our own. It is to help in the fulfilling of that task that this journal is being started.[7]

It is clear from these opening lines that *CJRT* was positioning itself less as an academic journal than as a religious one. This should not come as a major surprise, given that the line separating "religion" from "the study of religion" was, for all intents and purposes, almost invisible in Canada at this juncture. The journal also saw as part of its mandate the revivification of spiritual life in Canadian society through the creation of a new forum in which "religious thought" could be articulated.

The audience, then, was imagined to be not just theologians, but *all* Canadians – from professional theologians to priests and ministers to the laity – interested in the spiritual life of the young country. The editorial continues:

> The dominant interest in many religious quarters to-day is the search for reality, the conviction that life is not to be measured in terms of the things done, but in terms of man's participation in the eternal life. Consequently men are seeking the content of their faith and doctrine, in no narrow sense of that term, is coming to its own again. It is not something external to religion, but is the attempt to express in terms of reason the true inwardness of the Christian faith.[8]

It is worth considering that the first issue of the journal appeared in 1924, less than six years after the First World War, in which close to 61,000 Canadian soldiers perished and more than 172,000 were wounded. It was also the period after the Russian Revolution of 1917, which had brought the spectre of communism – the nemesis of theology – to parts of Europe. With this in mind, the inaugural editorial duly noted that

> the challenge of God to the church of to-day – a challenge which she is meeting through her systems of religious education more than in any other way – is to breathe into society such a spirit as will transform our machine industry, and humanize our "percentage" education, and vitalize our "insurance" religion and so share the enterprise of Him who came to proclaim "release the captives."[9]

At a time of spiritual malaise around the world, the editors were attempting to create a venue in which ideas could be discussed in a free and open environment. The editorial continued:

> The founders of this magazine desire that in its pages honest men may honestly say the things they believe without any mumbling or fear they cherish no cheap ambition to create a journal that shall be called radical or extreme, but they do hope to help in establishing of one that shall place a premium upon frank, straightforward, unequivocal presentation and discussion.[10]

It is by no means clear whether this policy of "honesty" was meant to include discussions of higher criticism. A perusal of the nine volumes that appeared shows little or no engagement with it. In volume 7, however, some Orientalists from the University of Toronto begin to write in its pages,[11] and, in the same volume, C.V. Pilcher of Wycliffe College, Toronto, translates a chapter of Hermann Gunkel's *Ausgewählte Psalmen.*[12] Gunkel (1862–1932) was a German scholar of the Old Testament and the founder of form criticism of the Bible, which maintained that written units of scripture can be traced to oral traditions.[13] In the context of the translated article, Gunkel does talk about the "corrupted" nature of some of the biblical texts and "errors of copyists."[14]

Perhaps what is most obvious about the journal, however, is its overwhelming (Protestant) Christian message. In this respect, the "religious knowledge" that the *CJRT* sought to produce for Canadians was largely Protestant. Where ecumenism was concerned, it was always, like the United Church of Canada, between Protestant denominations:

> It will be noted that the boards responsible for this journal have in their membership ministers and laymen from five of our Canadian Churches ... If the enterprise is to be carried on at all, therefore, it must be on broad and catholic lines ... It is expected that as these men work together in the task that has been committed to them, still greater things will be achieved to the Glory of God and for the progress of His Kingdom in the earth. God's Church is one and indivisible, and anything that will help it to speak for Him with one voice will help to make His name known in the earth. This magazine stands pre-eminently for the unity of faith in the bonds of peace.[15]

The journal, at least from this passage, viewed itself as carrying on the project that the United Church of Canada had inaugurated a few years earlier. The idea behind that union, and the ostensible goal of *CJRT*, was to encourage what seems to have been imagined as a uniquely Canadian response to unity among the various Protestant denominations.

The "editorial" sections reveal most clearly how the editors perceived the journal as relevant to the lives of Canadians. Most of these editorials focused not on one particular topic but on several at a time. A random example, from 1.4: 273–80, includes short editorial comments on the following broad range of topics: "Religious Education and the Public School" (273); "Fellowship" (273–4); "Summer Schools" (274–5); "Dr. Fosdick Again" (275); "The Vogue of 'Children's Week'" (275–6); "Conference of Social Work" (277); "Still to Study the Question," (277); "The British Association" (278–9); "Social Workers and the Church" (279); and "Social Dogma and Experiment" (280). In these editorials, we see on clear display a set of political and social concerns that the editors imagined were facing either Canada or the Church. In the aforementioned "Religious Education and the Public School," for example, we read that the journal "encourages the Religious Education Council of Canada (all denominations except Catholics) to get involved in religious education in public schools because 'the Church and the Church alone,' can perform adequately the task of religious instruction, and the next step will be to ask for a fair proportion of the educational life-time of the boy and girl for that important purpose."[16]

These editorials further show how Canadian theologians addressed what they considered to be pressing issues of the day from a religious perspective. They are not technical in any sense of the term, and they rarely engage in catechesis (which is found in the actual articles). Instead, they are rather prosaic accounts that seek to influence Canadians through the articulation of various issues arising in Canada along quasi-theological lines. These editorials, in other words, are not scholarly, but popular. This, of course, leads us to wonder who actually read the *CJRT*. There are no records of this, though the fact that the journal became insolvent after nine years suggests that its readership was negligible.

Trends

A perusal of the nine volumes of *CJRT* reveals certain trends that are indicative of the study of religion in Canada during the 1920s and '30s. When the journal talks about Church union, which it frequently does, it is solely in reference to Protestant union. In this context, a palpable "anti-Catholic" bias is clear. In his "Paul: The First Christian Protestant," for example, H.L. MacNeill argues that Paul's goal – presumably the goal of every good Christian – was to return to Jesus directly without seeking mediation. MacNeill, a professor of New Testament at Brandon College in Manitoba, and a teacher of the politician Tommy Douglas, further argued that "the truth of God in Jesus Christ is a sphere whose whole surface and content cannot be seen or comprehended by any single standpoint."[17] Such a position, however, did not mean that MacNeill was a literalist or a conservative thinker. Indeed, as we shall see later in this chapter, he would subsequently be charged by Baptist and other leaders, including William Aberhart, of being a proponent of higher criticism.

It is also fair to say that many of the articles in the journal are based less on rational or even historical argumentation than on the personal beliefs of the author. Such beliefs are then presented as if they were both natural and rational. There is thus a strong Christian bias throughout the journal. No one ever entertains the idea, for example, that people of other religions maintain the truth or veracity of their own religious knowledge; instead it is assumed that they wallow in ignorance because they have not accepted the salvific power of Jesus and Christianity. In "The International Situation and The Christian Ideal," for example, Newton W. Rowell argues that

> Europe's troubles are not primarily economic, but moral and spiritual ... The hope of the world lies in application of the teachings of the Prince of Peace to all the relationships of life, and the Christian Church – with all its weaknesses, and they are great, with all its mistakes, and there have been many – is the principal agency for making known the life and teachings of Christ to the men of every nation and of every land. The Church must strike the note of moral and spiritual leadership, or confess its failures in this hour of humanity's need.[18]

To blame the world's problems in 1924, six years after the end of the Great War and five years before the onslaught of the Great Depression, on a lack of spiritual leadership may strike us today as unfortunate. In keeping with this theme of the malaise of modernity as a correlative of spiritual decay, James Smyth, in an article titled "The Faith of Modern Man," writes:

> That the ideals of Jesus may prevail in society it is necessary to implant them in the minds of our young men and women at an age when there is a strong capacity for response to the heroic, and when the character is plastic. It is too late to talk of fellowship and brotherhood, and contempt for materialism and worldly power and applause, to men whose whole life has been inspired by motives far different.[19]

This homiletic tenor is reflected throughout the nine volumes' contents. The overwhelming assumption is that there are problems in the world on account of a spiritual malaise that has been caused by people either turning away from Christianity or not accepting it at all. In "The Living Truth," for example, Richard Davidson opines that "God reveals Himself in personality. All progress in religious knowledge springs from a humanizing of God. In Jesus of Nazareth, we find man's experience perfected."[20]

The journal is not all theological, however. In addition to the aforementioned types of devout and overly theological articles, there appear articles on other topics such as politics,[21] history,[22] and travel.[23] Each issue has a distinct section devoted to poetry, both Canadian and non-Canadian.[24] There is also a focus on new books by Canadian authors. Lorne Albert Pierce (1890–1961), the great Canadian publisher, editor at Toronto's Ryerson Press, and promoter of Canadian literature, developed and wrote irregularly sections titled "Memorabilia"[25] and "Fragmenta Litteraria,"[26] though nothing was particularly religious or theological about these. Pierce is perhaps best-known for imagining literature as an important aspect of unifying Canada and of promoting Canada's cultural development in the mid-twentieth century.

Other sections, beginning in volume 2, include "From an Expositor's Notebook" by William Manson, who was Chair of New Testament Language and Literature at Knox College, Toronto, and the author of books such as *Jesus the Messiah* (1943) and *The Way of the Cross* (1958). Titles in this section include "Christ the Light of the World," and the contents of these articles are fairly standard works of biblical exposition.[27] Volume 3 introduces "The Preacher's Page," edited by John Dow, a professor of New Testament at Emmanuel College in Toronto and a United Church theologian,[28] which offers various homilies and encourages readers to submit materials. There is a sense among the editors, in other words, that not only professional theologians should submit their work to *CJRT* – so too should pulpit ministers.

Even articles that would seem, at least by their titles, to signal a more critical approach to the study of religion, rarely do. If anything, other religions are treated with considerable scepticism, as is the use of humanities or social sciences to explain or understand religion or religions. In an article devoted to the psychology of religion and titled "Some Doubts about Psychology," the author laments that psychology cannot "truly interpret the spiritual life of man."[29] H.P. Whidden, in his article "What Is a Liberal Education," which again is not particularly religious, concludes as follows:

> Too frequently of late has the criticism been made that college graduates do not become practical men and women of affairs. While fully believing that statistics do not warrant such statements, I would urge that we address ourselves more seriously than ever to the task of giving the lie to every such charge by seeing to it that more and more the men and women who go out from college halls are educated to think and to be of practical service to the community, the nation, and the Kingdom of God.[30]

To sum up: *CJRT* was a Canadian periodical devoted almost exclusively, despite the name, to Christian theology and apologetics. Higher criticism and the use of other disciplines to study religion are largely avoided. Instead, the overwhelming emphasis is on homiletics, catechesis, and attempts to set a national religious conversation in public life along the principles of Protestant thought, which are imagined to be unified in the aftermath of the establishment of the United Church of Canada.

Historical Criticism

Most of the early volumes of the journal seem adamantly opposed to higher criticism of the Bible. This approach to scripture, as witnessed in the previous chapter, was perceived by its critics as undermining the sacred nature of the Bible, besides leading to a general state of irreligion and fear for the subsequent breakdown of society's moral fabric. A central figure in curtailing the excesses of such criticism was the German Rudolf Bultmann (1884–1976), who argued that historical analysis of the New Testament was both futile and unnecessary since the earliest literature produced by followers of Jesus was interested only in the fact that Jesus lived, preached, and was crucified. According to Bultmann,

> we can now know almost nothing concerning the life and personality of Jesus, since the early Christian sources show no interest in either, are moreover fragmentary and often legendary; and other sources about Jesus do not exist.Except for the purely critical research, what has been written in the last hundred and fifty years on the life of Jesus, his personality and the development of his inner life, is fantastic and romantic.[31]

For Bultmann and those who followed him, it was a fact that Jesus existed but all else was inconsequential. Many Canadian theologians, though perhaps not as technical or nuanced as Bultmann was in his complicated theological message, nevertheless shared his mistrust for higher critics. Writing in the first volume of the *CJRT*, William Manson declared:

> In an age when the solvent of historical criticism is at work on all beliefs, institutions, and principles coming down to us out of the past, and when not even the presuppositions of Christianity are safe against negation or dispute ... there are foundations which, though, temporarily submerged, are nevertheless not removed ... So even under the surge and wash of criticism there may exist unshaken foundations, broad enough and historical enough to support the Christian Church and the Christian ministry.[32]

Such foundations, for him, included that "Jesus existed historically," that "the impact of His personality on the lives of men created early Christianity," and that "primitive Christianity [cannot] be reduced to terms of the Old Testament or of Judaism, or of any other creed."[33]

Manson argues – without offering, as is typical of this literature, any historical proof – that just as Jesus built upon certain prophetic elements in the Old Testament, he was also unique in terms of world history and was in no way contained by previous or contemporaneous religious teachings. Though higher criticism may not be going away any time soon, believing students can nevertheless protect themselves so long as they are secure in their faith in Jesus and the Church:

> Like the Fatherhood of God and the Lordship of Jesus, the conception of the Spirit rests on an experience of authenticate truth, energy, and saving power ... The experience in question does not belong to an age, but is in its true nature timeless. For the same reason, it is not destructible by historical criticism. Having this assurance, the student of to-day will not be unduly disturbed by criticism, he may possess his soul in patience, for his foundations in the life of the spirit are not removed.[34]

Once again showing how anathema higher criticism was to so many Canadian theologians, yet another article in the opening volume is devoted to the subject. In "The Alleged Reaction in Old Testament Criticism," Arthur S. Peake proclaims that the higher critics not only have been misinformed, but as of late have even begun to doubt their own first principles. As a result, according to him, "the very foundation on which the critical analysis of the Pentateuch rests has been shattered: that archaeology has confirmed the sacred records and confounded the critics; and that some of the eminent scholars are already confessing the breakdown of critical theories and the re-establishment of traditional views."[35] Peake was the only non-Canadian who appeared in the first issue of the new journal. His views would seem to echo not only those of the editors, but also those of Canadian theological circles as a whole. This wishful thinking on his part, however, could not be supported by the growing popularity of higher criticism in general or by its increasing influence in Canadian biblical criticism in particular.

This adamant opposition to biblical studies, however, was not universally shared. In an interesting article titled "Evolution and Religion," J. Playfair McMurrich sought to differentiate between "man-made" Christianity that sought to suppress science and a more universal and knowledge-based Christianity. McMurrich, a graduate of Johns Hopkins University, a professor of anatomy, and Dean of the School of Graduate Studies at the University of Toronto, went on to argue that evolution had been developed through "a long period of incubation during which facts and theories were accumulating on the question of the mutability or permanency of species, until finally they were brought together by Charles Darwin and set in order so as to reveal beyond peradventure the law of organic evolution – for one may speak of it as a law just as one speaks of the law of gravitation."[36]

This argument is interesting in that the author, unlike others in the same issue, was not opposed to Darwinian evolution, but, like them, sought to carve out space for Christianity so that it could adequately address scientific principles. If it did not, according to McMurrich, then religion would crumble among thinking individuals. In this way he introduced a certain, albeit at this point rare, relativity into the conversation, one that would undoubtedly have made many of his theological colleagues uncomfortable. "We base our theology upon our Scriptures," he continues, "believing them to contain the revelation of God, but millions of people build up a very different theology based on the Koran, which they believe contains the revelation of the one God, through Mahomet, his prophet."[37] Unlike the theologians who contributed to the journal and who simply assumed that Protestant Christianity was the most sublime form of religious expression, McMurrich seems aware of the problems associated with such assertions. He has a problem with the historical record, yet he seems to have no problem with the spirit of God, which exists beyond history: "The acceptance of the doctrine of evolution may demand a revision of our doctrine of God. But does it not lead us to a far greater realization of His omnipotence?"[38]

He then tries to carve out space for science and scientific inquiry in the midst of dogmatic theology. He concludes: "A man-made theology has been built up around [the fundamental teachings of the Church], representing ideas of the cosmos long out of date, and serving only to obscure the truth. This it is what demands revision in light of the teachings of modern science, and that revision is bound to come. No amount of vituperation or ignorant opposition, no futile and childish legislation can retard it."[39]

McMurrich's article was an important precursor to the introduction of higher criticism in the journal. It is unclear, however, to just what extent it was causal. At any rate, in the journal's final volume we find an article by Ian F. MacKinnin of Dalhousie, New Brunswick, a United Church minister and not a professional theologian, that signals a reluctant acceptance of higher criticism, though not a full embrace. He writes: "The aim of this article is not to provide complete answers, but simply to indicate some of the conclusions on which members of the school are in agreement, to glance at some of the individual results attained and to ask the further questions – what is likely to be the future of this study? Will it have any determining influence on our conception of the person of Jesus Christ?"[40]

In charting the response to higher criticism over the nine volumes of the *CJRT* we sense a gradual change in attitude. While the journal begins in opposition to such criticism and indeed defines itself in that light, even hinting that those who developed its first principles have either changed their minds or are on the verge of doing so, by the end of the journal's run, in 1932, it is clear that this approach to the Bible not only is here to stay but also has made real inroads into seminaries and local parishes, to say nothing of its influence in more secular settings, such as departments of Semitic or Oriental studies, which at the time were largely confined to McGill and the University of Toronto.

Non-Christian Traditions

The *CJRT* was decidedly not interested in non-Christian religions. When and where they were mentioned, supersessionism or superiority was never far behind. In an article titled "Religions and Religion," Nathaniel Micklem, Chair in New Testament Language and Literature at Queen's Theological College, opens with the statement that "Jesus Christ is the Yea and Amen of all God's promises and all man's dreams."[41] Though the article acknowledges that there are different religions with their own unique historical and spiritual concerns, it quickly betrays any such relativity. Micklem concludes his "analysis" with these words: "Jesus Christ stands alone in history, and Christianity as the religion of Christ may, I believe, claim to be the final religion for the human race."[42]

We also encounter the odd article devoted to other places. J.D. MacRae –a graduate of the Universities of Manitoba and Glasgow, and Dean of the Faculty of Theology at Shantung Christian University – writes about the political revolution in China of 1911, but his historical examination is filtered through Christian concerns, when he asks, "Will China Become Christian?" His response is that "the last five years have seen some of the brightest minds address themselves to the greatest themes of our faith. Let us expect more light from the East."[43] Percy G. Price – a Torontonian, and superintendent of the East Tokyo Mission and chairman of the Social Service Committee of the Japan Methodist Church – writes in the same manner about Christianity in Japan in his "Japan and the Christian Movement."[44]

There tends to be a greater interest in Buddhism as a religion than in the countries where Buddhists are found. H.L. MacNeill, a graduate of the University of Chicago and professor of New Testament literature at Brandon College and subsequently at McMaster, who had also written the article on the "Protestantism" of Paul mentioned above, wrote several articles on Buddhism in which he presented a basic overview of it. His conclusion: the Buddha made "the tragic mistake of ignoring the value of life and self and personality, and of becoming altogether too negative in his thought and practice."[45] In his "Buddha as Pragmatist," he argues that "in fact, I make bold to say that historical Christianity in many of its forms, to-day as in the past, is in dire need of this earnest, constructive self-discipline of Buddhism, released as it can be from its blighting, negative, ultra-pessimistic [view] of life and its true goal."[46]

Interestingly, and as I noted earlier, MacNeill had been the subject of controversy and investigation at Brandon, not because of his teaching of Buddhism or anything we might call comparative religion, but on account of his liberalism and modernism, which was anathema in Baptist circles.[47] Indeed, MacNeill would later be credited with liberating the politician Tommy Douglas from "a literal interpretation of the scriptures."[48] *The Gospel Witness*, a newsletter published by the Baptist Church in Canada, reported in its 8 September 1932 edition that MacNeill had been investigated by a commission, then summarized the report of the commission, and concluded with the following statement:

> We need not occupy further space in discussing Professor MacNeill. That he is a Modernist of the Modernists there is not the shadow of a doubt. The law will be found to operate in university and denominational life, as in the life of an individual, "Whatsoever a man soweth, that shall he also reap." If the Denomination sows Modernism in the minds of its ministerial students, it will reap Modernism from its pulpits in the future. With such a man as Prof. H. L. MacNeill in the Chair of New Testament Interpretation in McMaster University it would be the sheerest hypocrisy for McMaster longer to contend that it has any sympathy with evangelical principles. The thing has come to pass which we predicted long ago, that McMaster was on the toboggan slide, and is descending with ever-increasing acceleration.[49]

This is an interesting case, because, though MacNeill is clearly a Christian thinker and certainly regards himself as such, his interpretation of Christianity was bothersome to the Baptist Church (recall that both Brandon and McMaster were initially Baptist institutions). This tension, and the growing unwillingness of places like McMaster to investigate such charges, would prove instrumental in the loosening of theological control and would contribute greatly to the formation of departments of religious studies in the coming decades. It is also interesting, though presumably not of interest to the Baptist Church, that MacNeill's liberalism led him to the study of Buddhism.

The Gospel Witness was highly critical of PhDs from the University of Chicago. Another such graduate was the Canadian Roy C. Bensen. A philosophy graduate, Bensen was subsequently hired – again, to the chagrin of *The Gospel Witness* – to head McMaster's philosophy department in 1932.[50] Bensen, who had served as a missionary in India, maintained that "it was impossible to have firm Christian convictions unless other religions were fully explored and understood."[51] To this end, he published "Karma and Transmigration" in the journal.[52] This idea that one could only fully appreciate one's own religion if one appreciated and understood those of other people would, as we shall see in the next chapter, prove to be a fundamental rationale for the secular study of religion in Canadian universities in the 1960s and '70s.

Again, figures like MacNeill and Bensen are important to our narrative because, despite (or indeed because of) their liberal views toward Christianity, they were able to understand and appreciate the world views of others. Though today we might find their language to be paternalistic or Orientalist, at the time they were revolutionary in the Canadian context. Thus, in hindsight, they represent an important transition from theology to secular religious studies.

Final Volume

The final volume of *CJRT*, 9.4, came out at the end of 1932. Its concluding editorial, titled "The End of an Episode," reflected on the past nine years and reiterated its inter-Christian ecumenism: "There has been no narrow denominationalism represented in the managing board and the editorial committee. The various Churches of Canada have always been included in their inevitably changing membership, and the unified aim of these executives has been constantly to help all sections of the religious and literary life of the land."[53] The editors go on to lament the current economic climate that has led to the journal's demise: "The cost of publication together with the steady decrease of the number of our subscribers in consequence of the prevailing depressions, has made the work increasingly difficult."[54] They continue:

> If some generous patron of disinterested benevolences could have found it possible to include this journal in the number of his clients, it might continue its distinctive and valued service in our Canadian life for an indefinite period. Our inability to find such a patron, after prolonged and persistent searching, means that we cannot see our way to go on any longer, and so, with great reluctance and keen regret, we are compelled to

announce that this number of the ninth volume of the *Canadian Journal of Religious Thought* is the last to appear in this form for the present.[55]

And with that concluding line the first foray into a Canadian journal devoted to religion came to an end.

The *Canadian Journal of Theology* (1955–70)

It would be twenty-three years before another periodical devoted to religion – again rather narrowly conceptualized as Christianity – appeared in Canada. Though it is certainly worth pointing out that, as mentioned in the previous chapter, the Canadian Society of Biblical Studies (CSBS) had begun publishing its *Bulletin* as early as 1935. In the words of John Macpherson, that bulletin was an important milestone because at the time, "those interested in following the development of Biblical scholarship in Canada had nothing to read except denominational and college announcements."[56] Macpherson also notes that with few exceptions "only a very few Canadian scholars had published in the available American professional journals."[57] The *Bulletin* thus served as a venue for publication between the two major journals discussed in this chapter, though it is worth noting that it was an annual and that it was devoted solely to matters of biblical interpretation and criticism, which included (though certainly not always) those of the form and redaction variety.

The new journal was titled the *Canadian Journal of Theology* (*CJT*) and focused solely on Christian theology. It was not interested, in other words, in any type of comparative theology. Indeed, the mandate was made clear in the journal's subtitle, *A Quarterly of Christian Thought*. The subtitle's emphasis on thought would seem to be a nod to its precursor. Indeed, the opening editorial, "The Purpose of the Journal," makes explicit the link between the two journals. In explaining to its readers why the new journal is necessary, the editors remark,

> In the first place, we are not so much starting a new periodical as seeking to recover and further the achievements of a predecessor. *The Canadian Journal of Religious Thought* had a successful career for a number of years. It was only the abnormal conditions of the great depression that brought it to an end. Since that day, the population of the country has increased, her material wealth has vastly expanded, and theology has had a new birth. If the former journal could thrive so well under less favourable conditions, we must not for very shame neglect the task of producing one today.[58]

The editors also note that their journal will positively contribute to the intellectual and cultural health of the country. Again, not unlike their predecessors at *CJRT*, they connect their journal to the religious and spiritual fate of the nation:

> In the second place, we belong to a nation that is rapidly achieving a splendid nationhood, progressive within and respected without. But we cannot grow wholesomely, deeply, and in a balanced way unless we develop among us all the organs of life and expression. Reflective journals are a prime necessity for intellectual and spiritual health. For this reason alone, there *must* be a Canadian Journal of theology. We are confident that every patriotic Canadian who has a sense of spiritual values will want to see our venture succeed.[59]

The editors also see it as their goal to encourage a distinctly *Canadian* practice of theologizing. Canadian Christians, once again, according to the inaugural editorial, are encouraged to develop a unique response to Jesus's message:

> In the third place ... We shall hear the Word of God only as we obey it in the Canadian milieu in which he has put it to serve him. Let no man be affronted by the word *Theology* in our name, as if it stood for dry, abstract, unpractical discourse. To us it means the Word or Truth of God yielded as we shape our decisions in live human issues in the light of Christ. We believe that the task of clarifying that Word and those issues in the service of the Church of Christ calls for a theological journal.[60]

As with its predecessor, there is very little reflection on other religious traditions and their practitioners. The focus is solely Christian, and a perusal of the contents quickly bears this out. This is made even more explicit in the editorial from the third issue of the first volume, which states the journal's aim as

> to discuss those issues of Christian faith and practice which bear directly on the life of the Church and on the thinking and action of the Christian believer, and to do this against the background of the past history and the present circumstances of the Christian communions of Canada. It is, in other words, essentially a journal of *theology*, devoted to the expression of Christian truth and to the clarification of the way of life which that truth involves.[61]

What is most striking about the new journal is that it is, again like its predecessor and the *Bulletin* of the CSBS, anglophone. The new journal was published by the University of Toronto Press with an initial subscription of 750,[62] which had jumped to 1,300 by volume 3.[63] Although more amenable to higher criticism, the journal still saw its primary mandate as being to advocate for Christian theological positions. "One of the most disturbing development of our time is the abandonment, by the individual, of moral responsibility," the editors write in a 1956 editorial, and "our situation has arisen because we have largely lost our theological concern for life."[64]

Despite this, and perhaps reflective of the winds of change in terms of the study of religion on Canadian campuses, there was a growing acknowledgment in *CJT* that matters had to change. Robert H.L. Slater, in an article titled "Christian Attitudes to Other Religions," begins this discussion:

> In situations complicated by local patriotism and new respect for indigenous cultures and traditions, must the Christian stand alone, apparently antagonistic, obliged to say an uncompromising "No" to every non-Christian belief? Can he not, and should he not, without disloyalty to Christ, say at times a more accommodating "Yes," acknowledging and welcoming basic agreements?[65]

Slater had a very interesting career.[66] Born in England and trained at Oxford, he went to Rangoon University in what is today Myanmar, where he spent sixteen years teaching Christian students philosophy. After the Second World War he received his PhD from Columbia in New York for a dissertation that was later published as *Paradox and Nirvana: A Study of Religious Ultimates with Special Reference to Burmese Buddhism.*[67] After teaching for two years at Huron College in London, Ontario, he was appointed as Professor of Systematic Theology at McGill, where he also served as the Principal of Montreal Diocesan Theological College and as Canon of Christ Church Cathedral. In the introduction to Slater's Festschrift, which appeared in the pages of the newly created *Studies in Religion / Sciences religieuses* (*SR*), its editor-in-chief, Joseph C. McLelland, quotes from a letter supplied by Slater's friend:

> Although his field is Comparative Religion, his adherence to his own faith has never been a matter of formality. Rather, because of his own depth of spirituality, he has been able to appreciate and respect the spiritual insights of others. At seminary he was regularly at the daily Eucharist and morning and evening offices. He was concerned to help men grow in a regular pattern of worship, for he himself was never ashamed to confess his own dependence on such a pattern.[68]

Slater was an ordained Anglican minister who specialized in Theravada Buddhism. His main goal, as the above passage makes clear, was to foster interfaith understanding. In 1958 he was hired by Harvard to be the first director of its Center for the Study of World Religions. This centre prided itself, as it still does, in cultivating inter-religious or interfaith dialogue. The goal of the centre, in the words of its anonymous donors, was to "help Harvard University maintain graduate and undergraduate courses in the religions of the world, to train teachers in this field, to give ministers a sympathetic appreciation of other religions, and to stimulate undergraduate interest in the religions of the world."[69] The *Harvard Crimson*, reporting in 1959, described the new centre as encouraging "spiritual communication between men of different religious faiths" by means of a "sympathetic study of the religions of the world" so that each scholar in the centre "may gain a clear insight and firmer faith in the truth of his own religion."[70]

While still highly theological, Slater is nevertheless interesting in that in him we witness, not unlike we did with George Monro Grant, a shift toward comparative – or, for lack of a better term, interfaith – theology for the sake of constructive dialogue between religions. This was another important step on the path toward the creation of departments of religious studies. While some could certainly argue that many such departments retain this model, there would gradually be more critical voices. Slater remained at Harvard until 1964, at which point another Canadian succeeded him – Wilfred Cantwell Smith, who will be discussed in more detail in the following chapter.

In 1959, in another article in the pages of *CJT*, John S. Conway made a plea for religious studies in universities. According to him,

> a department of Religious Studies could offer a course of studies as deep and as penetrating as any other in the university. Such a department would be able to attract students beyond the undergraduate level, for there is a growing demand among graduate students for courses in Religious Studies to complement and complete their work in related fields, such as history, psychology, or education ... It may be pointed out that there is a serious lack of advanced study and research in Religious Studies throughout English-speaking Canada. It is surely not too much to claim that if this branch of learning were given a larger place in university curricula, and accorded a larger share of academic resources, notable contributions could be made.[71]

My sense, though, is that Conway did not mean this in the sense of comparative religion that would later come to dominate departments of religious studies in the 1960s and '70s, but philosophy of religion, which is often synonymous with Christianity, a field that was very important in Britain. The university, at least on Conway's model, should not be the place to look at the historical and sociological (i.e., humanistic) dimensions of religious traditions, but the "place where ultimate questions are taken seriously."[72]

The need for such departments was echoed by the Rev. John W. Wevers. Wevers, professor of Hebrew at University College at the University of Toronto, made a plea for the establishment of departments of religion in the university: "The university is failing in its primary function, namely, to aid the student in thinking out for himself a satisfying view of thought and action. A Department of Religion is not a luxury; it is an imperative."[73] For Wevers, "a university serving and subsidized by a Canadian citizenry should be non-sectarian."[74] It was this desire, more than any court case or legal ruling, that would go on to make the academic study of religion possible in Canada.

Though we feel, at least from the above example, the winds of change in the air, the journal – given its mandate – remained devoted to Christianity and to theological method. An editorial from 1958 encouraged more pastors, ministers, and priests to contribute so that the journal might become more relevant to preaching activities.[75] One glaring instance of the journal's Christocentrism is the curious case of Ismail al-Faruqi, a scholar of Islam on the Comparative Study of Religion track in the Faculty of Divinity at McGill. In 1961 he wrote an article titled "On the Significance of Niebuhr's Ideas of Society," which is significant for at least two reasons. First, though a scholar of Islam, al-Faruqi could only appear in the journal if he wrote on a topic relevant to Christian theology. This in itself might not be surprising, however. The second reason, though, is jarring. Since al-Faruqi was not a Christian, the article had to be introduced by the editor, who writes that "it is not usual to preface a contribution to this journal with an introductory paragraph, but the article which follows has certain unusual features which perhaps justify an exception in this instance."[76]

Following this, the editor reassures his readers that al-Faruqi is, though not a Christian, at least a devout religious person: "Dr. Faruqi is a devout Muslim whose faith has impressed all his colleagues by its qualities of conviction and sincerity ... His present assignment is a critique of the Christian ethic from the Muslim point of view ... Not everyone will accept his estimate of Jesus and his teaching ... Nevertheless it is important that we in the West should discover how we appear to eastern eyes."[77]

Such a position would be increasingly untenable. Indeed, it would end in the following years as secular departments of religious studies began to spring up across Canada on university campuses. The final editorial, announcing the termination of *CJT*, makes this explicit. Therein, the Rev. Eugene R. Fairweather, the journal's last editor, writes: "Early in 1971 the University of Toronto Press will issue the first number of a new quarterly journal devoted to a wide range of religious studies, including those scholarly disciplines which have been regularly represented in the pages of this *Journal*."[78] This new journal, as mentioned, would be *SR*, to be discussed in greater detail in the following chapter. He calls the new journal "a fresh and promising venture in religious publishing."[79] He also notes, echoing my comments above, that

> in 1970 a Canadian university which fails to provide for religious studies, Christian and non-Christian, invites the criticism that its curriculum is anachronistic and inadequate. In 1970 the Canadian theological faculty or seminary which tries to work in isolation from the wider community of theological and religious scholarship is on the way to becoming the underprivileged exception to a recognized rule. We may reasonably hope that the coming decade will see an unprecedented flowering of religious and theological studies in the great academic centers of this country.[80]

Yet Fairweather also argues that, despite the current change in orientation, this does not rule out, at some future date, a new theological journal: "Now we yield our place to a journal designed to comprehend the diverse interests of Canadian theologians and students of religion in the 1970s. It may well be that, at some future date, a new periodical primarily devoted to Christian theology will be needed and demanded. But the forthcoming journal of religious studies clearly meets a present and urgent need. We welcome it and pledge our support."[81]

Conclusions

This chapter has surveyed the key publications developed in Canada over the course of roughly the first three-quarters of the twentieth century. It has examined some of the themes and authors and their concerns during that period. While decidedly theological in methodology and Christocentric in orientation, we see, especially during the last years of *CJT*, a paradigm shift: away from Christianity toward comparative theology and then toward comparative religion, from particularism to universalism, and from religious to secular and historical study. This process occurred over many years, and we see it reflected in the history, contents, and fates of these two journals. Indeed, this shift was also, as the following chapter will show in greater detail, the result of significant changes in Canadian society.

As Canadian society became increasingly diverse and as the federal government began to encourage such diversity, it was only a matter of time before the study of religion had to diversify. This is something that the closing editorial of *CJT* seemed to be aware of with great poignancy. Even during the height of *CJT*'s publication, advances were taking place behind the scenes. Departments of religious studies had begun to arise in select Canadian universities, scholarly organizations were beginning to develop, and *CJT*, as Fairweather duly noted, was becoming increasingly anachronistic. These new departments, moreover, increasingly sought out new methodologies as they set out to switch their purview to all religions and not just Christianity and its theological elaboration. The result was that the study of religion would now shift from the religious seminary to the secular university.

Chapter Seven

From Seminary to University

> Prior to the 1960s the theological colleges in Canada had no competition in the study of religion, but since then a larger proportion of the academic study of religion is taking place in undergraduate and graduate departments of religion which usually have no overt commitment to any specific religious traditions. The traditional theological disciplines of bible, church history and historical theology are increasingly dominated by religious studies approaches ... Consequently it has become clear in the 1980s that the seminaries are no longer the main institutional locus within higher education for the study of religion. They no longer set the agenda or the standards in the academic area and the trends in the scholarly study of religion no longer originate in the seminaries.[1]

Thus wrote N. Keith Clifford – professor of religious studies at UBC and former President of the Canadian Society of Church History[2] – in an article published in the pages of *SR* in 1990. It is no coincidence that Clifford penned his reflections on the demise of the importance of theology in the principal Canadian journal devoted to the non-theological and academic study of religion. *SR*, it will be recalled from the previous chapter, had replaced the much more narrowly focused *CJT*, a periodical that focused exclusively on Christianity and did so, moreover, as the title suggests, from a distinctly theological perspective. The switch in focus, scope, and methodology of *SR* both reflected and contributed to the institutional changes that Clifford noted. Indeed, by 1972, as Remus remarks, "virtually all religious studies departments in Ontario offered courses in non-Western religions, though often only at the generalist level."[3] The present chapter suggests that this formative change in the study of religion reflected a major change in Canadian society during these decades. As the ethnic and religious backgrounds of immigrants changed radically in the 1960s, the federal government began to fund programs that embraced the need to understand these groups. Moreover, young Canadian undergraduates of the 1960s and '70s, influenced by the global countercultural movement, became increasingly interested in other cultures and religions beyond the traditional Judeo-Christian.

Also in the background was the Fielding Report of 1966, which argued that there were too many small theological seminaries scattered throughout Canada that trained too few clergy.[4] The report recommended amalgamating these seminaries and concentrating them in specific cities. This led in the early 1970s to the creation of five major clusters in Halifax, Montreal, Toronto, Saskatoon, and Vancouver. In Halifax, for example, the Atlantic School of Theology was created through a combination of the Anglican, Catholic, and United churches; whereas the Vancouver School of Theology combined the Anglican and United churches, with the Presbyterians having an associate affiliation. Such clusters would have major repercussions for theological education and policy, given that each church would now have to initiate internal changes in negotiation with the other churches with which it was theologically affiliated.[5] It also meant that theology became increasingly involved with post-secondary education through affiliations in places like Vancouver and Halifax.[6] Even in those places that were not part of these clusters, closer affiliations with universities occurred. The University of Western Ontario, for example, saw affiliations with King's (a male Catholic liberal arts college) and Brescia (a female Catholic liberal arts college) in 1971, both of which were modelled on the university's earlier affiliation in 1956 with Huron College (Anglican).[7]

This diminution of theological education, as Clifford notes above, could then be juxtaposed with what would soon become a florescence of secular programs of religious studies at universities across the country during the late 1960s and early 1970s. This change from seminary to university was not just institutional; it was also curricular in that it reflected the way religion was understood in relationship to society. This new florescence of the secular study of religion manifested itself in a host of new ventures: the creation of a new and non-theological journal (*SR*); the rise of departments of religious studies, even in institutions with no previous interest in religion; and the establishment of scholarly societies devoted to the study of religion in general, and of religion in Canada in particular. This chapter seeks to contextualize this shift in orientation by focusing on the structural and institutional changes that facilitated it; the chapter that follows will look at the actual rise of such departments.

Behind the Scenes

Until the early 1960s, as we have seen, the primary place to study religion was in theological seminaries, and the main publishing forum was theological journals such as *CJRT* and *CJT*. Much, however, was happening intellectually and socially behind the scenes in Canada. By the late 1960s, secular departments of religion were beginning to take root, and *CJT* was increasingly seen as too parochial, too theological, and too Christocentric. All of this was occurring against a backdrop of demographic changes in Canada brought on by new immigration policies, which would radically alter the country's ethnic make-up. The 1960s thus proved to be a decade of change on a number of fronts.

These new departments of religious studies emerged either out of earlier programs in theology or, especially in the western provinces, *de novo*. The present chapter argues that demographic changes facilitated all of this. As immigrants made their way to Canada, and as multiculturalism became an official governmental policy, it became necessary to understand the beliefs and the customs of new Canadians. Newly formed departments of religious studies became the perfect place to research, teach, and disseminate an understanding of those religions of the globe that were now making a home for themselves in Canada.

The appearance of *SR* in 1970 was the direct result of these larger social, demographic, and intellectual trends in Canadian life. This is not to imply that Canada existed in a vacuum. It is probably no coincidence, for example, that in 1963 the United States Supreme Court, in its ruling on the *School District of Abington Township, PA v. Schempp*, declared school-sponsored Bible reading in American public schools to be unconstitutional.[8] The Court also differentiated between teaching religion and teaching *about* religion. In the words of Associate Justice Tom Clark:

> We agree that of course that the State may not establish a "religion of secularism" in the sense of affirmatively opposing or showing hostility to religion ... *It might well be said that one's education is not complete without a study of comparative religion or the history of religion and its relationship to the advancement of civilization*. It certainly may be said that the Bible is worthy of study for its literary and historic qualities. *Nothing we have said here indicates that such study of the Bible or of religion, when presented objectively as part of a secular program of education, may not be effected consistently with the First Amendment*. But the exercises here do not fall into those categories. They are religious exercises, required by the States in violation of the command of the First Amendment that the Government maintain strict neutrality, neither aiding nor opposing religion.[9]

This ruling would have a tremendous impact on the study of religion in the United States. For one thing its main society, the National Association of Bible Instructors (NABI), changed its name that same year, 1963, to the American Academy of Religion (AAR), in addition to changing the name of its main journal from *JNABI* to *JAAR*. Furthermore, since it was now legal to teach *about* religion in public institutions, state universities began opening departments of religious studies, including programs, in places like Virginia, North Carolina, Indiana, Iowa, and Florida.

Canada, however, had no such separation between church and state. If the reason for the change of institutional context in the United States was legal, in Canada it was demographic and the direct result of a more liberal immigration policy and the rise of multiculturalism as official federal policy. This is not to imply that the academic study of religion looked (or continues to look) different in Canada than it does in the United States or in other European countries. On the contrary, and much more modestly, it is only to suggest that the larger legal, demographic, and social conditions that facilitated such study are considerably different in the two countries.

Multiculturalism (1971)

The Canadian Parliament had, from its earliest years, enacted a number of restrictive immigration measures that targeted non-whites and non-Christians.[10] These included the Continuous Journey Regulation of 1908, which barred immigrants who were not travelling directly from their country of birth or citizenship by a "continuous journey." The intent was to block immigrants from India and South Asia, whose ships often had to stop at Japan or Hawaii.[11] This was in addition to such acts as the Chinese Immigration Act, renewed as late as 1923, which banned most forms of Chinese immigration to Canada.[12] Such legislation, however, had to be removed in 1947, the year that Canada signed the Declaration of Human Rights, which prevented discrimination based on race or religion. This was further facilitated by the Canadian Citizenship Act of 1946, which separated Canadian citizenship from British nationality.

Until the 1960s and '70s, Canadian immigration had largely favoured British, American, and European immigrants. However, immigration policies witnessed a tremendous liberalization under the Conservative government of John Diefenbaker (1957–63) and then the liberal government of Lester B. Pearson (1963–8).[13] The White Paper on Immigration, commissioned by Pearson in 1966, for example, stressed less country of origin and more the importance of skilled labour.[14] Though initially this would favour British and other European migration, it would soon set the stage for immigrants from other countries.

Key to the development of multiculturalism as official policy was the role of bilingualism and biculturalism in Canada. On 19 July 1963, Prime Minister Lester B. Pearson struck a Royal Commission on Bilingualism and Biculturalism in order "to recommend what steps should be taken to develop the Canadian Confederation on the basis of an equal partnership between the two founding races, taking into account the contribution made by the other ethnic groups to the cultural enrichment of Canada and the measures that should be taken to safeguard that contribution."[15] The commission, then, set out to examine the existing state of bilingualism and biculturalism in Canada with the aim of developing an equal partnership between the country's British and French elements. Implicit here, however, was the importance to the country of other "ethnic groups." The commission's goal was to "report on the role of public and private organizations, including the mass communications media, in promoting bilingualism, better cultural relations and a more widespread appreciation of the basically bicultural character of our country and of the subsequent contribution made by the other cultures; and to recommend what should be done to improve that role."[16]

The commission recommended, among other things, that bilingual districts be created in regions of Canada where members of the minority community, be they French or English, made up 10 per cent or more of the local population; that children be able to attend schools in the language of the parents' choice in regions where there was sufficient demand; that Ottawa become a bilingual city; and that English and French be declared official languages of Canada.

The commission was also tasked with considering the cultural contributions of other ethnic groups. In this context, it recommended that minority groups be given greater recognition and support in preserving their cultures.[17] Incoming prime minister Pierre Elliott Trudeau, who took office in 1968, used the commission's recommendations as a foundation for his new government's policy. In 1969, for example, the Official Languages Act / Loi sur les langues officielles made Canada officially bilingual.

Just as importantly, the report would serve as the government's official policy of multiculturalism.[18] In a speech to the House of Commons on 8 October 1971, Trudeau announced:

> It was the view of the royal commission, shared by the government and, I am sure, by all Canadians, that there cannot be one cultural policy for the Canadians of British and French origins, another for the original peoples

> and yet a third for all others. For although there are two official languages, there is no official culture, nor does any ethnic group take precedence over any other. No citizen or group of citizens is other than Canadian, and all should be treated fairly.[19]

Trudeau then proposed that the cultural freedom of all individuals be preserved and that the cultural contributions of diverse ethnic groups to Canadian society be recognized:

> The policy I am announcing today accepts the contention of the other cultural communities that they, too, are essential elements in Canada and deserve government assistance in order to contribute to regional and national life in ways that derive from their heritage yet are distinctly Canadian.[20]

The result was a policy of multiculturalism within a bilingual (but not multilingual) framework. This would mean:

> First, resources permitting, the government will seek to assist all Canadian cultural groups that have demonstrated a desire and effort to continue to develop a capacity to grow and contribute to Canada, and a clear need for assistance, the small and weak groups no less than the strong and highly organized.
>
> Second, the government will assist members of all cultural groups to overcome cultural barriers to full participation in Canadian society.
>
> Third, the government will promote creative encounters and interchange among all Canadian cultural groups in the interest of national unity.
>
> Fourth, the government will continue to assist immigrants to acquire at least one of Canada's official languages in order to become full participants in Canadian society.[21]

As of 1971, multiculturalism was official government policy. In 1982, when Trudeau repatriated the constitution from Britain, the Canadian government entrenched in it a Charter of Rights and Freedoms – that is, a bill of rights.[22] The charter guarantees certain political rights to Canadian citizens and civil rights to everyone in Canada in all areas and at all levels of the government. The charter's overarching goal is to unify Canadians around a set of principles that embody those rights. Section 27, for example, reads: "This Charter shall be interpreted in a manner consistent with the preservation and enhancement of the multicultural heritage of Canadians." This is generally seen as officially recognizing multiculturalism as a Canadian value.[23]

Finally, the Canadian Multiculturalism Act was enacted by Conservative prime minister Brian Mulroney in 1988. This act, "for the preservation and enhancement of multiculturalism in Canada,"[24] sets out in detail what multiculturalism policy involves:

> **3 (1)** It is hereby declared to be the policy of the Government of Canada to
>
> a. recognize and promote the understanding that multiculturalism reflects the cultural and racial diversity of Canadian society and acknowledges the freedom of all members of Canadian society to preserve, enhance and share their cultural heritage;
> b. recognize and promote the understanding that multiculturalism is a fundamental characteristic of the Canadian heritage and identity and that it provides an invaluable resource in the shaping of Canada's future;
> c. promote the full and equitable participation of individuals and communities of all origins in the continuing evolution and shaping of all aspects of Canadian society and assist them in the elimination of any barrier to that participation;
> d. recognize the existence of communities whose members share a common origin and their historic contribution to Canadian society, and enhance their development;
> e. ensure that all individuals receive equal treatment and equal protection under the law, while respecting and valuing their diversity;
> f. encourage and assist the social, cultural, economic and political institutions of Canada to be both respectful and inclusive of Canada's multicultural character;
> g. promote the understanding and creativity that arise from the interaction between individuals and communities of different origins;
> h. foster the recognition and appreciation of the diverse cultures of Canadian society and promote the reflection and the evolving expressions of those cultures;
> i. preserve and enhance the use of languages other than English and French, while strengthening the status and use of the official languages of Canada; and
> j. advance multiculturalism throughout Canada in harmony with the national commitment to the official languages of Canada.

Multiculturalism would, in turn, reflect and facilitate a new immigration policy in Canada. In 1967 a federal order-in-council (PC 1967-1616) established new standards for assessing potential immigrants and determining their admissibility.[25] The result was a points system, still in use today, in which potential immigrants are given a score in nine categories: education and training; personal character; occupational demand; occupational skill; age; prearranged employment; knowledge of French and English; the presence of a relative in Canada; and employment opportunities in their area of destination. Individuals receiving 50 points or more out of a possible 100 are admitted as independent immigrants, regardless of ethnicity or place of birth. After the implementation of this order-in-council, immigration from Asia, the Caribbean, Latin America, and Africa increased significantly.[26]

The Immigration Act of 1976 further contributed to this more inclusive pattern of immigration to Canada. For example, it was the first immigration act to include refugees – as defined by the UN's Convention Relating to the Status of Refugees – as a distinct class. It also sought to "[e]nsure that any person who seeks admission to Canada on either a permanent or temporary basis is subject to standards of admission that do not discriminate on grounds of race, national or ethnic origin, colour, religion or sex."

As a result of all this, in the 1960s and '70s Canada underwent a momentous demographic change. Up until then the country had been largely white, European, and Christian. Afterwards it became increasingly multicultural, multiethnic, and multireligious. This would have a tremendous effect both on the country and, important for this study, on the study of religion within it. It is no coincidence, for example, that the main journal of religion in Canada prior to 1970 had focused entirely on Christian theology, whereas after that year it transformed itself into a secular journal that used non-theological methodologies and that opened its pages to *all* religions. Here we should, once again, keep in mind the words of Fairweather in his final editorial in the *Canadian Journal of Theology*: "In 1970 a Canadian university which fails to provide for religious studies, Christian and non-Christian, invites the criticism that its curriculum is anachronistic and inadequate."[27] This statement wonderfully sums up the situation. Christian theology was quite quickly being replaced by non-denominational and secular religious studies, something echoed by the quote from Clifford with which I began this chapter. Federal legislation on multiculturalism, for example, demanded that the beliefs, customs, and religions of others be taken seriously. This meant that a journal that focused narrowly on Christianity would not, for example, be eligible for federal financial support. The articulation and defence of Christian truth-claims was coming to be seen as "anachronistic and inadequate" when it came to addressing the changing ethnic and religious make-up of Canada. This is not to say that Christian theological institutions ceased to exist. It does mean, however, that they became – to return us again to the quotation from Clifford – increasingly irrelevant for the majority of Canadians.

In their stead, a broad-based network of societies and organizations formed in the 1960s and '70s that would shape the study of religion in Canada into the present. It is no coincidence, then, that virtually all of the major scholarly associations devoted to the study of religion were founded in the 1960s and '70s. The main outlier to this was the Canadian Society of Biblical Studies (CSBS), which, as we saw in a previous chapter, was created in 1933. Below I provide brief histories of these scholarly organizations, which paved the way for the florescence of departments of religious studies throughout the country.

First, though, it is worth noting that these scholarly societies were part of an ongoing process in the 1960s of nationalizing the study of religion in Canada by making it relevant to specifically Canadian concerns and interests. The formation of these societies was intimately connected to a larger process of establishing a Canadian scholarly identity in general and one that involved the study of religion in particular. Without their own societies and without their own journal, Canadian scholars of religion, like Canadian scholars more generally, risked being swallowed up by the much larger American academy and all of the scholarly and publishing institutions associated with it. Indeed, as the Canadian Church historian John Grant argued in 1955, just prior to the formation of the Canadian Society of Church History (CSCH), there was a "subtle temptation to write into Canadian church history assumptions derived from the study of other countries," with the result that "we may easily be led to overlook differences that are as striking as the similarities and sometimes even more significant."[28] The scholarly societies discussed below were attempts to ameliorate just this situation.

Scholarly Organizations Devoted to the Study of Religion

Canadian Theological Society (CTS)

The Canadian Theological Society was founded at Emmanuel College in the University of Toronto in 1955. Its sole aim was to promote theological reflection and writing in a Canadian context.[29] It will be recalled from the previous chapter that 1955 was the same year the *Canadian Journal of Theology* was founded. The society and the journal must be seen as interconnected: both were committed to theologizing from a distinctly Canadian perspective. Though what exactly theologizing "from a Canadian perspective" meant was not always clear. It seems to have meant using Christian theology to address the spiritual and other issues facing Christian Canadian society. The society, not unlike the journal, was originally Protestant in orientation, but both would eventually include more Catholic and Orthodox voices, especially the former after the Second Vatican Council, which would liberalize the Catholic Church over the following decade.

The minutes from the initial meeting (where no papers were read) list the following in attendance: Very Rev. George C. Pidgeon, Rev. Pres. A.B.B. Moore, Rev. Prin. W.R. Coleman, Rev Prof. R.J. Williams, Bishop S.C. Steer, Rev. Prof. William O. Fennell, Rev. Prin. A.D. Matheson, and Rev. George Boyle. At that meeting a constitution was developed, which included the following raison d'être: "to promote interest in the study of theology in Canada."[30] The first annual meeting was held the following year at the Faculty of Divinity at McGill, and from 1961 until 1969, the CTS met conjointly with the CSBS and the Canadian Society of Church History (CSCH) (see below). As Fennell, one of its earliest members, notes, joint programs were developed and presidential addresses were presented to sessions that included all three societies.[31] In 1969 the three societies all agreed to meet with the conglomerate Learned Societies, with the first such meeting held the following year. The "Learneds" had been established in 1930 (it would be renamed the Congress of the Humanities and Social Sciences in 1996), with the aim of encouraging collaborative and interdisciplinary research across the humanities and social sciences.[32]

Canadian Society of Church History (CSCH)

In 1960 the Canadian Society of Church History (CSCH) was founded as a non-denominational association with the aim of promoting and encouraging research in the history of Christianity, particularly in the context of Canada. According to N. Keith Clifford, quoted at the beginning of this chapter, though it was meant as a parallel to the American Association of Church History – which had been founded much earlier, in 1888 – it had a distinctly nationalist aim, that being "a search for the uniqueness of the Canadian experience."[33] Again, though, we see how this experience, at least for this society, largely meant Canada's *Christian* experience – which should not surprise us, given the society's mandate.

Société canadienne de théologie (SCT)

The Société canadienne de théologie, the francophone counterpart to the Canadian Theological Society, was founded in 1963. Its goal, according to its website, "comme mission initiale et essentielle de favoriser le développement des études théologiques au Québec et au Canada français."[34] Many anglophone societies had by then emerged and subsequently focused on developing a nationalist scholarly agenda; francophone societies did the same, only their "nationalist" agenda was French Canadian. In the case of SCT, it involved articulating a uniquely Québécois or French Canadian theological perspective.[35] Given the importance of the Catholic Church in Quebec, this has meant a predominant though by no means exclusive grounding in and attachment to Catholicism. Though it is worth noting that this Catholic approach, including Catholic biblical interpretation, also takes place within the confines of the Association catholique des études bibliques au Canada (ACÉBAC).

Canadian Society for the Study of Religion / Société canadienne pour l'étude de la religion (CSSR/SCÉR)

The Canadian Society for the Study of Religion / Société canadienne pour l'étude de la religion (CSSR/SCÉR) was founded in 1965 by George Grant (McMaster),[36] Boyd Sinyard (Sir George Williams, subsequently Concordia), and William Nicholls (UBC), with the assistance of Sheila McDonough (Sir George Williams/Concordia) and Eugene Combs (McMaster).[37] The goal of the new society was to open up the study of religion to other (i.e., non-Christian) religions and to develop non-theological methodologies. Within ten years of the founding of *CJT*, then, the academic study of religion was slowly gaining traction. It was this society, moreover, that pushed for the creation of a new journal that would supersede its more narrowly focused predecessors.

Importantly, CSSR was intended to serve as a point of reference for Québécois scholars who sought to stress the humanistic study of religion (*sciences de l'homme*) over catechesis at a time when the Quebec government was itself trying itself to differentiate between these two approaches.[38] In this context, it is also worth noting that CSSR/SCÉR was also the first society dealing with the study of religion in Canada to, at least in theory, adopt an official policy of bilingualism.[39]

In 1965, CSSR/SCÉR applied successfully for admission to the Learned Societies (discussed above); it was the first society dealing with religion to do so.[40] Reflecting the multicultural moment and perhaps also echoing the rise in ecumenical theology found in some of the later issues of *CJT*, its founders based their argument on the importance of understanding those who practise different religions. Admission to the Learned Societies was a milestone in the academic study of religion in Canada because it meant that, as of 1965, religious studies now existed as an independent field of study, and in a manner that could be clearly differentiated from theology on the one hand and cognate fields such as philosophy and history on the other. The following year, the society gained a representative on the Humanities Research Council (HRC), an umbrella organization that helps fund and promote the humanities in Canada. This further cemented religion as a field of study in the humanities. With funding from the Canada Council, the federal government agency that funds research in the arts broadly defined, the HRC assists in the publication, travel, and research activities of its constituencies.

As mentioned, from the start, CSSR/SCÉR set out to be a bilingual organization, and members were encouraged to speak and/or write in their first language. Its first meeting was held in 1966 at the Learned Societies Conference in Sherbrooke, Quebec. It was CSSR/SCÉR, more than any other organization, that contributed to the broadening of studies of religion beyond Christianity in Canada. Moreover, it fostered, more than any other organization, the increasingly non-Christian focus of newly forming departments of religious studies across Canada.[41]

Société québécoise pour l'étude de la religion (SQÉR)

Despite the rhetoric of bilingualism encountered in CSSR/CSÉR, it was anything but for francophone scholars. As Rousseau and Despland note in their "State-of-the-Art" volume devoted to Quebec, "le fait brutal de l'unilinguisme de la majorité des universitaires anglophone" with the result that the CSSR and other orgaizations "n'a pas réussi depuis sa fondation à offrir aux francophones un espace de communication satisfaisant."[42] This meant, in practice, that anglophones did not need to learn French and that annual meetings tended to favour, given the sheer numbers, English over French. To rectify this situation, Rousseau, Despland, and others proposed a francophone society devoted to the study of religion, which they called the Société québécoise pour l'étude de la religion (SQÉR). In its May 1989 meeting, the Section des sciences religieuses of the Association canadienne-français pour l'avancement des sciences (ACFAS) voted in its favour, which meant that the new society would meet annually with the aim of bringing together "tous les Québécois partageant ses objectifs, francophones et anglophones et tous les francophones canadiens qui souhaitent se relier ainsi avec se foyer distinct de l'espace scientifico-culturel au sein du grand ensemble canadien."[43]

SQÉR subsequently applied for, and received, admission to the Canadian Corporation for Studies in Religion / Corporation canadienne des sciences religieuses (CCSR) (see below). Thus, SQÉR, like all of the other learned societies devoted to religion in Canada, served as a venue for maintaining cultural identity and independence. So while there existed American and European societies devoted to the study of religion, church history, theology, patristics, and so on, these distinctly Canadian societies marked distinctly Canadian boundaries. Moreover, in the case of francophone societies, it also established distinctly Québécois ones.

Canadian Corporation for Studies in Religion / Corporation canadienne des sciences religieuses (CCSR)

In 1970, CSSR/SCÉR, CSBS, CSCH, and CTS together created an umbrella organization, the Canadian Corporation for Studies in Religion, which became recognized by a federal charter the same year.[44] The goal of this larger organization was to aid in "publishing a journal and other materials to serve the needs of scholars working in both the French and English languages in Canada in all fields of the academic study of religion." Though, as we saw with the need on the part of francophone scholars of religion in Canada to form their own society, SQÉR, this genuflection to bilingualism tended to be, at least in the early years, primarily in name only.

A subsequent goal of the corporation was, in the words of Harold Coward, to "effectively represent [the study of religion's] interests to SSHRC and the Humanities and Social Sciences Federation."[45] The Social Sciences and Humanities Research Council of Canada (SSHRC) had been created by an act of Parliament in 1977 as a federal funding agency to promote and support post-secondary research and training in the humanities and social sciences.[46] SSHRC sets policy, creates budgets, and directs research priorities through a committee established by the federal government. Today it reports directly to the Minister of Innovation, Science and Economic Development.

Most fundamentally at the beginning, however, the corporation was responsible for founding the new journal *SR* (discussed below). In addition, it was responsible for funding and publishing the *Guide to Religious Studies in Canada*, prepared by Charles Anderson, which underwent three editions (1967, 1969, and 1972). These guides, published with grants from the Canada Council, were, as will be recalled from the Introduction, intended to "document some aspects of the recent history of the discipline," primarily by providing statistical and logistical overviews of the various departments of religious studies in Canada, "now in its second decade."[47]

The list of constituent organizations would grow to include the SCT and CSPS, though CSCH would drop out of the consortium in 2010, arguing that its needs were not being met by the corporation-sponsored journal, *SR*.[48] In addition to *SR*, the corporation created and maintained six book series to meet the needs of its various members. These were *Editions SR*;[49] *Comparative Ethics Series / Collection d'Ethique Comparée*;[50] *Dissertations SR*;[51] *Studies in Christianity and Judaism / Études sur le christianisme et le judaïsme*;[52] *The Study of Religions in Canada / Sciences religieuses au Canada*;[53] and *SR Supplements*,[54] all published by Wilfrid Laurier University Press (WLUP).[55]

Studies in Religion / Sciences religieuses (*SR*)

In 1970, *CJT* morphed into *SR*, which published its first volume in 1971. The change in name and focus perfectly encapsulates the profound changes that occurred in the study of religion in Canada during the 1960s. *SR*, subtitled *A Canadian Journal / Revue canadienne*, was one of the initial publication ventures of the recently created Canadian Corporation for Studies in Religion through its publication wing, the Corporation for the Publication of Academic Studies in Religion in Canada. It was initially published by the University of Toronto Press before moving to Wilfrid Laurier University Press, and then to Sage Publishers with volume 39 in 2010.

The new journal's inaugural editor was William Nicholls (UBC), a former Anglican chaplain and the founder of the Department of Religious Studies at UBC.[56] The managing editor was John Webster Grant (Emmanuel College), a United Church minister and church historian. The associate editors were Michel M. Campbell (Université de Montréal), a theologian, and Gordon Harland (University of Manitoba), a specialist in church history and contemporary Christian thought. As is evident from the fields of interest of the new editorial team, the areas represented were not significantly different from those of *CJT*. Because of this, neither were the contents of the first few volumes of *SR*.[57] According to Donald Wiebe, one reason for this initial blurring of boundaries between *SR* and *CJT* was that the latter, "experiencing financial difficulties and being unable to secure Canada Council funding because of its 'religious character,' signed away its existence to [*SR*] that was able to secure such government funding. In return, however, the *Canadian Journal of Theology* group received assurance from William Nicholls, the first editor of *SR*, that the new journal would not abandon its theological readership."[58]

Wiebe is certainly correct to note that whereas *CJT* was not eligible for public funds, *SR*, which defined itself as a more humanistic and scientific journal, was. However, the quasi-theological tenor of the new journal may well have had more to do with the fact that there was simply no natural pre-existing set of contributors to produce non-theological scholarship on the academic study of religion in the late 1960s and early 1970s. Of the twenty-four articles published in volume 1, for example, only two dealt explicitly with non-Christian religions.[59]

Unlike its predecessor, *SR* was (and still is) a largely bilingual journal, with articles and book reviews appearing in both official languages. In the inaugural edition, Nicholls explained the focus of the new journal and its relationship to its predecessor:

> The editors of *Studies in Religion / Sciences religieuses* have accepted the task of creating a Canadian journal to cover the whole field of the academic study of religion. As the successor to the *Canadian Journal of Theology*, *SR* will continue to serve scholars in the various theological disciplines who formally looked to *CJT* as an organ for the publication of their work. But the special interest of these scholars will now take their place in a wider context of academic study of religion and religions by a variety of methodologies.[60]

Nicholls continued by noting that, whereas *CJT* had been largely fed by scholars and editorial boards in or near Montreal and Toronto, *SR* would aim for a "geographically diffuse representation" aided by "the considerable advances which have been made in Canadian universities in recent years in the study of religion."[61] In terms of its contributors and its readers, Nicholls acknowledged that there would have to be a fine line between theology and more academic study: "*SR* has inherited from its predecessor an obligation to ... scholars working in theology, church history, the study of the Old and New Testaments, and other related disciplines, and will continue to publish their work, as well as that of Jewish scholars working on their own faith and history."[62]

In addition to this constituency, which seems to have transferred naturally over from *CJT* – though the number of "Jewish scholars working on their own faith and history" was certainly negligible – Nicholls also announced a new constituency:

> The religions of our own culture are here examined in the context of the study of all the other religions of the world, and of the attempt to understand the nature of the religious phenomenon wherever it appears in human existence. This new methodological approach to Christianity and Judaism is still under development, and there is a regrettable scarcity of books reflecting it. As we learn to understand "our own" religions by the same methods we use in understanding "other" religions such as Hinduism and Buddhism, new light will inevitably be shed on both.[63]

While vague as to the contours of the new methodologies, Nicholls nevertheless is intimating here that *SR* should – and again we hear echoes of the old *CJT* – "be most significant and creative if it sheds light on the questions of human existence which religion has always tried to confront."[64] He then goes a step further, arguing that this quest must not be tantamount to "edification," but that there must be "a rigor and a detachment, a disciplinary and scientific basis, appropriate to true scholarship in religion as in every other field."[65] Though, it should be noted, he nowhere spells out how a detached perspective might shed such light on universal questions.

Recall that when Eugene R. Fairweather wrote the final editorial for *CJT*, he hoped "it may well be that, at some future date, a new periodical primarily devoted to Christian theology will be needed and demanded."[66] His hopes proved to be well-founded, for in 1985 there appeared a new journal housed at the Toronto School of Theology, an ecumenical centre composed of the various religious colleges affiliated with the University of Toronto (see chapter 2). This new journal, the *Toronto Journal of Theology*,[67] in the words of Jean-Marc Laporte, its inaugural editor, was the direct result of the lacunae *SR* presented for theological reflection: "Canadian scholars of many denominational affiliations lost a forum of more specific theological character in which they could converse with each other and with the educated public of the Canadian Churches. Moreover in the intervening years the Canadian theological scene has expanded considerably. With the *Toronto Journal of Theology* we intend to provide an additional opportunity for theological discourse within Canada, and thus fill a real need."[68]

The appearance of the *Toronto Journal of Theology* revealed – or, perhaps better, exacerbated – a certain tension in the study of religion in Canada. Because of the historically close connections between denominational colleges and public universities in Canada, this tension did not simply disappear with the appearance of religious studies as an academic field of study. If anything, this tension worsened. *SR*, as we shall see in the following section, now became the venue where this tension was put on full display.

Religious Studies vs. Theology

The anxiety over whether the new study of religion should be theological, objective, or some combination thereof appeared fairly early in the pages of *SR*, and a brief focus on it will illumine some of the issues at stake in these early years. In an article titled "The Reconvergence of Theology and Religious Studies," originally presented as a paper at the annual meeting of the Canadian Society for the Study of Religion in 1974, Charles Davis of Concordia University boldly declared that "the distinction between theology and religious studies has served its purpose. It is now outdated."[69] A "reconvergence" of theology and religious studies, in Davis's view, would introduce "greater clarity and honesty into the procedures of both."[70] He seemed to mean that if theology would return as a central focus of the study of religion, as it had been in medieval Scholasticism, instead of being repudiated by it, then said study would be able to articulate better the truth-claims of religion in general and specific religions in particular. Davis concluded:

> There is no reason to continue a distinction in principle (politically it may still be necessary at certain times and in certain places) between theology and religious studies. Religious studies is a *mélange* that requires unmixing – above all, by a clear distinction between historical and systematic studies. The systematic study of religion, whether scientific or philosophical, could learn much from theology, which might help it turn program into achievement, theology on its part has to acknowledge that it can no longer operate with the data or the authority of a single tradition if it wishes to keep its theoretic status.[71]

The journal's editors must have anticipated a heated exchange, so they invited a number of other scholars to reply to Davis's assertions in his lead article.[72] While these responses were largely themselves theological in nature, it was Donald Wiebe, then at Brandon University in Manitoba (and later at Trinity College at the University of Toronto), who responded most forcefully to Davis's challenge from the perspective of the academic study of religion. "The mere fact that religious phenomena have become the subject of academic and scholarly investigation," wrote Wiebe, "hardly implies the existence of a 'science' of religion – unless by that phrase one means simply the growth of a body of knowledge, the accumulation of factual data, about particular religious traditions."[73] Instead, Wiebe found fault with Davis and, in particular, with another Canadian scholar of religion, Wilfred Cantwell Smith, whom I shall discuss in more detail below. According to Wiebe, like Davis,

> Smith refuses to countenance the categorical schemas of the academic study of religion as of any value in understanding faith (real religion) although he admits its value in the scrutiny of "external tradition." To study religion (faith), then, one would have himself to be, in some sense at least, religious, for there is a *uniqueness* in the religious experience that is impossible to capture in rational, scientific concepts. Thus Smith insists that "one

of the things needed in a comparative study of religion is an ability to see the divine which I call faith."[74]

Here Wiebe was arguing that so-called methodologies used in the academic and ostensible secular study of religion have a propensity to fall back on the insider language and categories of theology. Wiebe here was articulating a fundamental tension in the study of religion: though religious studies desires to be a respectable academic field, it can only study – according to the likes of Cantwell Smith (echoing the language of non-Canadian scholars such as Rudolph Otto and Mircea Eliade) – the external expression of highly subjective inner experiences. Claims to a "science of religion," according to Wiebe, were unsubstantiated. As a means to break with this nebulousness, Wiebe called for a more critical study:

> The study of religion, if it is to be characterized as "scientific," must proceed without the assumption of the intellectual, or perhaps better, cognitive superiority of the world view of either the "outsider social scientist" or of the "uncritical inner participant." Whereas the former excludes any possibility of the truth of the "supernatural explanations" of religion (i.e., religion's interpretation of itself by means of reference to transempirical realities), the latter rejects all possibility of the correctness or truth of the "reductionistic explanations" of the social sciences.[75]

For Wiebe, the study of religion was less a discipline than a field of study. This debate would echo and reverberate in the pages of *SR* throughout the next decade. In 1984, Davis and Wiebe again clashed over the proper way to study religion. In an essay titled "Failure of Nerve in the Academic Study of Religion," Wiebe argued that, despite the call on the part of those like Davis who wanted a "reconvergence" of theology into the academic study of religion, such a reintroduction would be unfortunate and counterproductive to developing a secular and scientific approach. The "study of religion," Wiebe argued, "gained a political identity within the academic community (i.e., the scholarly-scientific community), precisely by distinguishing itself from theology."[76] This explicit re-establishment of theology constituted, he maintained, "a rejection of the scientific/academic goals [the academic study of religion] originally espoused and, therefore, constitutes a massive 'failure of nerve' by the academic community in religious studies."[77] Wiebe, then, argued that Davis was mistaken in his understanding of theology:

> His claim that systematic theology is concerned essentially with the ordered exposition of the doctrines of a particular tradition which rests on

> revelation and authority seems contradicted by his further claim that the science of religion is simply a more advanced stage of systematic theology and not something essentially different while still maintaining that he has kept the term theology simply to refer to "reflection" upon religion and *not* for the process of expression and communication belonging to religion as such.[78]

For Wiebe, then, there existed a real "failure of nerve" on the part of scholars of religion to differentiate a science of religion from confessional study. Though the latter had traditionally been carried out in denominational institutions, he maintained that it had simply morphed into secular departments of religious studies.

This, perhaps not surprisingly, engendered a response from Davis, which he titled "Wherein There Is No Ecstasy."[79] Therein, Davis accused Wiebe of engaging in a passionate "display of rationality" in the favour of the "strident voice of secular humanism."[80] Davis clarified that

> I am not asking that the study of religion should directly evoke a religious experience – though it may indirectly do so. I am saying simply that the student of religion – if possessed of a reasonable measure of competence – should evince some awareness or, even better, some familiarity with the distinctive features of such experience. Whether to make that requirement is to be unfair to the unecstatic Wiebe and his like depends upon the assumptions one is prepared to accept as valid in this context.[81]

Davis then declared that religious faith or experience is "accessible as an object of study only to those capable of grasping that prior meaning."[82] The crux of their argument, thus, takes us again to the heart of the tensions within the field of religious studies. Is its goal to study human and social forms of expression or interior forms of experience? One could argue that the exchange between Wiebe and Davis has never really disappeared from the pages of *SR*. Though a "roundtable" was published on this matter in a subsequent volume,[83] the terms and problematics of the debate have carried into the present: individuals continue to debate the nature and purpose of the academic study of religion. Taken as a whole in the present context, however, the debate puts on clear display just what was at stake in the study of religion in Canada in the first decades of its migration from theological seminaries to secular settings.

In the time that remains in this chapter I would like to focus on a few individuals who were instrumental to the formation of the academic study of religion in Canada in the 1960s and '70s. Wiebe might object that these individuals further confused the scientific and confessional study of religion; that said, they were among the most important players on the Canadian scene at a formative moment in the field's development.

George P. Grant (1918–1988)

George Parkin Grant was the paternal grandson of George Munro Grant, who had been instrumental in secularizing Queen's in the first part of the twentieth century.[84] Grant was a philosopher, a nationalist, and a political conservative, as well as the founder of the Department of Religious Studies at McMaster University in 1961. Recall that prior to becoming a provincial (and thus public) university in 1957, McMaster was a church-affiliated college (Baptist), all of whose students had to take a course in the New Testament with its president, George P. Gilmour, a Baptist minister.[85] When Grant arrived, he sought to expand the curriculum to include other religions, but in such a manner that the perennial questions of human existence – Who am I?, Where do I come from?, and so on – would remain central to the life of the university as opposed to being marginalized at the expense of the hard sciences.

Grant was a regular commentator on CBC Radio, and on his programs he often combined philosophy, religion, and political thought. In 1965, he published *Lament for a Nation*, in which he predicted Canada's inevitable cultural absorption by the United States. He argued that this would come at the expense of Canadian cultural nationality.[86] In other works and radio addresses, Grant was critical of what he viewed as modernity's dark underbelly, such as unharnessed technological advancement and the concomitant loss of moral foundations to guide humanity.

As head of the new secular department – one of the first in Canada – Grant emphasized the academic study of religion over theology, was critical of reducing religion to other phenomena (such as politics or society), and took a broad view of religion to include non-Western ones. In an essay titled "The Academic Study of Religion in Canada," he argued that one purpose of a university "is to attempt to understand the nature of what is, and as some form of religion seems to be coeval with man, it is necessary to try to understand religion."[87]

In his rationale for setting up the department, Grant argued that at the very least, a student must acquire "some knowledge of the religious history of the West" and "must investigate some other great tradition which answers some of the religious questions in at least a superficially different way."[88] For Grant, this meant either Hinduism or Buddhism, but not Islam, "because of its common Semitic roots with Judaism and

Christianity"; nor did such a comparative framework mean that the religious history of the West should be "compared with some fairly parochial religion which makes little claim to universality" (e.g., Indigenous traditions).[89]

Grant, then, thought that the focus of a department of religious studies should be on these "big questions." For him, this was the field's raison d'être: "If the department is to be more than a set of disparate specialisms this common interest in universal questions must be present. If one wishes merely to produce area specialists, this is best done in such bodies as the Institute of Islamic Studies or in departments of Near Eastern studies."[90]

Grant's first hires, as Remus notes, were in Bible (Eugene Combs), patristics (A.A. Stephenson), and "Eastern" religions (J.G. Arupa and Paul Younger).[91] Like other scholars in this early period, he strongly emphasized the importance of dialogue between religions, seeing this as "the crucial activity of a department of religion."[92]

Wilfred Cantwell Smith (1916–2000)

Probably the best-known Canadian scholar of religion, Cantwell Smith was born in Toronto in 1916 and graduated from the University of Toronto in 1938. He then spent six years in India (1940–6), during which he taught Indian and Islamic history at Forman Christian College in Lahore. In 1948 he received his PhD in Oriental languages from Princeton, whereupon he began teaching at McGill as the Birks Professor of Comparative Religion. In 1952, he founded the university's Institute of Islamic Studies. In 1964, he moved to Harvard, where he was named director of the Center for the Study of World Religions, replacing the recently retired Robert H.L. Slater (a fellow Canadian). In 1973, he moved to Dalhousie University in Halifax, Nova Scotia, where he founded the Department of Religion in that institution; he then returned to Harvard. Cantwell Smith at various times was president of the American Academy of Religion (1983), the American Society for the Study of Religion, the Middle East Studies Association (1978), and the Humanities and Social Sciences section of the Royal Society of Canada.[93]

The Institute of Islamic Studies was the first of its kind in North America. It was, as Charles J. Adams notes, the fruit of Cantwell Smith's vision:

> He determined that the Institute should be a joint Muslim-Western enterprise, an effort to interpret Muslim faith and civilization in a manner true both to the faith itself and to the Western critical university tradition. Islam was to be discussed in the presence of both Muslims and non-Muslims by

> a staff and student body that were to be similarly composite. It was hoped in this manner to institutionalize the conditions for communication and to avoid the negative aspects of the "Outsider's view" that had been so characteristic of much of Western orientalism.[94]

Guiding Cantwell Smith's vision for the institute, and his oeuvre more generally, was an emphasis on faith and the importance of inter-religious or interfaith dialogue. He argued, for example, that the key to the study of religion was an appreciation of the inner faith that believers encounter in their religion. Religions might differ in their beliefs, Cantwell Smith maintained, but in faith they share a remarkable set of similarities. It was on this level, he maintained, that comparison must reside. Cantwell Smith wrote the very first article in the newly founded *SR*, titled "A Human View of Truth," in which he argued that "the locus of truths is persons ... It is not statements that are true or false but the use of them by individuals."[95] The study of religion must take the personal, inner faith at face value and not impose conditions on it. Cantwell Smith continued: "In my field of Orientalist studies, there is a type of research practiced by remote observers, chiefly westerners writing only or in principle for a western audience. In this type of study, the outsider's formulations are never meant to be checked by Asians to see whether the impersonal, the so-called objectivist truths are also existentially true, or can become so, in terms of those Asians' personal lives."[96] This argument, as he would expatiate in other writings, meant that when we write about other religions we must consider the beliefs and faith commitments of those about whom we write. He also contended that what we say about others has to be verified by them.

Whether we agree with this methodology or not, there can be no doubt that the institute, founded in 1952, represented an important milestone in the development of the non-Christian study of religion in Canada. While not a department of religious studies per se, it nonetheless created space in the Faculty of Divinity in which other religious traditions could be studied. As early as 1948, for example, Cantwell Smith held the Birks Chair of Comparative Religion at McGill. Even though he did so in a Faculty of Divinity, his position and indeed his vision represented one of the earliest iterations of a comparative approach to religion, albeit one that had predecessors in the likes of George Monro Grant, Louis H. Jordan, and especially Cantwell Smith's own colleague at McGill, Robert H. L. Slater. Though, as Wiebe would argue, Cantwell Smith's approach to religion – especially its emphasis on faith and inner experience – retained the confessionalism of old. What his approach did *not* include was supersessionism or Christocentrism.

Klaus K. Klostermaier (1933–)

A native of Germany, Klaus K. Klostermaier obtained a PhD in philosophy from the Gregorian University in Rome in 1961. An ordained Catholic priest, Klostermaier then spent several years as a missionary and theologian before receiving another PhD in Indian history and culture from the University of Bombay in 1969. He moved to Canada and joined the faculty of the University of Manitoba in 1970 to teach "Asian religions."[97]

Like Grant and Cantwell Smith, Klostermaier stressed the importance of civilizational and religious dialogue. In an article in the second volume in *SR* titled "Hindu-Christian Dialogue: Its Religious and Cultural Implications," for example, he writes that "Hindu-Christian dialogue may become more and more necessary for Christendom as such in the attempt to find a new and legitimate self-understanding in the wider horizons of our world. One may venture to suggest that the encounter with Hinduism could give new impulses to Christian theology that reach greater depth, are more meaningful, and would prove to be longer lasting than most of the recent popular departures."[98]

For Klostermaier, then, a large part of the need for studying religions other than one's own is to appreciate better both self and other. Such dialogue, he continues, "presupposes a recognized and accepted difference between the partners and a willingness on both sides to respect the 'otherness' of the other."[99] This appreciation, in turn, facilitates the growth of each of the participants, or traditions, engaged in the dialogue. Klostermaier, again like Grant and Cantwell Smith, sees the academic and ostensibly secular study of religion as being able to articulate and subsequently provide solutions to human questions that transcend specific religions and that are of universal significance.[100] Moreover, and like the other two scholars discussed in this section, he seems to equate the academic study of religion with interfaith dialogue.

Conclusions

The 1960s and '70s witnessed a sea change in the way the study of religion was configured. Perhaps nowhere is this more clear than in the journals devoted to the study of religion in Canada. *CJRT* and *CJT* were theological journals that assumed Christian truths to be self-evident and universally applicable. The treatment of other religions was non-existent at best or paternalistic and supersessonist at worst. By 1971, *CJT* had been replaced by *SR*, a new journal devoted to comparative religion, which included non-Western traditions from an ostensibly objective perspective.

As Canada grew in terms of both its population and the places from where new immigrants came from, it became clear that a theological journal could no longer serve the needs of an increasingly multicultural and multireligious population. The study of religion now began to shift from denomination-affiliated schools and colleges to secular departments of religious studies. Initially, this manifested itself, at least topically, as a shift from the articulation of Christian truth-claims toward a stronger emphasis on interfaith dialogue and conversation. Though some, most notably Donald Wiebe, would contest this renewed confessionalism, there can be no doubt that it became an important part of the way in which the academic study of religion was configured in Canada.

This emphasis on dialogue was, I suggest, a direct result of multiculturalism being instituted as a federal policy in the 1960s. Because it was now seen as important to appreciate different cultures and religions, universities and colleges began to emphasize the mediation of such differences in their curricula. Grant, Cantwell Smith, and Klostermaier, among others, began to emphasize the importance of faith and of the shared spiritual life, so it was perhaps natural that they all regarded the academic study of religion as a means to help articulate and solve universal human problems. That they all helped shape some of the earliest departments of religion in Canada based on this understanding reveals something of the changing attitudes toward the study of religion in Canada.

Indeed, their visions would pave the way for the florescence of religious studies in Canada over the next few decades – a topic to which the following chapter turns.

Chapter Eight

Florescence

The story from seminary to university is a complicated one that encompasses numerous historical, sectarian, legal, sociological, and economic factors. That story, moreover, is as regional as it is national, for each of Canada's regions confronted its own distinct set of forces involving fundamental questions: Where should religion be taught? By whom should it be taught, and to whom? And, just as importantly, how should religion be taught, and under what auspices? Today the line separating academic and theological studies of religion tends to be quite obvious, but that has not always been the case. This is not to say that theology cannot be an academic activity. But it is to say that it has a different set of intellectual investments than does the academic study of religion.

My goal in this study has been to trace the transition of the study of religion in Canada from its originary seminary setting to its subsequent university one. I do not claim that this transition was either necessary or evolutionary. Nor do I claim that religious studies is always distinct from ecumenical and theological concerns, nor do I argue that theology has been superseded by the academic study of religion. Indeed, theology is still being taught in many places outside the context of the secular university. A perusal of any of the State-of-the-Art volumes reveals the names, places, and types of courses offered in such institutions. Neither time nor space permits a review of these here. In any case, my primary goal has not been curricular or departmental; rather, it has been to show how the academic study of religion developed in Canada at the national and regional levels.

The present chapter examines the rise of distinct departments of religious studies. These departments began to emerge in the 1960s based on features described in the previous two chapters. It is not my intention here to retell the stories of each department's creation and rise. This has been done ably in the volumes associated with the State-of-the-Art series as well as in Coward's memoir. My goal, on the contrary, is both simpler and more complex. In terms of the former, I seek to tie up some of the loose threads from the previous chapters by showing how secular departments of religious studies were created, either *de novo* or from existing theological programs, and how they gained in popularity and importance at the expense of the theological study of religion, which increasingly became relegated to the margins of post-secondary education. In terms of the latter, I seek to examine in considerably more detail than the State-of-the-Art volumes the reasons – social and institutional – for this florescence. That florescence did not occur overnight; on the contrary, it was a slow process that in many ways mirrored the reasons why *SR* replaced *CJT*. This, it will be recalled from the end of chapter 7, was based on the fact that theology was increasingly becoming anachronistic and too Christocentric for Canadians in general, and for Canadian undergraduates in particular. The 1960s witnessed many changes that would strongly influence the rise of academic and largely secular departments of religious studies from UBC in the west to Memorial University of Newfoundland in the east.

As Canadians became less religious, as immigration patterns changed, and as the government determined what could and could not be funded by federal dollars, it was perhaps inevitable that how, where, and by whom religion was studied would change. Those changes reflected larger changes in Canadian society,[1] such as immigration, increased social mobility, and access to university education, a growing desire among young Canadians to learn more about the "spiritual traditions" of the East, and, of course, the related countercultural movement associated with the 1970s. All of these events would make their mark on post-secondary education in general and on the academic study of religion in particular. Religious studies programs would be greatly altered by these decades; they would be transformed from marginal departments at which more entrenched disciplines looked askance, into an integral part of humanities curricula at Canadian universities.

As Anderson notes in his *Guide*, the breakthrough that led to this florescence of departments of religious studies in the 1960s and '70s occurred when university administrators grew more aware and accepting of the distinction between religious study of religion and secular study of religion.[2] This was a difficult distinction to draw, because of the often vitriolic struggle faced by Canadian universities to maintain their independence once they had wrested it from ecclesiastical control. Anderson writes:

> The study of religion was acceptable when conducted under university auspices, but a degree of distrust accompanied its treatment by a theological faculty. University decision makers perceived, rightly or wrongly, a conflict of interest between the commitments appropriate to the university and some of those necessarily held by a faculty of theology. Despite the fact that religion was being increasingly recognized as an important and legitimate field of inquiry, there was little hope that Canadian universities would sanction any significant development in the study of religion unless a new pattern was found.[3]

This new pattern, as will be increasingly clear in this chapter, was one wherein non-Christian religions were studied in a manner never encountered before in the country. "Eastern" religions, especially Buddhism and Hinduism, became popular as unprecedented numbers of young Canadians gravitated to these courses.[4] And they were taking these courses not as part of ministerial training but rather as part of an arts curriculum that increasingly stressed diversity. The methodology these new courses followed tended to stress comparison and increasingly tended to privilege other cognate disciplinary fields, such as anthropology and psychology. In addition to all this, the topics in such courses were new, and included ritual, belief, customs, and experience.

What was novel about these new departments of religious studies that sprang up around the country was that they lacked connection to any particular denomination. Instead of being housed in affiliated theological schools, which were becoming more and more marginal to the modern university, these new departments were located at the very heart of the university, in arts faculties and other humanistic and social scientific departments. Religious studies was now becoming an autonomous field of study that could take its place alongside other departments such as history, English, and classics. This process was accompanied by changes in funding and institutional support. Of course, none of these other disciplines had to undergo quite the same trials and tribulations to be taken seriously by administrators and fellow colleagues.

We might well ask ourselves, who inhabited these newly created institutional spaces? Where did the faculty members who cohabited in these new departments of religious studies come from? Since there were no departments in Canada to train these faculty, it should come as little surprise that, not unlike in the early days of theology in Canada, faculty, at least in the beginning, often had to be trained elsewhere. Some – like Wilfred Cantwell Smith and Robert H.L. Slater – had been trained in American graduate schools (such as the University of Chicago or Harvard), where non-Western religions were increasingly being studied using appropriate historical, textual, and philological approaches. Others, like George P. Grant, had been trained in the United Kingdom (especially at Oxford or Cambridge), where philosophy of religion was more common when it came to religious studies. Yet others had been trained in cognate fields such as Near Eastern studies or East Asian studies. While some were still being trained in Biblical studies (e.g., William Nicholls, the first chair of the Department of Religious Studies at UBC), the overwhelming majority of these new scholars specialized in non-Western religions. Significant here is that these initial faculty, most if not all trained abroad, would be responsible for the subsequent creation of graduate programs in Canadian universities – programs that in turn would develop a new generation of Canadian-trained scholars of religion. This would lead to the further indigenization of the field on Canadian soil, though of course in such a manner that it was and indeed would continue to be in conversation with larger trends in the field emerging in and emanating from other countries.

Another prominent feature that aided in this florescence of departments of religious studies was the growing awareness, again on the part of university leaders, that a public university should attend to the perennial questions of human existence. Universities, in other words, were not simply to be places where students learned historical facts and read the great works of English and other literatures. They were, instead, as George P. Grant remarked, places where ethical teaching was to raise society from the inhumanity of technological encroachment. Many of these perennial questions, not surprisingly, were linked to or believed to be linked to the world's religious traditions. The study of non-Western religions, in other words, was seen by many as a way to understand other ways of knowing that were connected to civilizations much older than the one Canada knew. Certainly connected to this was the growing dissatisfaction on the part of many students with traditional religious (read: Christian) institutions – a dissatisfaction combined with a thirst for some sort of "spiritual" meaning beyond such institutions. Newly formed departments of religious studies and their course offerings in non-Christian religious traditions became a perfect place for young Canadians to explore religious truths in non-dogmatic and secular settings.

The present chapter is an attempt to move on from some of these larger considerations toward more micro ones, which are often unique to specific departments situated within idiosyncratic bureaucratic and administrative cultures. The reasons articulated above bear on the creation of *all* departments of religious studies, but they play out differently at each given university. Most universities were figuring out just how to create the institutional space for the study of religion, a topic that had been avoided by most departments either intentionally (as in the case of western Canada) or as a consequence of earlier sectarian debates (as in Ontario and Atlantic Canada). Faculty, for starters, had to be convinced that religious studies was not tantamount to the reintroduction of theology or superstition into the university curriculum under the cloak of objectivity. This often meant revisiting initial charters to make room for the study *of* and *about* religion as opposed to studying religion. It also meant the search for faculty to occupy the new departments, which often had to sit uncomfortably, at least initially, with cognate faculty in divinity at affiliated theological colleges. The result was a grand administrative dance, whose end product was the creation of a national field of study.

What follows is not an exhaustive analysis of either every department of religious studies in Canada or even of those that are examined. That task has been done, as already mentioned, in the various State-of-the-Art volumes and in Coward's memoir. Instead, I have chosen to focus on certain departments that provide what I consider to be interesting case studies that offer yet another window onto the many ways the field of religious studies came to be included within arts curricula associated with post-secondary education in Canada. To reiterate, there was no one-size-fits-all paradigm for the creation of such departments. On the contrary, as Ronald E. Miller notes in his state-of-the-art chapter devoted to Saskatchewan, "every university has a particular set of circumstances that produces a certain development. Within that development, also, every university department is marked by its own stamp that reflects varieties of disciplinary philosophy, personnel, financial support, and so on."[5] To this, we could certainly add that the formation of each department was also contingent on an idiosyncratic set of internal administrative desires and, not infrequently, external community pressures to ensure that religions were both taught and taught in a manner with which they agreed. Almost every provincial university in the 1960s and '70s acknowledged the need to include the academic study of religion as part of its arts curriculum, yet it was often more mundane issues, as Miller notes, that necessitated the formation of individual departments. The dates in parentheses mentioned below are those of actual departmental formation as opposed to either initial administrative fiat or initial hire.

McGill (1949)

McGill had always had a complex relationship to the study of religion.[6] As early as the late nineteenth century, a number of theological colleges in Montreal had affiliated with the university,[7] and, by 1912,

Congregational, Diocesan, Wesleyan, and Presbyterian colleges had developed a cooperative theological education with a joint curriculum, but one that nonetheless permitted each to provide its own professional training for Christian ministry.[8] The main ideological impetus behind this was the increased desire for church unification (which would happen within a few years, with the United Church), and the main driver for such cooperation was William Massey Birks, a wealthy Montreal merchant and someone with a great interest in ecumenicism. It was Birks who brought to Montreal for a set of lectures, also in 1912, A.G. Fraser, an Anglican minister and Principal of Trinity College in Kandy, Ceylon. That college was of interest to Birks because it had successfully combined seven denominational schools under one administratively ecumenical canopy. Birks was also interested in the non-denominational Union Theological Seminary in New York, whose president, Francis Brown, he also invited to Montreal to consult.[9] Montreal, thus, became an important city, with its epicentre in McGill, of inter-Protestant cooperation.

The principals of the four cooperating colleges, as they were known, would rotate among themselves, on an annual basis, the deanship of the program and the administration of the curriculum. The experiment was roundly praised for its willingness to move beyond sectarianism, which by then had gripped post-secondary education in the young country; some, however, objected. Dr. J. Paterson-Smyth, Rector of St. George's Church in the city, was on record saying that he would never agree to a situation in which church history taught to Anglicans would be taught by a non-Anglican.[10] This sentiment, not surprisingly, was the biggest impediment to the academic study of religion, and it would not diminish to a significant enough degree to allow for such study until the 1960s. Yet many dissenters apparently acknowledged that the cooperative theological program, whatever the respective differences in understanding the Sacrament, was an important way to bring the instruction of religion (read: Christianity) into the curriculum of McGill.

This difference in respective theological programs would be mediated to some extent with the formation of the United Church of Canada in 1925, after which three of the affiliated colleges became affiliated with the new church. Since continuing Presbyterians kept Presbyterian College, the three former colleges now affiliated with the United Church needed a new building, which led to the building of Divinity Hall in 1931, renamed the Birks Building in 1972. This relationship among the colleges and between them and the university would lead to the founding, in 1948, of a Faculty of Divinity.[11] This was, in many ways, the natural telos of the cooperative theological program.

The new faculty was to have six chairs: Old Testament Language and Literature, New Testament Language and Literature, History of the Christian Church, Systematic Theology, Philosophy and Psychology of Religion, and Comparative Religion. Though appointments were to be made by the Board of Governors of McGill, appointments to the first four of the aforementioned chairs would have to come from a nominating committee on which all participating colleges were equally represented.[12] Note that the last two of these chairs were, at least in theory, non-denominational. It was those two chairs that would set the course for more secular religious studies at McGill.

The inaugural appointment in Comparative Religion was Wilfred Cantwell Smith, discussed at the end of the previous chapter. Cantwell Smith – and I think this is symptomatic of the early comparative or non-theological study of religion in Canada in these years – was still strongly invested in inter-religious understanding.[13] Indeed, the Chair in Comparative Religion would soon be referred to as the Birks Professorship in Comparative Religion, revealing to just what extent ecumenicism was imagined to be a part of it. Cross-cultural or inter-religious understanding is an important part of the religious studies curriculum today, but it is now by no means its sole concern, and the field has expanded considerably from it. Indeed, we might even say that interfaith dialogue is more comparative theology than it is comparative religion, even though it was (and still is) called by the latter name.[14] Nevertheless, it is necessary to appreciate just what intellectual changes had to happen in order for Christian theology to transform itself into comparative religion or even comparative theology. This emphasis on ecumenicism at the faculty is also visible in the inaugural appointment of the aforementioned Robert H.L. Slater to the Chair of Systematic Theology.[15]

In 1970, the name of the Faculty of Divinity was changed to the Faculty of Religious Studies in order to reflect the new emphasis on the academic study of religion. The emphasis was now on understanding the world's religions through the methodological lens of comparison, which, as we have noted several times, was perhaps a natural step from theology. If theology was an attempt to work out the truth-claims of specific Christian denominations, comparison – or, alternatively comparative religion – was an attempt to show how truth-claims worked in different religious contexts from what, at least in theory, was a value-neutral perspective.[16] Comparison, then, was about taking religion seriously and not about reducing it to specific human contexts.[17] Nevertheless, the change in nomenclature is surely significant in the annals of the study of religion in Canada, for it signalled that the faculty would now be in the business of educating students who were not interested in entering the ministry. This change in natural constituency would generate further significant changes down the line.

Another significant event at McGill was the opening of the Institute of Islamic Studies in 1951.[18] This was the brainchild of Cantwell Smith, who hoped the new institute would provide a broader and less Christocentric venue for the study of religion. He was, again as the Birks Professor of Comparative Religion, interested in facilitating a forum for mutual understanding between the Islamic world and the West. His goal, which he largely achieved, was to have the program staffed by both Western and Muslim scholars. This institute was first housed in the Faculty of Graduate Studies before being moved to the Faculty of Religious Studies for the 1973–4 academic year.[19]

McMaster (1960)

McMaster University ended its affiliation with the Baptist Church and became a secular, provincial university in 1957. The university was now non-denominational, but there were still Baptist theologians on the faculty, and though they were increasingly associated only with McMaster's Divinity School, students could still take courses in that tradition. In 1960, Paul Clifford, a Baptist theologian, was assigned the task of developing a department of religious studies, for reasons outlined above: to examine and appreciate the religious aspects of human meaning, and to do so on neither a Christian nor a theological basis. It was Clifford who hired George P. Grant,[20] who was instrumental in building the new department using the model examined in chapter 7. Grant insisted on students learning both the religious history of the West and another "great" tradition. Here, the comparative model – as with Cantwell Smith at McGill, earlier on – was again paramount. However, Grant did not want to refer to this model as "comparison," because for him, implicit in that word was the notion of Western superiority, either "the superiority of Christianity or (more recently) of the progressive West."[21] As Coward notes, to correct this notion Grant encouraged faculty and students – much like Cantwell Smith had done at the Institute of Islamic Studies – to "have first-hand contact with representatives of the religious traditions they are studying."[22] Implicit in this model was that students needed to study the religious texts of others from teachers of those traditions.[23]

This requirement to study with living representatives of another tradition would come to figure highly in many Canadian departments. It works on the assumption that the only way for a student (undergraduate or graduate) to understand or appreciate the religious traditions of the world is to study them with those who are both learned *in* the particular tradition and *of* the tradition. This, of course, can cause problems, for many traditions are diverse and encompass many different viewpoints. For example, can a Sunni Muslim address objectively the topic of Shi`i Islam, or vice versa? The assumption was being made that an Indian man (and they often were men in these early years) can serve as an adequate metaphor or metonym for an entire subcontinent. Another feature of the Canadian system was that unlike in American universities, which tended to focus heavily on American religious forms, Canadian departments were much more outward-looking. This was no doubt connected to multiculturalism, which celebrated diversity as opposed to anything uniquely Canadian.

Almost from the beginning, the focus at McMaster was on so-called Asian religions, particularly those of South Asia (i.e., India) and East Asia (i.e., China). This was, as Remus duly notes, part of Grant's view that institutions in Ontario should cooperate rather than compete with one another.[24] Thus, since the study of Islam was being treated at Toronto (and McGill), Grant chose to focus the McMaster program on Asia, the West, and the philosophy of religion. This tripartite division would subsequently be reproduced by alumni of McMaster, who would go on to found or direct other programs in Canada. In this regard, one of its most successful graduates was Harold Coward, who would play an important role in the founding of the Department of Religious Studies at the University of Calgary in 1976.[25] That department, under his direction, was modelled on McMaster's, with the three main areas of study being "Western religions," "Eastern religions," and the catch-all "nature of religion."[26]

UBC (1964)

The earliest secular department – and one not created out of past theological iterations – to devote itself solely to the academic study of religion without any precursors was the one established at the University of British Columbia in Vancouver. Brian J. Fraser notes in his State-of-the-Art review that the creation of the department was precipitated by the problem of how to transfer credits between the numerous theological colleges in BC and UBC.[27] Courses that transfer students wanted to use for credit at UBC were often regarded as too theological or sectarian for university credit. While this would eventually precipitate the rise of secular religious studies, which explicitly sought to avoid precisely such issues as encountered at other institutions, many faculty and colleagues were – and this is certainly not unique to

UBC – becoming increasingly mistrustful of such overtures. For many of these people, the study of religion was indistinct from theology, and it was unclear to them how the academic study of religion broke from sectarian theological colleges and seminaries, which were predicated on both the articulation and the verification of religious truth-claims. In other words, university administrators and faculty would have to be made aware of the differences between the academic and the religious study of religion. The main way to do this, as noted above, would be to show how the world's religions rather than just a particular denomination of Christianity, when understood historically and textually, contributed positively to the search for meaning.

In 1955, UBC's senate decided that a course offered by a local theological college titled Foundations of Christianity violated university policy and had to be rejected on those grounds. A lawyer for the university argued that "a generalized approach to religion is not in error under our Statute [i.e., Section 99 of the University Act] but the teaching of any such subject should not be carried out in such a manner as to indoctrinate or inculcate into the mind of the student, any particular religious creed or dogma."[28] Section 99 further stipulated that "the University shall be strictly non-sectarian in principle, and no religious creed or dogma shall be taught." The report thus concluded that a course devoted specifically to Christianity, presumably from a particular sectarian perspective and with an ostensible agenda, could not be taught under the administrative auspices of UBC.

To correct this situation and to avoid similar issues in the future, UBC in 1956 decided to establish a secular Department of Religious Studies. The department would not materialize for several years; even so, this early date – the mid-1950s – put UBC at the forefront of the national discourse on the academic study of religion. Except for the one provided by McGill, there were very few paradigms for how such a department would materialize or indeed what it would teach or even look like. Administrators did, however, seem to be aware that such a department would contribute positively to students' humanistic (as opposed to theological) education, and that the proposed department would "provide not only electives for undergraduates, but also the possibility of doing majors and honours work at the undergraduate level and ultimately both an MA and a PhD program at the graduate level."[29] In 1958 a committee was struck to find a suitable candidate to create such a department, and in 1961 William Nicholls, a former Anglican chaplain at the University of Edinburgh and a Christian theologian, was hired. Despite his theological credentials, Nicholls would play a major role in the founding of the Canadian Society for the Study of Religion (CSSR) and *SR*.[30]

Nicholls set about trying to get Section 99 of the University Act amended, and in 1963 an amendment was finally passed that replaced "taught" with "inculcated" so that it now read, "no religious creed or dogma shall be *inculcated*." Faculty were subsequently hired, and the Department of Religious Studies came into official existence in 1964. For this department to be established, however, previous courses, indicative of an earlier time, devoted to the topic of "religious knowledge" and taught by affiliated theological colleges, would have to be removed. These colleges, according to an arts faculty committee struck in 1965, could propose their own courses for credit in the faculty, but these would have to be approved by the relevant department or departments.[31]

Université de Montréal (1969) and Université du Québec à Montréal (1972)

The history of the study of religion in Quebec differs significantly from that in the rest of the country, owing to its unique history in terms of Catholicism and the place of that religion, perceived or otherwise, in the province. This meant that an overwhelming propensity in francophone universities was toward theology. Only the late 1960s, reflecting larger trends in the country, do we begin to see the emergence of the more secular "sciences des religieuses" – or "religiologie," as it was called at Université du Québec à Montréal – which tended to be more comparative in method and focused more broadly on Eastern religions.[32] As with other provinces, however, such an approach had to emerge out of *théologie* or *sciences confessionnelles,* and was again connected to the changes brought about by multiculturalism[33] and the growing disillusionment with traditional religion in the province.[34] The 1950s and '60s, as Benoit Lacroix notes, saw a more historical approach to religion gradually appear alongside Catholic theology and catechesis. This was the direct result of larger changes in Quebec society, not the least of which was the weakening of the Catholic Church.[35] The gradual diminution of the theological paradigms in Quebec universities led, as Rousseau suggests, to new paradigms – both new methodologies and the appreciation of other religious traditions – for the study of religion.[36]

One feature that distinguishes Quebec from the rest of Canada is the interest there in the role of religion in the province.[37] This has involved examining either specific religions in the province or the place of secularism therein.[38] In 1968, according to Louis Rousseau, a group of faculty at the Collège Ste-Marie in Montreal who were interested in non-confessional approaches to religion decided to name their enterprise "religiologie."[39] Although other Québécois universities had developed centres devoted to religion – such as the Centre de recherches en sociologie religieuse, which opened at Laval in 1958 – they were still largely interested in "requêtes pastorales."[40] Religiologie signalled the end of this and the emergence of a more critical and non-theological study. In 1969 the Collège Ste-Marie merged into the newly formed Université du Québec à Montréal (UQAM). The Université du Québec system had been established in 1968 in response to widespread student protests that had broken out in the autumn of that year; it was part of an effort to extend education to more Québécois students. Just as importantly, it created religiously neutral institutions that were not invested in Catholic ideology.[41]

The same year that UQAM opened its doors, the education ministry held a colloquium on the place of non-confessional religion in the province.[42] In 1972 the Département des sciences religieuses was created and took its place alongside other disciplines to study the humanities (*sciences humaines*). The Département des sciences religieuses at UQAM was the most important department for the new approach to religion, but other universities in the Université du Québec system – such as at Chicoutimi, Trois-Rivières, and Rimouski – created similar departments with the same emphasis.[43]

The Université de Montréal (1969) offers another paradigm. Unlike the Université du Québec system, which was able to take a non-sectarian approach to religion, the Université de Montréal had always had a Faculty of Theology, which, like all francophone faculties of theology in the province, was heavily Catholic. Indeed, the former faculty was one of the founding faculties when the university was established in 1878 as the Montreal branch of Université Laval.[44] Although Madeline Sauvé notes that as early as the 1960s the term "sciences religeuses" was beginning to be employed, it tended primarily to denote courses devoted to Christianity.[45] Indeed, this seems to have been the primary reason why UQAM decided to employ the term "religiologie" – it was a way to differentiate what they sought to do.

As Michel Campbell notes in his 1972 study, the faculty reorganized its programs in 1969 to allow for greater diversity in its offerings.[46] Though he does not mention it, it is probably no coincidence that several years earlier, in 1965, the Second Vatican Council had promulgated *Nostre aetate*, which sought to clarify the Church's relationship to other religions and which encouraged interfaith dialogue.[47] The two main programs became "nouvelle introduction aux études théologiques" (NIET) and "année de réflexion en études patorales" (AREP).[48] Though theology and catechesis were both still at the centre, epistemic space was increasingly carved out for less confessional programs in biblical studies and in sciences religieuses, the latter of which was created in the 1974–5 academic year as a certificate program in the faculty.[49]

University of Manitoba (1968)

The University of Manitoba decided in 1967 to create a Department of Religion the following year. Interestingly, and certainly relatedly, it had established a Department of Judaic Studies as early as 1950 – the oldest such department in the country.[50] Rabbi Arthur Chiel, director of the local B'nai B'rith and presumably paid through its auspices, would teach courses in modern Hebrew and Jewish history at no cost to the university.[51] Though as Harland and Badertscher note in their State-of-the-Art review volume, this scenario – a person external to the university being paid by non-university funds to teach for-credit courses in a university – caused some administrators unease.[52] To rectify this, the local Jewish community raised funds for a private Maimonides College, which would function as an affiliated college to the university not unlike the affiliated Christian colleges. The proposed college never materialized even though the university had reserved land for it. Instead, in 1964 the local Jewish community offered to "pay the salary of a full time professor to be approved by the University authorities for the Judaic Studies department."[53] New in this language was that the candidate, unlike Rabbi Chiel, would have to be vetted and approved by the university rather than the local Jewish community. The same year, the university hired Rabbi Zalman Schachter as professor and head of the department. Eventually, the university would pay the salaries of the faculty associated with Judaic Studies, which subsequently became known as the Department of Near Eastern and Judaic Studies.[54]

I mention Judaic studies in this context not only because it is singular in terms of the Canadian context in both its mandate (i.e., offering courses in non-Christian religion) and date (i.e., 1950s),[55] but also because this department helped drive the study of religion at the university. As Gordon Harland, the first professor of religion at Manitoba, writes, when the Department of Religion came into existence, while new, it was not unheralded at the university: "Important resources for the task were present both in the Department of Judaic Studies and in those faculty members who had taught religious studies courses in the colleges."[56] To mark the break with the colleges and their more theological concerns, the new department would be housed in the Faculty of Arts, not a college.[57]

The subsequent use of faculty members from the theological college revealed a potential tension, and perhaps further blurred the line, between the theological study and the academic study of religion. If members of the former could suddenly have their courses counted toward the latter, the question could well be asked just how different the two approaches were in theory or indeed in praxis. Was it the role of the university to hire scholars of non-Christian religions for departments of religious studies, on the assumption that Christianity would be covered by various Christian theologians associated with affiliated colleges or seminaries? Such a model occurred more frequently in Canadian universities than one might suspect, and indeed continues to be followed in the present.[58]

The Department of Religion at the University of Manitoba was behind Canada's first International Association for the History of Religions (IAHR) meeting in 1980. Instrumental in the planning of this meeting – the primary international forum for the critical study of religion[59] – was William Klassen, but especially Donald Wiebe, who would shortly move to Trinity College in Toronto, where he would become the major force for attracting the same conference to Toronto in 2010.[60]

University of Toronto (1969)

As we have seen at several points in this study, the University of Toronto provides a particularly acute case study with which to chart the history of the academic study of religion in Canada – both its early tensions and its subsequent possibilities. In terms of the academic study of religion, a delicate balance had to be struck between the "godless" University College on the one hand and the affiliated colleges on the other.[61] As early as 1909, the Faculties of Divinity at the affiliated colleges began to group their courses devoted to Christianity under the general rubric "Religious Knowledge."[62] In 1960, as Watson notes, the University of Toronto began transforming all teaching departments in the colleges into university departments, with the only exception being Religious Knowledge. This tended to reinforce the rather strange position the study of religion had within the university in the early years.[63] Note, moreover, that administrative and ideological barriers prevented students from taking Religious Knowledge courses outside of their own college. This further exacerbated the sectarian divisions that had plagued the university from the beginning; it also further blurred the distinction between university and seminary that the early framers of the university had sought to overcome.

Things gradually began to change, at least on the ecumenical front, in the mid-1960s as representatives from the affiliated colleges sought to dismantle such barriers with the aim of creating a Department of Religion.[64] Though this was met with considerable mistrust on the part of university administrators, who, perhaps on account of the history of the study of religion at that institution, feared that it would lack objectivity and overinvest in theological polemics.[65]

Not unlike at McGill and Manitoba, faculty of the affiliated colleges' Religious Knowledge courses began to reach out to what were perceived to be cognate departments within University College: Islamic Studies, Near Eastern Studies, and East Asian Studies. Religious Knowledge now began to imagine itself as a "combined" unit and began to appoint one colleague to be the director of the unit on a basis of rotation.[66] This would, in due course, lead to cross-appointments between these departments and the affiliated colleges.[67] This would further loosen the colleges' investment in theology and begin the process of introducing the study of religion to the University of Toronto curriculum.

By 1969, faculty who taught Religious Knowledge in the various affiliated colleges had been brought together with other cognate faculty in the university's Near Eastern Studies, Islamic Studies, and East Asian Studies departments as the Combined Departments of Religious Studies.[68] By 1975 the university had entered into a memorandum of agreement with the colleges that individual departments housed in colleges would become departments of the university; with this fiat, the Department of Religious Studies was created.[69] Though, as can be imagined, despite the change in name, the new department still largely consisted of the same names and maintained the same focus on Christianity. Yet as Remus well notes, "the appointment of newer faculty – trained in religious studies – meant that the move toward religious studies in Ontario universities would proceed."[70]

In 1976 the university created a separate graduate Centre for Religious Studies with the aim of providing a more scientific and history-of-religions approach to data. This was done over administrators' fears that Christian studies would be unduly represented.[71] The graduate centre and the undergraduate department were amalgamated in 1992.[72]

University of Alberta (1973)

The University of Alberta offers yet another interesting case. From its inception, this institution wanted very little to do with religion and insisted (see chapter 4) on firm lines of separation between itself and its two church-based affiliated colleges, St. Stephen's (United) and St. Joseph's (Catholic). So there was very little history at the University of Alberta for religious studies, biblical studies using higher criticism, or even Near Eastern or Oriental studies.

The Department of Religious Studies did not come into existence until 1973; but as Neufeldt makes clear in his State-of-the-Art volume, discussions about the need to teach about the place and role of religious meaning in human societies began as early as 1960.[73] In a 1961 memo, a senate committee acknowledged that "knowledge of religious teachings and writing is essential for a proper understanding of much that is studied in many disciplines."[74] Again we see university administrators increasingly aware in the 1960s that an arts curriculum ought to pay some attention to the religious quest for meaning, albeit not using the traditional and narrow theological parameters of the affiliated colleges, but in a way that examined all religions (but especially non-Western ones) from a value-neutral perspective. The committee envisioned "courses that might be taught in such a department": "the Judeo-Christian religion with its literature and history; the religions of the world, their literature, their founders, and their main ideas and tenets; contemporary living traditions, their philosophy, ethics, and main concerns."[75]

Clearly, then, the university was interested in precisely the same type of department that so many Canadian universities were interested in developing during this period. The department would not be created until 1973, though as early as 1967 the university had made it clear that, should such a department form, the aforementioned theological colleges would play no part in it, so as to maintain a clear distinction between the academic and the theological study of religion.[76] Despite this attempt at a distinction, however, many courses from these two colleges, not unlike at Manitoba, have been cross-listed by the department and vice versa over the years.

Dalhousie (1973)

Atlantic Canada, as seen in a previous chapter, was a hotbed of religious sectarianism in the nineteenth century, so much so that when the University of New Brunswick was founded, its charter explicitly rejected the study of religion in any form.[77] Most of the universities and colleges in the region, with a few notable exceptions, were established as Christian institutions with particular denominational concerns. Bowlby and Faulkner note that even as these institutions became provincialized and as departments of theology transformed themselves into departments of religious studies, "many of the faculty originally appointed and tenured in the theology department continued their appointments in the religious studies department."[78] The result, as they also note, meant that the secular study of religion in Atlantic Canada retained a distinctly Christian bias.

One exception to all this was Dalhousie University in Halifax. Founded in 1818 as an iteration of the Pictou Academy, Dalhousie, at least at first, tended not to accept Catholic or Anglican students.[79] The tendency not to accept the former led to the creation of distinctly Catholic colleges (e.g., Mount Saint Vincent, St. Mary's, St. Francis Xavier) in the region.

In 1973, a Department of Comparative Religion was established at Dalhousie. As the name implies, it intended to focus on comparison by putting at least two religions in counterpoint with one another. Wilfred Cantwell Smith was hired from Harvard to lead the fledgling department.[80] Unlike other cognate departments in Atlantic Canada, the one at Dalhousie was geared toward a history-of-religions program that, in the words of Bowlby and Faulkner, "was hierarchically structured, beginning with courses on the traditions and culminating in a thematic, comparative seminar."[81] In so doing, it was, in many ways, like McGill shaped by the ecumenical program of Cantwell Smith, which compared the religious faiths of believers. Cantwell Smith returned to Harvard five years later.

University of Regina (1974) and University of Saskatchewan (1984)

I lump these two institutions together not because they are, obviously, both located in Saskatchewan, but because they represent a paradigm for the creation of religious studies not seen in the other provinces. At both universities, religious studies reflected the theological colleges' desire to create a more inclusive approach to religion as opposed to that of more secular universities. Unlike the University of Alberta, which set out to exclude the affiliated colleges from the new department (albeit with mixed success), the University of Regina and the University of Saskatchewan welcomed the support, both financial and intellectual, of such colleges.

As early as 1969, while it was still a campus of the University of Saskatchewan,[82] a motion was presented at what would become the University of Regina to create a secular Department of Religious Studies the following year.[83] The proposal, however, went nowhere until 1974, when a program was developed that would include relevant faculty at Campion (Catholic) and Luther (Lutheran) Colleges.[84] This, however, led to charges of Christian bias in the curriculum and, concomitantly, the usual set of fears on the part of other faculty. After changes enacted by the Curriculum Committee, a revised program was developed to examine five major divisions: religious figures and thinkers; religious system; religious issues; aspects of religious life and practice; and interdisciplinary and integrative studies.[85] From the beginning at Regina, staffing was one of the major issues, as was not uncommon at other Canadian institutions. Since there had always been a limited number of actual hires into religious studies, most of the faculty came from other departments or, more commonly, from Luther and Campion colleges.

As noted in chapter 5, religion had always been taught at the University of Saskatchewan in the context of seminary training at the numerous theological colleges affiliated with it. Needless to say, many administrators and faculty in the Faculty of Arts and Sciences worried that should the study of religion migrate into the secular university it would be tantamount to Christian studies and engage in catechesis as opposed to scholarly inquiry. They were in no hurry to devote scarce resources to its inclusion even at a time when most other Canadian universities had opened their own religious studies departments.[86]

As Miller notes, pressure came from a rather different source: the separate school system. As early as 1964, the two teaching colleges in the province became part of the university, and the role of religion would become important to the training of teachers for the separate school system.[87] In such a system, teachers would need to be taught the fundamentals of Catholic theology, and to this end, the Catholic Women's League petitioned the university to develop credit classes in theology.[88] This led to the desire on the part of many to develop an ecumenical school of theology. The proposal, however, was not supported by the president of the Lutheran Theological Seminary, who argued that what the university most needed was a religious studies department as opposed to a school of theology. The former side won by a narrow margin at a vote in the university's senate on 29 May 1971.[89]

This failure set off the motion to create a secular religious studies program at the university. The various theological colleges and the Department of Far Eastern Studies supported a proposal to create such a program. In December of the following year, the university's senate formally approved plans to create a *School* of Religious Studies. As Miller notes, however, "the resources of the new School of Religious Studies basically constituted a re-ordering of what was already present. The faculty established for the school comprised nominees from the existing staff members of the affiliated theological colleges."[90] In 1975 the university approved a class in world religions, but all the other classes were in biblical Judaism and Christianity. A subsequent external review recommended that religious studies at the University of Saskatchewan be "brought in harmony" with other Canadian universities and recommended the formation of a *department* (as opposed to a school) with a major and an honours degree.[91] This did not happen until 1984.

Conclusions

This chapter has examined several institutional histories of how religious studies came to be with an eye toward better understanding the complexities associated with the academic study of religion on Canadian campuses. Virtually every institution of post-secondary education in Canada made a conscious decision in the 1960s and early 1970s to include religious studies. This was done, as we have seen, under the guise of making the arts curriculum more multicultural, in addition to introducing alternative (read: non-Western) takes on enduring questions of human existence, such as Who am I? Where do I come from? What is good and bad? And what is the nature of human flourishing?

University administrators, in other words, increasingly realized that the study of religion could take place *within* the university as opposed to being a peripheral topic taught by clerics at affiliated theological colleges. This movement from periphery to centre coincided with a change in Canada's demographics, the growing importance of multiculturalism, and, perhaps most importantly, the appearance at universities of students who, while interested in issues of spirituality and meaning, were increasingly uninterested, like the overwhelming majority of Canadians, in mainline churches in Canada.[92]

For this sociological change to manifest itself in secular universities, however, a number of things had to happen. First, faculty and university administrators had to be willing to include the study of religion as part of their curricula. Second, and perhaps most importantly, firm lines had to be drawn between theological and academic study. This was arguably the most difficult task, especially since at many universities there was no history of the secular study of religion and it was taught only in the affiliated theological colleges, which had their own vested interests in the subject matter. Moreover, many faculty in other departments were initially extremely sceptical of the introduction – or in some places, reintroduction – of religion into what was perceived to be a secular curriculum. Indeed, as witnessed in places like UBC, there was even explicit language in the charter that prevented such teaching that had to be changed.

Conclusions

The teaching and study of religion in Canada has had a long and convoluted history, just as in other countries. As this volume has shown, that history has been intimately connected to Canada's birth and subsequent development. While today we may take the existence of theological seminaries or departments of religious studies for granted, when we do so we overlook the manifold contexts and struggles that contributed to their founding and ongoing presence. Departments of religious studies did not simply appear in the same manner that departments of history or philosophy did. This is on account of the role, both overt and subterranean, that religion has played in the modern nation-state. Religion has long been an integral part of a nationalist strategy, as we saw on clear display, for example, in attempts to define Upper Canada along strictly Anglican lines, and more recently in how more secular departments of religious studies promote a form of inter-religious dialogue. I have tried to argue that discourses on religion cannot be delinked from discourses on nationalism since the very idea of the liberal individual (be it as citizen or as consumer) functions as the cornerstone of the nation.

The study of religion, be it confessional or non-confessional, accordingly is heavily invested in the modern nation-state. That investment points to a number of decidedly non-academic contexts – demographic, social, political, legal – that define how we talk about, or want to talk about, religion in the public sphere. Those contexts subsequently help structure the way religion is envisioned nationally and how it is studied institutionally.

Religion, then, is imagined, constructed, and situated within specific national frames of reference. The present study has made the case that we need to take seriously the various localized contexts in which modern nation-states come into existence simultaneously with the production of various discourses on religion. The anxieties generated as a result of this coexistence constantly reappear in the way religion is taught – where, by whom, to whom, and about what. This is not to imply that there are not transnational concerns that help define the study of religion in a global context. But it *is* to state that every liberal, Western democracy has its own specific and unique concerns and anxieties over religion that determine where and how it ought to be located and that structure religion's place within legal and political systems.

Because of this anxiety over religion, very few academic fields of study have experienced the same type of scrutiny and resistance in the contemporary university. The study of religion had to contend with this resistance twice: at the beginning, when theological seminaries were synonymous with institutions of higher learning; and then again in the 1960s and '70s, when more humanistic religious studies programs were introduced to now secular universities.

The latter resistance has been the direct result of the fact that the teaching of religion has, for most of the past two millennia, been caught up in catechesis, exclusion, bigotry, and, ultimately, the creation of often elaborate discourses for constructing self and other. The young Canada was certainly no different in this regard than other countries in Europe. Seminaries were associated with institutions of higher learning that were understood, at least initially, along sectarian lines. This exacerbated tensions between Anglicanism and other Protestant denominations, between French and English Canadians, and between European Canadians and Indigenous populations. Denominations had their own seminaries and, especially in eastern Canada, these seminaries functioned as the precursors to the modern university. The ensuing skirmishes and struggles are perhaps most visible in the story of how the University of Toronto emerged out of the ashes of King's College. Yet that story is not unique, but only exemplary of struggles witnessed at other institutions as they sought to shed their commitment to theological education and the training of clergy.

It was only during the 1960s that this tradition began to change, at first slowly and then rapidly. This was sparked by changing immigration patterns, declines in church attendance, the rise of counterculture and the concomitant interest in non-Western religions, and changes in the official Catholic positions on non-Christian religions. It is certainly no coincidence that in the same decade that these larger changes were occurring, secular departments of religious studies began to emerge – either *de novo* or out of existing theological programs. And just as importantly, they were now imagined as an integral component in arts curricula across the country. As religion began to be defined more broadly and not just along Christian lines, university administrators began to envision secularly reconstituted religious studies as offering alternative solutions to enduring and universal questions. Despite initial resistance on the part of some faculty, departments formed, scholarly societies were created, and the main journal devoted to the study of religion in Canada removed the word "theology" from its title and reinvented itself as a journal devoted to the study of religion – *all* religions, not just those that comprised Protestant Christianity.

This metamorphosis, as I hope should be clear by now, was not simply the result of changes in the United States or Europe. Faculty and ideas certainly travelled freely across international borders, but how religion was thought about was ultimately a nationalist concern. In this, Canada was and is no different from any other liberal democracy. If anything, and at the risk of repetition, the present study has tried to argue that this metamorphosis occurred under intellectual, social, historical, and political conditions that were unique to Canada. While I do not want to claim that religion causes the nation, or vice versa, I do make the point that discourses on religion cannot be understood adequately outside their national contexts. In other words, the study of religion in Canada cannot simply be reduced to the anxieties concerning religion and its role in the public sphere, as apparently happened in other countries.

Indeed, and to revisit my introduction, the present volume had its genesis when, during a meeting with young Canadian graduate students, one of them suggested to me that the *School District of Abington Township, PA v. Schempp* case heard in the United States Supreme Court had a direct bearing on the situation in Canada. I disagreed. Yet I had never really thought about this in any detail, so I began researching what would eventually become the present volume. Instead of reducing the rich texture of the study of religion in Canada to the legal debates over religion in the United States,[1] this study has sought to situate the study of religion, both theology and religious studies, within the *longue durée* of Canadian history. That included placing this study in the context of colonial Great Britain, Confederation, the expansion of the country through the CPR, and Canada's increased national self-confidence after the First World War. None of these individual factors exerted a simple or inextricable influence on Canadian theology – or theology carried out in a Canadian context – but taken together, they formed the backdrop against which scholars plied their trade and thought about matters they perceived to be relevant to Canada and to Canadians. In hindsight we certainly might think that their attempts were unduly Christocentric; nevertheless, they represented a distinctly Canadian take on thinking about religion. Their thinking was theological to be sure, but they undertook such activities in distinctly Canadian institutions, namely, the seminaries associated with specific denominations. Some of these denominations would join forces in the early twentieth century to form the United Church of Canada (see chapter 5). That union led to a diminution of dogmatic orthodoxy, and when combined with the rise and dissemination of higher biblical criticism to seminaries and universities, it helped create an environment in which a more secularly academic approach could flourish.

The transformation from theology to religious studies, and the movement from seminary to university, that occurred in the 1960s was precipitated by larger global forces, such as the Second Vatican Council, whose *Nostra aetate* stressed the importance of dialogue with and understanding of other religious traditions. This was especially the case in Quebec, where the Catholic Church had always had a powerful influence. There were also, of course, many other national forces, most notably the rise of multiculturalism and the subsequent changes in immigration policy that radically altered Canada's demography. These global and more local forces would play out in the institutional configuration of how religion was understood and subsequently taught.

Harold Coward ends his memoir on an optimistic note, stating that religious studies has a bright future that will propel it "into the twenty-first century and make strong contributions to both human knowledge and the public good."[2] Yet the statistics, especially over the past few years, do not necessarily lead to that optimistic conclusion. Indeed, the "death of the humanities" would seem to point in the opposite direction. While the intent of the present volume has been historical as opposed to predictive, it cannot be gainsaid that the study of religion in Canada has been greatly impacted by the current trend when it comes to provincial funding for universities, not to mention by students who are increasingly turning their backs on the humanities and social sciences.

While this is not the place to prognosticate about where the long-term repercussions of such myopia will lead, it is safe to say that it has had a direct impact on the study of religion in Canada. Recent years, for example, have seen the amalgamation of departments at UBC (now the Department of Classical, Near Eastern, and Religious Studies), Calgary (Classics and Religious Studies), and Alberta (Interdisciplinary Studies). It is uncertain – and this is especially germane for the two institutions in Alberta – what the future will hold as faculty retire and are increasingly not being replaced. The Faculty of Religious Studies at McGill has recently been transformed into the School of Religious Studies within the Faculty of Arts. This undoubtedly is a means to enable McGill to reign in the costs associated with having a separate faculty for religious studies, for which, as witnessed above, there were real and historical reasons.

Regardless of these modern transformations, which may be only fleeting, there is no denying that the study of religion will, once again, undergo major shifts in emphasis. As students look for more "practical" majors and as enrolments in religious studies decrease, religious studies will increasingly have to change to meet the changing needs of Canadian students in the twenty-first century. Anderson began his analysis of religious studies in 1972 with the claim that "before the second half of the 1960s was far advanced, religious studies had demonstrated that it had a sizeable potential clientele."[3] More than five decades later, it is unclear whether such a locution rings true. If Anderson wrote about the florescence of religious studies and his *Guide* certainly bequeaths that to us, course offerings actually seem to be shrinking at many universities across Canada.

This may well be on account of multiculturalism being such an integral part of the Canadian fabric that different cultural backgrounds and contexts are simply insignificant or irrelevant to most Canadians. Or it may be the result of the fact that the second generation of those Canadians who had eschewed mainline Protestant churches are no longer interested in other venues for exploring "timeless questions." Or it may be the result of the further diminution of the influence of the Catholic Church in Quebec and its replacement by a secularism that is no longer interested in the study of religion regardless of institutional context. Or, then again, it may be the result of more institutional forces, such as departmental politics that are exacerbated by shrinking arts budgets. Most likely, it is some combination of all of these factors.

Once again, however, we see quite clearly how the study of religion remains contingent on a set of broader forces and local contexts. In keeping with the general tenor of this study, it seems safe to conclude that the study of religion – whether as theology or as religious studies – has played a prominent role in the shaping of Canada. Its transformation from seminary to university was not a simple transition but was instead the result of the numerous forces recounted above. An account of this institutional history reveals something about the growth and development of Canada, especially its changing relationship to religion and the role of religion in the public sphere. It also reveals something about the larger context of the study of religion and how such study is intimately connected to the modern nation-state.

Notes

Introduction

1 Others have proposed alternatives. Most notable are Carlin A. Barton and Daniel Boyarin, who put it in late antiquity. See Barton and Boyarin, *Imagine No Religion*. Steven M. Wasserstrom locates it in the heresiographical literature associated with medieval Islam. See Wasserstrom, "Islamicate History of Religions." Guy G. Stroumsa puts it later in early modern Europe and the Age of Empires. See Stroumsa, *A New Science*.

2 For historical precedents, see Waardenburg, *Classical Approaches to the Study of Religion*; Sharpe, *Comparative Religion*; Capps, *Religious Studies*.

3 See, for example, the criticisms of McCutcheon, *Manufacturing Religion*; Wiebe, *The Politics of Religious Studies*; Fitzgerald, *The Ideology of Religious Studies*. While I am aware of and sympathize with the theoretical approaches of many listed above, they largely remain offstage in footnotes. In what follows my goal is to provide a historical as opposed to a sociopolitical analysis of the material.

4 See Nongbri, *Before Religion*.

5 This is perhaps best put in the language of Jonathan Z. Smith, who provocatively stated – perhaps the most often cited locution in the field – that "*there is no data for religion*. Religion is solely the creation of the scholar's study" (his italics). See the introduction to his *Imagining Religion*, xi.

6 See further McCutcheon, *Manufacturing Religion*, 127–57; Fitzgerald, *The Ideology of Religious Studies*, 3–32; Dubuisson, *The Western Construction of Religion*, 99–114.

7 Hughes, *Abrahamic Religions*; idem, *Rethinking Jewish Philosophy*.

8 I say "Western country" because the academic study of religion is, by and large, a Western initiative.

9 For an attempt to divide this along regional lines, see the essays collected in Alles, ed., *Religious Studies*. Though it is worth noting that neither Canada nor North America is mentioned therein.

10 See, for example, Imhoff, "The Creation Story."
11 This is often done by the State-of-the-Art volumes to be discussed shortly.
12 Later to become the Canadian Corporation for Studies in Religion (CCSR). More information on the make-up of this corporation may be found in chapter 7 below.
13 From the CCSR website at http://ccsr.ca/history.
14 From the 1972 volume's Foreword by Walter H. Principe, President of the Corporation for the Publication of Academic Studies in Religion in Canada, in Anderson, *Guide to Religious Studies in Canada*, 4.
15 Anderson, *Guide to Religious Studies in Canada*, 6.
16 Ibid., 7.
17 Neufeldt, *Religious Studies in Alberta*.
18 Rousseau and Despland, *Les sciences religieuses au Québec depuis 1972*.
19 Remus, James, and Fraikin, *Religious Studies in Ontario*.
20 Badertscher, Harland, and Miller, *Religious Studies in Manitoba and Saskatchewan*.
21 Fraser, *The Study of Religion in British Columbia*.
22 Bowlby with Faulkner, *Religious Studies in Atlantic Canada*.
23 See, especially, chapter 8 below.
24 Coward, *Fifty Years of Religious Studies in Canada*.
25 E.g., ibid., x, 4, 84, 199.
26 Ibid., 84.
27 Hillary Kaell, "Introduction," in Kaell, *Everyday Sacred*, 9.
28 See Voisine, *Histoire de l'Église catholique au Québec*, 20–3; Rousseau and Remiggi, *Atlas historique des pratiques religieuses*, 2–6.
29 I would, however, direct the interested reader to the following studies in addition to the State-of-the-Art review by Rousseau and Despland mentioned above: Lacroix, "Les origines ou la naissance des sciences humaines de la religion au Québec"; Campbell, "Notes sur la conjoncture des sciences religieuses au Canada français"; Partikan and Rousseau, *La théologie québécoise contemporaine*; Rousseau, "De fierté, d'espoir et d'inquiétude." More recently, see the collection of essays in Rousseau, ed., *Le Québec après Bouchard-Taylor*.

1. Inauspicious Beginnings

1 For general background, see Eccles, *The Canadian Frontier*, 1–34; Bumstead, *A History of the Canadian Peoples*, 1–30.
2 See Greer, *The People of New France*, 3–10.
3 More generally, see Greer, ed., *The Jesuit Relations*, 1–18.
4 Biggar, ed., *The Voyages of Jacques Cartier*, 26.
5 Grant, *Moon of Wintertime*, 3.

6 Biggar, ed., *The Voyages of Jacques Cartier*, 68.
7 Havard, "'Protection' and 'Unequal Alliance,'" 113–38.
8 Though for a more sanguine reading, see True, *Masters and Students*, 3–26.
9 On the role of slavery in New France, see Rushforth, *Bonds of Alliance*, 15–72.
10 Hayes, *Anglicans in Canada*, 11–49; see further Fahey, *In His Name*, 1–36.
11 More generally, see Anderson, *Crucible of War*; Baugh, *The Global Seven Years War*, 1–72.
12 For requisite background, see Lanctot, *A History of Canada*, vol. 3.
13 Conrad, *A Concise History of Canada*, 80–106. More generally, see Conrad and Hiller, *Atlantic Canada*.
14 Bothwell, *The Penguin History of Canada*, 149–99.
15 Qtd. in Burwash, "Origin and Development of the University of Toronto," 9.
16 Qtd. in Friedland, *The University of Toronto*, 5.
17 Qtd. in ibid., 5.
18 For general history, see Taylor, *The Civil War of 1812*; Stagg, *The War of 1812*.
19 Wallace, *The Family Compact*, 1–7. More recently, see Earl, *The Family Compact*; Patterson, "An Enduring Canadian Myth"; Mills, *The Idea of Loyalty in Upper Canada*, 3–10.
20 *Report on the Affairs of British North America*, 46.
21 General background on the Church of England in Canada may be found in Fahey, *In His Name*. On Strachan in particular, see Boorman, *John Toronto*.
22 Qtd. in Friedland, *The University of Toronto*, 6.
23 Qtd. in ibid., *The University of Toronto*, 8.
24 See Read and Stagg's essay collection, *The Rebellion of 1837 in Upper Canada*. On the rebellion in Lower Canada, see Schul, *Rebellion*.
25 *Report on the Affairs of British North America*, 46.
26 The full Report may be found at http://www.canadiana.ca/view/oocihm.32374/1?r=0&s=1.
27 Lee, *The Canada Company and the Huron Tract*.
28 *Report on the Affairs of British North America*, 12.
29 Ibid., 12–3.
30 The full act may be consulted at http://www.solon.org/Constitutions/Canada/English/PreConfederation/ua_1840.html.
31 Bothwell, *Penguin History of Canada*, 183–6.
32 Indeed, to try to ameliorate these tensions, it was arranged for leadership of the new province to be shared by an anglophone from Canada West and a francophone from Canada East.
33 A readable biographical sketch is in Saul, *Louis-Hippolyte Lafontaine and Robert Baldwin*, 27–61.

34 See ibid., 63–87.
35 Ibid., 152–60.
36 See, for example, Remus, "Religion and Religious Studies in Ontario," 9–11.
37 See Simmons, *Keepers of the Record*, 13–40.
38 Vroom, *King's College*, 2–3; Dewolf and Flie, *All the King's Men*, 6–14.
39 On its history, see Provost, "Les Origines éloignées du Séminaire de Québec"; idem, "Historique du Séminaire de Québec."
40 Kaell, "Introduction," 9.
41 Ibid., 9.
42 Ibid., 9. See further Voisine, *Histoire de l'Église catholique au Québec*, 6–12.
43 Provost, *Le Séminaire de Québec*.
44 Bureau, "Le Petit Séminaire de Québec."
45 Bounadère, *Aperçu historique sur les petits séminaires*, 3–5.
46 See, for example, Miller, *Residential Schools and Reconciliation*, 3–10.
47 Truth and Reconciliation Committee of Canada (hereafter TRC), *Canada's Residential Schools: The Final Report*, vol. 4.
48 Harris, *A History of Higher Education in Canada*, 14–18.
49 See Chidester, *Savage Systems*, 1–11; idem, *Empire of Religion*, 3–24.
50 In the opening to his *Elementary Forms of the Religious Life*, for example, Émile Durkheim writes: "In this book we propose to study the most primitive and simple religion which is actually known, to make an analysis of it, and to attempt an explanation of it. A religious system may be said to be the most primitive which we can observe when it fulfils the two following conditions: in the first place, when it is found in a society whose organization is surpassed by no others in simplicity; and secondly, when it is possible to explain it without making use of any element borrowed from a previous religion" (13).
51 Grant, *Moon of Wintertime*, 10.
52 For recent attempts to think through these legally, see the essays collected by Macklem and Sanderson in *From Recognition to Reconciliation*.
53 TRC, *Summary of the Final Report*, 50. http://www.trc.ca/websites/trcinstitution/File/2015/Findings/Exec_Summary_2015_05_31_web_o.pdf.
54 Université Laval and the Séminaire de Québec now have no legal affiliation. The *séminaire* became an independent institution in 1970, and Petit Séminaire, now a private Roman Catholic secondary school, became independent in 1987.
55 Frost, *McGill University*, vol. 1, 173.
56 Qtd. in Alfred G. Bailey, "Early Foundations, 1783–1829," 15.
57 On Paine and the Loyalists more generally, see Bell, *Loyalist Rebellion in New Brunswick*, 10–12.
58 Bailey, "Early Foundations, 1783–1829," 16.
59 Ibid., 18.

60 Firth, "King's College, Fredericton," 22.
61 Ibid., 23.
62 Vroom, *King's College*, 38.
63 Firth, "King's College, Fredericton," 28.
64 Raymond, *The Genesis of the University of New Brunswick.*
65 Keirstead, "University of New Brunswick Past and Present."
66 MacKirdy, "The Formation of the Modern University," 33.
67 Ibid., 34.
68 See my comments in *Comparison: A Critical Primer.*
69 Friedland, *The University of Toronto*, 8.
70 Thomas, "The Early Days of King's College."
71 Vroom, *King's College*, xi.
72 Qtd. in Vroom, *King's College*, 21.
73 Qtd. in ibid., 37.
74 Qtd. in ibid., 37.
75 See Akins, *A Brief Account.*
76 The articles are reproduced in Vroom, *King's College*, 39–42.
77 Ibid., 40.
78 Ibid., 41.
79 Ibid., 42.
80 Friedland, *The University of Toronto*, 10.
81 His biography may be found in Frost, *James McGill of Montreal.*
82 Frost, *McGill University*, 30.
83 Ibid., 35–6.
84 Ibid., 21.
85 Qtd. in ibid., 49.
86 Ibid., 50.
87 Ibid., 58.
88 Ibid., 86.
89 See further Maheux, "Pourquoi l'Université en 1852?," 381–7.
90 Frost, *McGill University*, 173.
91 His ideas will be discussed in greater detail in the context of chapter 3 below.
92 On the history of the study of religion at McGill, see chapter 9 below.
93 Qtd. in Calvin, *Queen's University at Kingston*, 16.
94 Qtd. in ibid., 20.
95 Qtd. in ibid., 21.
96 Qtd. in ibid., 32.
97 I shall talk more about him as an early Canadian scholar of religion in chapter 3.
98 Qtd. in Calvin, *Queen's University at Kingston*, 149.
99 There were certainly precursors, such as the Canada Baptist College, which existed from 1838 to 1849, in Montreal. This institution had hoped

to affiliate with McGill, but the latter institution was not interested, since it was, as witnessed above, pretty Anglican at this point and not interested in affiliating with other Protestant denominations.

100 See Vining, ed., *Woodstock College Memorial Book.*
101 Unlike Americans, who sought to put colleges in the countryside, far from cities, Canadians seemed content to put them in urban environments. Unlike many of the other individuals discussed in this chapter, Fyfe had been educated in the United States rather than in Britain.
102 Johnston, *McMaster University*, vol. 1, 20.
103 Ibid., 18.
104 Qtd. in ibid., 31–2.
105 Qtd. in ibid., 35.
106 See Masters, "The Rise of Liberalism in Canadian Protestant Churches."
107 Qtd. in Johnston, *McMaster University*, vol. 1, 52.
108 Qtd. in ibid., 60.
109 See Thomson, "McMaster University."

2. The University of Toronto: A Case Study

1 Harris, *A History of Higher Education in Canada*, 27–36. Though Harris's volume is an important attempt to move beyond the history of individual institutions and instead offer a synthetic account of post-secondary education in Canada, he is unfortunately rarely interested in the theological underpinnings of the endeavour.
2 Hodgins, *Documentary History of Education in Upper Canada*, 12.
3 Harris, *A History of Higher Education in Canada*, 27.
4 Qtd. in Vroom, *King's College*, 10.
5 Remus, "Religion and Religious Studies in Ontario," 7.
6 Robinson, *Canada and the Canada Bill*, 44.
7 Qtd. in Remus, "Religion and Religious Studies in Ontario," 7.
8 Qtd. in Burwash, *The University of Toronto and Its College*, 508.
9 Qtd. in Burwash, "Origin and Development of the University of Toronto," in *The University of Toronto and Its Colleges*, 10.
10 Wilson, *The Clergy Reserves of Upper Canada*, 3–5.
11 *Charter of the University of King's College*, University of Toronto Archives. Qtd in Friedland, *The University of Toronto*, 8.
12 Harris, *A History of Higher Education in Canada*, 29.
13 Roper, "The Anglican Episcopate in Canada."
14 See Spragge, "John Strachan's Contribution to Education."
15 The religious nature of universities was at this time a growing concern in England. In 1826 the University of London had been established as a non-sectarian institution, but not by a Royal Charter, so it could not grant

degrees. The Commons supported the granting of degrees, but the House of Lords rejected it (by a vote of 8–9). Finally in 1836, it was allowed to do so. The University of London would subsequently function as the prototype for the University of Toronto.

16 Qtd. in Burwash, "Origin and Development of the University of Toronto," 11.
17 Spragge, "John Strachan's Contribution to Education," 155–6.
18 Burwash, "Origin and Development of the University of Toronto," 12.
19 See Howard, *Upper Canada College*, 1–29.
20 Qtd. in Burwash, "Origin and Development of the University of Toronto," 16.
21 Jones, "Higher Education in Ontario," 137–40.
22 Burwash, "Origin and Development of the University of Toronto," 19–20.
23 Friedland, *The University of Toronto*, 19.
24 Qtd. in Burwash, "Origin and Development of the University of Toronto," 25. See also Hodgins, *Documentary History of Education in Upper Canada*, 152.
25 Qtd. in Burwash, "Origin and Development of the University of Toronto," 26–7.
26 Recall the statement of Christopher Hagerman, a leader of the Family Compact, quoted in the previous chapter.
27 Qtd. in Burwash, "Origin and Development of the University of Toronto," 188.
28 See Rawlyk and Quinn, *The Redeemed of the Lord Say So*, 4–10.
29 See Clifford, "The History of Protestant Theological Education in Canada." More generally, see Masters, *Protestant Church Colleges in Canada*, 1–12.
30 Saul, *Louis-Hippolyte Lafontaine and Robert Baldwin*, 153–72.
31 See Schneider, "The Habit of Deference."
32 Gidney, "Centralization and Education."
33 Qtd. in Friedland, *The University of Toronto*, 28.
34 Remus, "Religion and Religious Studies in Ontario," 9.
35 Qtd. in Friedland, *The University of Toronto*, 35.
36 Henri Pilon, "The Founding of the University of Trinity College," 4.
37 Strachan, *Church University of Upper Canada*, 3.
38 Henderson, "The Founding of Trinity College," 11.
39 Qtd. in Friedland, *The University of Toronto*, 66.
40 Sissons, *A History of Victoria University*, 133.
41 Qtd in Friedland, *The University of Toronto*, 101.
42 See Smith, "Federation and Fullness," 17–44. See, albeit briefly, Watson, *Religious Studies in the University of Toronto*, 8–12.
43 Qtd. in Friedland, *The University of Toronto*, 105.

3. Late Victorian Scholarship and the Rise of Higher Criticism

1 For relevant context, see Frei, *The Eclipse of Biblical Narrative*. For an overview of the Canadian context, see Moir's important work, *A History of Biblical Studies in Canada*, 25–51.

2 Note that whereas even Oxford could make exceptions to hiring Jews, King's could or would not.

3 See, for example, *The Collected Mathematical Papers of James Joseph Sylvester*, 4 vols.

4 Friedland, *The University of Toronto*, 23.

5 For brief biography and relevant context, see Langton, "The University of Toronto in 1856."

6 [Anon.], "Review of *Elements of Natural Philosophy*," *The English Review*, 192.

7 [Anon.], "Review of *Elements of Natural Philosophy*," *The Gentleman's Magazine and Historical Review*, 70.

8 On the English approach to the study of religion, see Preus, *Explaining Religion*.

9 On his work in geology, see, for example, Dawson, *Acadian Geology*.

10 Qtd. in Frost, *McGill University*, vol. 1, 183.

11 Qtd. in ibid., 184.

12 On the formation of the Royal Society, see Harris, *A History of Higher Education in Canada*, 93–102.

13 For larger context, see the essays in Paradis and Postlewait, eds., *Victorian Science and Victorians Values*; Levine, "Defining Knowledge."

14 Dawson, *The Origin of the World*, i.

15 Ibid., 9–10.

16 Ibid., 10.

17 Ibid., 338.

18 Ibid., 343.

19 Ibid., 343.

20 Dawson, *Facts and Fancies in Modern Science*, 5.

21 Ibid., 5.

22 Ibid., 221–2.

23 Though, as witnessed in the Introduction, some scholars would argue that very little has changed today.

24 For his biography, see Grant and Hamilton, *George Monro Grant*.

25 See Calvin, *Queen's University at Kingston*, 90–115.

26 Grant's great-grandson, Michael Ignatieff, writes about this journey in *True Patriot Love*.

27 Grant, *Ocean to Ocean*, 17.

28 Ibid., 23.

29 Grant, *Advantages of Imperial Federation*, 5.

30 Calvin, *Queen's University at Kingston*, 97.
31 Ibid., 101.
32 Ibid., 108.
33 Ibid., 114. Though, it is worth noting, that this would not actually happen until 1910.
34 I quote from the enlarged edition of 1895: Grant, *The Religions of the World in Relation to Christianity*, vii.
35 Ibid., vii.
36 Ibid., vii.
37 Ibid., viii.
38 See the comments in Remus, "Religion and Religious Studies in Ontario," 35.
39 Grant, *The Religions of the World in Relation to Christianity*, 1.
40 Ibid., 2.
41 Ibid., 4.
42 Ibid., 4.
43 Ibid., 5.
44 Ibid., 5.
45 See Remus, "Religion and Religious Studies in Ontario," 36.
46 Cochrane, ed., *The Canadian Album*, 451.
47 See Remus, "Religion and Religious Studies in Ontario," 36.
48 Jordan, *Comparative Religion*, x.
49 It is a loaded methodology, to be sure. See my criticisms in *Comparison*, 25–50.
50 Jordan, *Comparative Religion*, x.
51 Ibid., xiii.
52 Ibid., 580.
53 Much of my analysis in what follows relies on Moir, *A History of Biblical Studies in Canada*.
54 Masters, "The Rise of Liberalism," 27–39.
55 For relevant context, see Hill, "Early Hebrew Printing."
56 Moir, *A History of Biblical Studies in Canada*, 7.
57 See Menkis, "'The Voice of the Minister." On de Sola's larger economic activities, see Tulchinsky, "'Said to Be a Very Honest Jew.'"
58 For relevant context, see Saperstein, "The Academic Study of Canadian Jewish Preachers."
59 "de Sola, Abraham," in *Dictionary of Canadian Biography*, vol. 11 (1881–1890). http://www.biographi.ca/en/bio/de_sola_alexander_abraham_11E.html.
60 Adams, *A History of Christ Church Cathedral*, 98–100.
61 Ibid., 100.
62 I have relied on the account of the affair as described in Abbot-Smith, "Frederick Julius Steen." http://anglicanhistory.org/canada/bheeney/3/2.html.

63 Johnston, *McMaster University*, vol. 1, 90.
64 Foster, *The Function of Religion*, 13.
65 Johnston, *McMaster University*, vol. 1, 93.
66 Ibid., 93.
67 Qtd. in ibid., 99.
68 Ibid., 94.
69 Ibid., 104.
70 Qtd. in ibid., 104.
71 Qtd. in ibid., 105.
72 Moir, *A History of Biblical Studies in Canada*, 14–15.
73 Jordan, "The Higher Criticism in Canada."
74 Moir, *A History of Biblical Studies in Canada*, 15.
75 Ibid., 15.
76 McCurdy, *Aryo-Semitic Speech*, 1.
77 Ibid., 5.
78 Qtd. in Jordan, "The Higher Criticism in Canada, 37.
79 Moir, *A History of Biblical Studies in Canada*, 57–8; Remus, "Religion and Religious Studies in Ontario," 21.

4. Westward Bound

1 See, for example, Cairns, "The Governments and Societies of Canadian Federalism"; Friesen, "The Evolving Meanings of Region in Canada."
2 Savoie, "All Things Canadian are Now Regional."
3 Constitution Act of 1867, http://laws-lois.justice.gc.ca/eng/Const/page-1.html#h-3.
4 Relevant histories dealing with this include Bothwell, *The Penguin History of Canada*, 187–212; Conrad, *A Concise History of Canada*, ch. 6; Morton, *A Short History of Canada*, 7th ed., 88–98. More recently, see Krikorian et al., eds., *Roads to Confederation*.
5 The Métis are of mixed Indigenous and Euro-American ancestry; however, the name tends to be used specifically to designate a group of such people who in the nineteenth century inhabited the areas around the Red and Saskatchewan rivers in what is today known as Manitoba. Métis peoples are recognized as one of Canada's Aboriginal peoples under the Constitution Act of 1982, along with First Nations and Inuit peoples.
6 Space does not permit me to focus much on this event, except briefly in the context of the founding of the University of Manitoba (see below). On Louis Riel, see Charlebois, *The Life of Louis Riel*. For full-blown studies of the Riel Rebellion, see Boyden, *Louis Riel and Gabriel Dumont*. For more technical studies, see Stanley, *Birth of Western Canada*. For an eyewitness account, see McDougall, *In the Days of the Red River Rebellion*.

7 This term was removed upon completion of the Confederation Bridge in 1997.

8 See Kelley, *The Transatlantic Persuasion*; more specifically to the Canadian context, see Christian and Campbell, *Political Parties and Ideologies in Canada*, 3–17.

9 John A. Macdonald, "On Canadian Confederation," http://www.bartleby.com/268/5/1.html.

10 Grant, *Ocean to Ocean*, 23–4. See also Fleming, *Report and Documents*.

11 For a general history of the CPR, see Stevens, *History of the Canadian National Railways*; Lamb, *History of the Canadian Pacific Railway*.

12 See Eagle, *The Canadian Pacific Railway*, 1–15.

13 Ibid., 148–72.

14 Ibid., 149–55.

15 The act may be read online at https://www.ourdocuments.gov/doc.php?flash=false&doc=33&page=transcript.

16 On the early history of Saskatchewan, see Anderson, *Settling Saskatchewan*, 12–30.

17 King, *The First Fifty*, 27.

18 On francophone immigration into the province in these early years and their need to set up their own institutions, see Lapointe and Tessier, *The Francophones of Saskatchewan*, 1–42.

19 For a general survey on higher education in Saskatchewan, see Muir, "Higher Education in Saskatchewan." More specifically, see Kerr, "Building the University of Saskatchewan."

20 See Murray, "The Early History of Emmanuel College."

21 In Morton, *Saskatchewan*, 5–8.

22 King, *The First Fifty*, 27.

23 Murray, "The Early History of Emmanuel College," 83–7. See also Thomas, "The Church of England and Higher Education."

24 Roland E. Miller, "Religious Studies at the University of Saskatchewan: Its Origin and Development," in Badertscher, Harland, and Miller, *Religious Studies in Manitoba and Saskatchewan*, 101.

25 King, *The First Fifty*, 11. According to King's statistics, roughly 6 per cent of graduates of Arts and Sciences went into divinity (by comparison, 4 per cent went into law, 9 per cent into medicine, and 25 per cent into teaching and primary school education).

26 See Murray, "The Contest for the University of Saskatchewan." In Ontario, the University of Toronto established its agricultural school in Guelph (now the University of Guelph).

27 Qtd. in King, *The First Fifty*, 29.

28 King, *The First Fifty*, 26.

29 Murray, "The Early History of Emmanuel College," 97–101.

30 King, *The First Fifty*, 26.
31 Ibid., 64.
32 Pitsula, *As One Who Serves*, 23–47.
33 Ibid., 250; Topping, "Catholic Studies in Canada."
34 Pitsula, *As One Who Serves*, 250.
35 Ibid., 252.
36 Ibid., 255.
37 Ibid., 259.
38 Brennan, "'The Autonomy Question'"; Russell, "Rhetorics of Identity."
39 Thomas, *The Liberal Party in Alberta*, 1–10.
40 For a biography, see Babcock, *Alexander Cameron Rutherford*.
41 Alexander, *The University of Alberta*, 5.
42 For a biography, see Corbett, *Henry Marshall Tory*.
43 Alexander, *The University of Alberta*, 6
44 For a general, more recent, survey on higher education in Alberta, see Andrews, Holdaway, and Mowatt, "Postsecondary Education in Alberta since 1945."
45 Corbett, *Henry Marshall Tory*, 51–64; see also Macleod, *All True Things*, 1–2.
46 Corbett, *Henry Marshall Tory*, 21–7.
47 Macleod, *All True Things*, 6. For his comments about mediocrity, see Corbett, *Henry Marshall Tory*, 87.
48 Corbett, *Henry Marshall Tory*, 93–100.
49 Qtd. in Macleod, *All True Things*, 6.
50 Corbett, *Henry Marshall Tory*, 110–21.
51 Macleod, *All True Things*, 10–11.
52 Johns, *A History of the University of Alberta*, 1–19.
53 Macleod, *All True Things*, 14.
54 Ibid., 27.
55 See Johns, *A History of the University of Alberta*, 61–8.
56 Macleod, *All True Things*, 53.
57 Johns, *A History of the University of Alberta*, 66–8.
58 Bumstead, *St. John's College*, 1.
59 Morton, *A History of the Canadian West to 1870–71*, 1–21. On Lord Selkirk, see Bumstead, *Lord Selkirk*, 255–77.
60 Bumstead, *St. John's College*, 3.
61 On the Hudson's Bay Company more generally, see Ruggles, *A Country So Interesting*, 18–22, 74–86.
62 Bumstead, *St. John's College*, 6–7.
63 Ibid., 13.
64 For general survey on higher education in Manitoba, see Gregor, "Higher Education in Manitoba."
65 Qtd. in Bumstead, *St. John's College*, 17.

66 Baird, "The History of the University of Manitoba."
67 Morton, *One University*, 5–12.
68 Bumstead, *St. John's College*, 28.
69 Ibid., 76.
70 Barman, *The West Beyond the West*, 99–128.
71 Damer and Rosengarten, *UBC*, 3.
72 For general survey on higher education in British Columbia, see, Denison, "Higher Education in British Columbia."
73 See Harris, "Locating the University of British Columbia."
74 Damer and Rosengarten, *UBC*, 5.
75 Ibid., 5.
76 Ibid., 7.
77 Ibid., 9.
78 Ibid., 9.
79 Harris, "Locating the University of British Columbia," 115–18.
80 Damer and Rosengarten, *UBC*, 13.
81 Elliot and Miller, *Bible Bill*, 7.
82 On Scofield, see Trumbell, *The Life Story of C.I. Scofield.*
83 See, for example, Boone, *The Bible Tells Them So*, 77–99.
84 Elliot, "The Devil and William Aberhart," 325–30.
85 Sandeen, *The Roots of Fundamentalism*, 224.
86 Elliot and Miller, *Bible Bill*, 13.
87 On the Moody Bible Institute and its larger context, see Carpenter, "Fundamentalist Institutions." More generally, see Sandeen, *The Roots of Fundamentalism*, 1–15.
88 Elliot and Miller, *Bible Bill*, 16.
89 On the Plymouth Brethren, see most recently Introvigne, *The Plymouth Brethren*, esp. 8–17.
90 Elliot and Miller, *Bible Bill*, 27.
91 Ibid., 32–3.
92 Ibid., 36.
93 See Elliot, "The Devil and William Aberhart," 330–7.
94 Qtd. in Elliot and Miller, *Bible Bill*, 38.
95 See Elliot, "Anti-Semitism and the Social Credit Movement."
96 Qtd. in Elliot and Miller, *Bible Bill*, 110.
97 Elliot and Miller, *Bible Bill*, 103.
98 Ibid., 167.
99 Qtd. in ibid., 116. Though interestingly, Major Douglas disagreed with Aberhart's conception of Social Credit.
100 On Social Credit in Alberta more generally, see Irving, *The Social Credit Movement in Alberta*; Calderola, "The Social Credit in Alberta."
101 Elliot and Miller, *Bible Bill*, 31.

102 Requisite biographies may be found in Shackleton, *Tommy Douglas*; Margoshes, *Tommy Douglas*; Lam, *Tommy Douglas*.
103 For relevant context, see Masters, *The Winnipeg General Strike*.
104 Lam, *Tommy Douglas*, 27–8.
105 See chapter 6 below.
106 On the Social Gospel, see Allen, "The Social Gospel and the Reform Tradition in Canada"; Riddell, *Methodism in the Middle West*, 200–25.
107 CSIS still has an 1,100-page file on Douglas from as early as when he was a preacher in Weyburn. They still refuse to release it. See Lam, *Tommy Douglas*, 219.
108 He did, however, complete an MA in sociology by correspondence at McMaster. His thesis was titled "The Problems of the Subnormal Family," and it argued for eugenics. See Shevell, "A Canadian Paradox."
109 Lam, *Tommy Douglas*, 49.
110 For relevant background, see Horn, "Frank Underhill's Early Drafts."
111 Qtd. in Lam, *Tommy Douglas*, 109–10.
112 Qtd. in Shackleton, *Tommy Douglas*, 49. A nice selection of his speeches may be found in Lovick, ed., *Tommy Douglas Speaks*.
113 In 2004 the CBC called for Canadians to nominate their greatest Canadian. Ten finalists were chosen, each with an advocate. After this, Tommy Douglas was voted "greatest Canadian of all time."

5. Battle Lines

1 Grant, *The Canadian Experience of Church Union*, 7.
2 See, for example, Allen, *The British Industrial Revolution*, 1–22.
3 Buckner, "Whatever Happened to the British Empire?" More generally, see Campey, *The Scottish Pioneers of Upper Canada*.
4 Grant, *The Canadian Experience of Church Union*, 9.
5 Ibid., 9–10.
6 Patterson, *Memoir of James MacGregor*, 409.
7 Moir, *A History of Biblical Studies in Canada*, 22.
8 There were certainly other precedents, such as the unions that created the Church of South India and the Church of North India. On the Canadian context, see Silcox, *Church Union in Canada*, 3–23; Grant, *The Canadian Experience of Church Union*, 7–8; Schweitzer, "Introduction," xi–xix at xiv.
9 Grant, *The Canadian Experience of Church Union*, 17–18.
10 Qtd. in ibid., 18.
11 Silcox, *Church Union in Canada*, 125–64; Grant, *The Canadian Experience of Church Union*, 19–30; McIntire, "Unity among Many."
12 Grant, *The Canadian Experience of Church Union*, 25.

13 The United Church continued to be a "uniting" church. In 1930 the Synod of the Wesleyan Methodist Church of Bermuda became part of the United Church of Canada's Maritime Conference. The Evangelical United Brethren Church became part of the United Church of Canada in 1968. In addition, various individual congregations from other Christian communions have become part of the United Church over the years.

14 United Church of Canada, "The Basis of Union (1925)," 2, online at http://www.united-church.ca/sites/default/files/resources/basis-of-union.pdf, General Precepts.

15 McIntire, "Unity among Many," 23.

16 Grant, *The Canadian Experience of Church Union*, 27.

17 United Church of Canada, "The Basis of Union (1925)."

18 McIntire, "Unity among Many," 8.

19 Ibid., 5.

20 Ibid., 26.

21 Ibid., 26–7.

22 See Stebner, "The 1930s," 40.

23 Qtd. in McIntire, "Unity among Many," 23.

24 Qtd. in ibid., 23.

25 Qtd. in ibid., 24.

26 United Church of Canada, "Basis of Union," II.3 (I).

27 Ibid., 5.

28 Moir, *A History of Biblical Studies in Canada*, 15.

29 Watson, *Religious Studies in the University of Toronto*, 8–11; Remus, "Religion and Religious Studies in Ontario," 19–22.

30 Moir, *A History of Biblical Studies in Canada*, 25.

31 Ibid., 26; Remus, "Religion and Reigius Studies in Ontario," 21.

32 Moir, *A History of Biblical Studies in Canada*, 28.

33 See the comments in Sinclair-Faulkner, "Theory Divided from Practice."

34 Ibid., 327–9.

35 Moir, *A History of Biblical Studies in Canada*, 34; see further Horn, *Academic Freedom in Canada*, 25–35.

36 Sinclair-Faulkner, "Theory Divided from Practice," 329–30.

37 Moir, *A History of Biblical Studies in Canada*, 35.

38 Sinclair-Faulkner, "Theory Divided from Practice," 331–3; Horn, *Academic Freedom in Canada*, 27–30.

39 Qtd. in Moir, *A History of Biblical Studies in Canada*, 36.

40 For requisite biographical details, see Greenlee, *Sir Robert Falconer*.

41 Moir, *A History of Biblical Studies in Canada*, 39–41.

42 Qtd. in ibid., 40.

43 See Horn, *Academic Freedom in Canada*, 78–82.
44 Qtd. in Moir, *A History of Biblical Studies in Canada*, 63.
45 Qtd. in ibid., 29.
46 See Watson, *Religious Studies in the University of Toronto*, 11–13.
47 Moir, *A History of Biblical Studies in Canada*, 29.
48 Qtd. in Moir, *A History of Biblical Studies in Canada*, 30.
49 Watson, *Religious Studies in the University of Toronto*, 13–14.
50 Qtd. in Moir, *A History of Biblical Studies in Canada*, 31.
51 I shall discuss this in greater detail in chapter 8.
52 Martin and Wiebe, "Documenting the Delusion," 321.
53 Ibid., 322.
54 Remus, "Religion and Religious Studies in Ontario," 21.
55 Moir, *A History of Biblical Studies in Canada*, 67.
56 Qtd. in ibid., 67.
57 Remus, "Religion and Religious Studies in Ontario," 21.
58 Moir, *A History of Biblical Studies in Canada*, 67–8.
59 MacPherson, "A History of the Canadian Society of Biblical Studies," 2.
60 Remus, "Religion and Religious Studies in Ontario," 22.
61 http://www.csbs-sceb.ca/Bulletin.html.

6. Venues of Dissemination

1 For example, Moore, "Fate and Free Will."
2 [Editors], "The Purpose of the Journal: An Editorial," *Canadian Journal of Theology*, 2.
3 Perhaps this is best symbolized by Canada's success in the Battle of Vimy Ridge. On the battle itself, and the repercussions for Canadian identity, see the essays in Hayes, Iarocci, and Bechtold, eds., *Vimy Ridge*. On the legacy, see Cook, *Vimy*.
4 [Editors], *Canadian Journal of Religious Thought* 1.1 (1924): 90. The context of this quotation is in the biography section of the first issue, under Arthur Peake, who is described as "a professor of biblical exegesis at Manchester University in England."
5 Flatt, *After Evangelicalism*, 12–14.
6 Ibid., 35.
7 [Editors], "The Purpose of the Journal," *Canadian Journal of Religious Thought*, 1.
8 Ibid., 3.
9 Ibid., 5.
10 Ibid., 1.
11 For example, Mercer, "An Expedition to Abyssinia."
12 Pilcher, "Hermann Gunkel on Psalms 42, 43."

13 See, for example, Gunkel, *The Legends of Genesis.*
14 Pilcher "Hermann Gunkel on Psalms 42, 43," 319.
15 [Editors], "The Purpose of the Journal," 2.
16 [Editors], "Religious Education and the Public School."
17 MacNeill, "Paul: The First Christian Protestant," 199.
18 Rowell, "The International Situation and The Christian Ideal," 25.
19 Smyth, "The Faith of Modern Man," 70.
20 Davidson, "The Living Truth," 159.
21 For example, Ernest Thomas, "The Significance of Political Groups," 71–81.
22 For example, Gifford, "Christianity in the British Isles before Augustine."
23 For example, Rose, "Travelling Europe."
24 Including a regular column titled "Poet's Page." See, for example, *CJRT* 1.1 (1924): 82–3. See also Phelps, "An Approach to Contemporary Poetry."
25 For example, *CJRT* 1.1 (1924): 84–5.
26 For example, ibid., 88–9 and 1.3 (1924): 266–7.
27 Manson, "From an Expositor's Notebook," 165–6.
28 The author of, among other things, Dow, *This Is Our Faith.*
29 Scott, "Some Doubts about Psychology," 106.
30 Whidden, "What is a Liberal Education," 39.
31 See, for example Bultmann, "Jesus and the Eschatological Kingdom," 94–5.
32 Manson, "Foundations Which Are Not Removed," 16.
33 Ibid., 17.
34 Ibid., 23.
35 Peake, "The Alleged Reaction in Old Testament Criticism," 40.
36 McMurrich, "Evolution and Religion," 464.
37 Ibid., 470.
38 Ibid., 471.
39 Ibid., 472.
40 MacKinnin, "'Formgeschichte' and the Synoptic Problem," 190.
41 Micklem, "Religions and Religion."
42 Ibid., 27.
43 MacRae, "The New Tide in China," 520.
44 Price, "Japan and the Christian Movement."
45 MacNeill, "The Course of Buddhism in India," 54.
46 MacNeill, "Buddha as Pragmatist," 343.
47 See Burkinshaw, *Pilgrims in Lotus Land*, 97–9.
48 Scott, "Brandon College and Social Christianity," 144.
49 "How Will Ontario and Quebec Baptists Receive Prof. H.L. MacNeill," *The Gospel Witness* col. 11, no. 17, 8 September 1932, 3.
50 Johnston, *McMaster University*, vol. 2, 69.

51 Ibid., 70.
52 Bensen, "Karma and Transmigration."
53 [Editors], "The End of an Episode."
54 Ibid.
55 Ibid.
56 Macpherson, "A History of the Canadian Society of Biblical Studies," 3.
57 Ibid., 3–4.
58 [Editors], "The Purpose of the Journal: An Editorial," 1.
59 Ibid., 1.
60 Ibid., 2.
61 [Editors], "Theological Scholarship," 139.
62 [Editors], "Editorial," *CJT* 1.2 (1955): 67.
63 [Editors], "Editorial," *CJT* 3.2 (1957): 68.
64 [Editors], "A Theological Need," 125.
65 Slater, "Christian Attitudes to Other Religions," 215.
66 The following biographical materials come from McLelland, "Editorial," *SR* 6.5 (1976–7): 483–4.
67 Slater, *Paradox and Nirvana* (University of Chicago Press, 1950).
68 McLelland, "Editorial," 484.
69 https://cswr.hds.harvard.edu/about/history.
70 Welch, "New Building Will House Church Study." http://www.thecrimson.com/article/1959/11/20/new-building-will-house-church-study.
71 Conway, "The Universities and Religious Studies," 270.
72 Ibid., 270.
73 Wevers, "Canadian Universities and the Teaching of Religion," 162.
74 Ibid., 161.
75 [Editors], "Editorial," *CJT* 4.3 (1958), 163–4.
76 [Editors], "On the Significance of Niebuhr's Ideas of Society," 99.
77 Ibid., 99.
78 Fairweather, "Editorial: Canadian Journal of Theology, 1955–1970," 127.
79 Ibid., 127.
80 Ibid., 128.
81 Ibid., 128.

7. From Seminary to University

1 Clifford, "Universities, Churches and Theological Colleges," 3–4.
2 Discussed in greater detail below.
3 Remus, "Religion and Religious Studies in Ontario," 38. He bases his data on the 1972 edition of Anderson, *Guide to Religious Studies in Canada*.
4 See, for example, Fielding, "Twenty-Three Theological Schools"; more generally, see idem, *Education for Ministry*.

5 Clifford, "Universities, Churches and Theological Colleges," 6.
6 See Fraser, *The Study of Religion in British Columbia*, 28–31. The Atlantic School of Theology is unfortunately left out of Bowlby and Faulkner, *Religious Studies in Atlantic Canada*.
7 See Gwynne-Timothy, *Western's First Century*, 12–33.
8 See Imhoff, "The Creation Story," 466–72.
9 http://en.wikisource.org/wiki/Abington_School_District_v._Schempp_(374_U.S._203)/Opinion_of_the_Court (my italics).
10 For a general survey, see Hawkins, *Canada and Immigration*, 89–118.
11 Kelley and Trebilcock, *The Making of the Mosaic*, 316–51. On more specific populations, see Ralston, "Canadian Immigration Policy in the Twentieth Century." And for a documentary, see Kazimi, *Undesirables*.
12 Bangarth, "'We Are Not Asking You [...]'" See also Taylor, "Racism in Canadian Immigration Policy."
13 Hawkins, *Canada and Immigration*, 139–75.
14 The White Paper on Immigration may be found at https://www.pier21.ca/research/immigration-history/white-paper-on-immigration-1966.
15 *Report of the Royal Commission on Bilingualism and Biculturalism*, Appendix 1: *The Terms of Reference* (1963), 173. http://epe.lac-bac.gc.ca/100/200/301/pco-bcp/commissions-ef/dunton1967-1970-ef/dunton1967-70-vol1-eng/dunton1967-70-vol-part2-eng.pdf.
16 Ibid., 174.
17 Wayland, "Immigration, Multiculturalism and National Identity in Canada"; Hawkins, *Critical Years in Immigration*, 218; Temelini, "Multicultural Rights, Multicultural Virtues: A History of Multiculturalism in Canada."
18 Forbes, "Trudeau as the First Theorist of Canadian Multiculturalism."
19 Rt. Hon. P.E. Trudeau (Prime Minister), "Announcement of Implementation of Policy of Multiculturalism within Bilingual Framework," 8 October 1971. https://www.pier21.ca/research/immigration-history/canadian-multiculturalism-policy-1971.
20 Ibid.
21 Ibid.
22 http://publications.gc.ca/collections/Collection/CH37-4-3-2002E.pdf.
23 And it is often combined with Section 15, which reads:

> 15.(1) Every individual is equal before and under the law and has the right to the equal protection and equal benefit of the law without discrimination and, in particular, without discrimination based on race, national or ethnic origin, colour, religion, sex, age or mental or physical disability.
>
> (2) Subsection (1) does not preclude any law, program or activity that has as its object the amelioration of conditions of disadvantaged

individuals or groups including those that are disadvantaged because of race, national or ethnic origin, colour, religion, sex, age or mental or physical disability.

24 http://laws-lois.justice.gc.ca/PDF/C-18.7.pdf.
25 https://www.pier21.ca/research/immigration-history/immigration-regulations-order-in-council-pc-1967-1616-1967.
26 Whitaker, *Canadian Immigration Policy since Confederation*, 19.
27 Fairweather, "Editorial," 128.
28 Grant, "Asking Questions of the Canadian Past," 98.
29 A short and convenient overview of the society may be found in Fennell, "The Canadian Theological Society."
30 Ibid., 410.
31 Ibid., 411.
32 It changed its name from the "Learned Societies" (aka "Learneds") to the "Congress of Humanities and Social Sciences" in 1996. Recent years, however, have seen some Canadian organizations meet outside the auspices of the congress, though none of those that make up the Canadian Corporation for Studies in Religion (CCSR – see below) do.
33 Clifford, "Religion and the Development of Canadian Society," 521.
34 https://theocan.org/page-d-exemple/qui-sommes-nous-mission.
35 See Strykman, "Présentation," 13–15.
36 For more on Grant, see below.
37 See the convenient account in Combs, "Learned and Learning," 357–63.
38 Desrosiers, "Notes épistémologiques sur la religiologie"; see also Rousseau and Despland, "Introduction," in *Les sciences religieuses au Québec*, 11–21.
39 Anderson, *Guide*, 9.
40 Ibid., 9.
41 Also worth mentioning in the present context is the Canadian Society of Patristic Studies / Association canadienne des études patristiques (CSPS), founded in 1975, which encourages and contributes to the study in Canada of everything to do with the patristic era (c. 100 to 750 CE).
42 Rousseau and Despland, *Les sciences religieuses au Québec*, 141.
43 Rousseau, unpublished memorandum on the foundation of SQER, qtd. in Remus, "Religion and Religious Studies in Ontario," 85.
44 Walter H. Principe, "Foreword," in Anderson, *Guide*, 5.
45 Coward, *Fifty Years of Religious Studies in Canada*, 78.
46 It is one of three major federal granting agencies, the others being the Natural Sciences and Engineering Research Council (NSERC) and Canadian Institutes of Health Research (CIHR). Together these are frequently referred to as "the tri-council."

47 Both quotations come from Anderson, *Guide*, 6.
48 This information comes from private conversations I had with the various constituent societies when I was managing editor of *SR* from 2000 to 2009.
49 From the WLUP website: "This omnibus series published original monographs in particular religious traditions; on themes or topics that intersect a number of traditions; and that incorporate any number of theoretical and/or methodological approaches." Online, including list of titles, at https://www.wlupress.wlu.ca/Series/E/Editions-SR.
50 From the WLUP website: "This series published original monographs that deal with ethics broadly defined." Online, including list of titles, at https://www.wlupress.wlu.ca/Series/D/Dissertations-SR.
51 No description on the WLUP website, but a list of titles may be found at https://www.wlupress.wlu.ca/Series/C/Comparative-Ethics.
52 From the WLUP website: "This series published monographs on Christianity and Judaism in the last two centuries before and the first six centuries of the common era, with a special interest in studies of their relationship or the cultural and social context within which they developed." Online, including list of titles, at https://www.wlupress.wlu.ca/Series/C/Comparative-Ethics.
53 From the WLUP website: "The Study of Religion in Canada / Sciences Religieuses au Canada series was 'A State-of-the-Art Review' of religious studies in Canada. Each volume covered a particular geographic region and presents a descriptive and analytical study of courses, programs and research undertaken in the field of religious studies in Canada." Online, including list of titles, at https://www.wlupress.wlu.ca/Series/S/Study-of-Religion-in-Canada.
54 No description on the WLUP website, but a list of titles may be found at https://www.wlupress.wlu.ca/Series/S/SR-Supplements.
55 Though, perhaps as a sign of the times, in 2015 these six series were folded into two – *Advancing Studies in Religion* and *Studies in Christianity and Judaism* – which are now published with McGill–Queen's University Press.
56 Fraser, *The Study of Religion in British Columbia*, 13.
57 The journal has been digitalized, and the contents of all volumes may be found at http://journals.sagepub.com/home/sir.
58 Wiebe, "The Failure of Nerve in the Academic Study of Religion," 420. The essay, in addition to a number of essays that "think" with it, is reprinted in Arnal, Braun, and McCutcheon, eds., *Failure and Nerve in the Academic Study of Religion*.
59 Guenther, "Buddhist Metaphysics and Existential Mysticism"; Kinsley, "'The Taming of the Shrew.'"
60 Nicholls, "Editorial," 1.

61 Ibid., 1.
62 Ibid., 2.
63 Ibid., 2.
64 Ibid., 3.
65 Ibid., 3.
66 Fairweather, "Editorial," 128.
67 The journal describes its mandate on its webpage: "*Toronto Journal of Theology* is a progressive, double-blind refereed journal of analysis and scholarship, reflecting diverse Christian traditions and exploring the full range of theological inquiry: Biblical Studies, History of Christianity, Pastoral Theology, Christian Ethics, Systematic Theology, Philosophy of Religion, and Interdisciplinary Studies." http://www.utpjournals.press/loi/tjt.
68 Laporte, "Editorial," 412.
69 Davis, "The Reconvergence," 205.
70 Ibid., 205.
71 Ibid., 205.
72 These responses, published in the same volume and issue, were by Gregory Baum (St. Michael's at the University of Toronto and later McGill), Kenneth Hamilton (Winnipeg), William O. Fennell (Emmanuel College), Paul Younger (McMaster), and William Hordern (Lutheran Theological Seminary, Saskatoon).
73 Wiebe, "Is a Science of Religion Possible?," 5.
74 Ibid., 5 (his italics).
75 Ibid., 16.
76 Wiebe, "The Failure of Nerve."
77 Ibid., 402.
78 Ibid., 404.
79 Charles Davis, "Wherein There is No Ecstasy," *SR* 13.4 (1984): 393–400. Though, as can be seen by the page numbers, Davis' response actually appears before Wiebe's article. It might be worth noting that Davis had been the editor of *SR* and that this issue was the first issue of his successor, Roland Chagnon.
80 Davis, "Wherein There Is No Ecstasy," 393.
81 Ibid., 394.
82 Ibid., 394.
83 They appeared, along with responses by both Wiebe and Davis, in *SR* 15.2 (1986).
84 See chapter 3 of this volume.
85 Remus, "Religion and Religious Studies in Ontario," 44.
86 Grant, *Lament for a Nation*. In 2005 the Literary Review of Canada recognized the work as one of the hundred most important Canadian books.
87 Grant, "The Academic Study of Religion in Canada," 60.

88 Ibid., 62–3.
89 Ibid., 63.
90 Ibid., 64.
91 Remus, "Religion and Religious Studies in Ontario," 44.
92 Grant, "The Academic Study of Religion in Canada," 67.
93 A full biography may be found in these two volumes, among others: Hughes, *Wilfred Cantwell Smith*; Aitken and Sharma, eds., *The Legacy of Wilfred Cantwell Smith.*
94 Adams, "The Development of Islamic Studies in Canada, 187.
95 Smith, "A Human View of Truth," 6.
96 Ibid., 17.
97 See Badertscher, Harland, and Miller, *Religious Studies in Manitoba and Saskatchewan*, 74–5.
98 Klostermaier, "Hindu-Christian Dialogue," 83.
99 Ibid., 84.
100 Ibid., 97.

8. Florescence

1 For an excellent work that quantifies and explains Canadians' drift from engagement with religious institutions, see Clarke and Macdonald, *Leaving Christianity*, 27–71.
2 Anderson, *Guide to Religious Studies in Canada*, 8.
3 Ibid., 8.
4 Ibid., 11–12.
5 Roland E. Miller, "Religious Studies in Saskatchewan," in Badertscher, Harland, and Miller, *Religious Studies in Manitoba and Saskatchewan*, 81.
6 See chapter 1 in this volume.
7 See Markell, *The Faculty of Religious Studies, McGill University*, 2.
8 Ibid., 2–3.
9 Ibid., 2.
10 Ibid., 4.
11 Ibid., 17–24.
12 Rousseau and Despland, *Les sciences religieuses au Québec depuis 1972*, 48–9; Markell, *The Faculty of Religious Studies*, 27.
13 Indeed, Wiebe would still say it is. See, for example, the discussion in the previous chapter.
14 See, for example, my *Comparison*, 42–5.
15 See chapter 6 in this volume.
16 Though see my *Comparison*, 14–18.
17 Recall Wiebe's complaints in chapter 7 in this volume.
18 Rousseau and Despland, *Les sciences religieuses au Québec depuis 1972*, 49.

19 Ibid., 49.
20 See chapter 7 in this volume.
21 Grant, "The Academic Study of Religion in Canada," 64.
22 Coward, *Fifty Years of Religious Studies in Canada*, 33.
23 In religious studies this is known as the insider/outsider problem. For background, see McCutcheon, *The Insider/Outsider Problem in the Study of Religion.*
24 Remus, "Religion and Religious Studies in Ontario," 45.
25 See Neufeldt, *Religious Studies in Alberta*, 5–6; Coward, *Fifty Years of Religious Studies in Canada*, 20–2.
26 I was a member of this department from 2001 to 2009.
27 Fraser, *The Study of Religion in British Columbia*, 12.
28 "Interim Report of the Legal Sub-committee on the Senate Committee on Religious Studies," *Minutes of the Faculty of Arts and Sciences*, 3 August 1955 (Senate Record, box 32, file 8), qtd. in Fraser, *The Study of Religion in British Columbia*, 13.
29 Fraser, *The Study of Religion in British Columbia*, 12–13.
30 Coward, *Fifty Years of Religious Studies in Canada*, 18.
31 Fraser, *The Study of Religion in British Columbia*, 15.
32 Anderson, *Guide*, 52
33 Michel Campbell, "Notes sur le conjonctore des sciences religieuses," in Anderson, *Guide*, 21–2.
34 Kaell, "Introduction," in *Everyday Sacred*, 3–12.
35 See Lacroix, "Les origins ou la naissance des sciences humaines." See also Campbell, "Notes sur le conjoncture des sciences religieuses," 24–5.
36 Rousseau, "De fierté, d'espoir et d'inquiétude," xix–xxiv.
37 Campbell, "Notes sur le conjoncture des sciences religieuses," 27.
38 Larouche and Ménard, "Présentation," in *L'étude de la religion au Québec*, 3–5.
39 Rousseau, "La religiologie à l'UQAM," 85.
40 Ibid., 85.
41 Ibid., 86–7.
42 Published in Ryan, ed., *L'enseignement et la recherche.*
43 Campbell, "Notes sur le conjoncture des sciences religieuses," 26–7.
44 Sauvé, *La Faculté de théologie de l' Université de Montréal*, 21; more generally on the creation, see 21–35.
45 Ibid., 346–7.
46 Campbell, "Notes sur le conjoncture des sciences religieuses," 28.
47 See, for example, Bulman, "The Historical Context." See also my *Abrahamic Religions*, 66–70.
48 Campbell, "Notes sur le conjoncture des sciences religieuses," 28.
49 Sauvé, *La Faculté de théologie de l' Université de Montréal*, 332–4, 350–3. See also Rousseau and Despland, *Les sciences religieuses au Québec depuis 1972*, 50–1.

50 *Winnipeg Free Press*, 5 May 1950.
51 Gordon Harland and John M. Badertscher, "Religious Studies in Manitoba," in Badertscher, Harland, and Miller, *Religious Studies in Manitoba and Saskatchewan*, 25–6.
52 Harland and Badertscher, "Religious Studies in Manitoba," 26.
53 Memo of Rose B. Rady, Chair of the Board of Governors of Maimonides College, to Dr. H.H. Saunderson, President of the University, 25 May 1962, in University of Manitoba Archives, 27-35-26. Qtd. in Harland and Badertscher, "Religious Studies in Manitoba," 26.
54 The department was subsequently suspended in 1989, and its faculty were folded into the Department of Religion. This would also have the effect of bringing the study of Judaism into the Department of Religious Studies.
55 McGill would not establish its Department of Jewish Studies until 1968. The University of Toronto has a centre, not a department.
56 Harland and Badertscher, "Religious Studies in Manitoba," 26.
57 See chapter 4 in this volume.
58 In addition to the University of Manitoba, at, for example, the University of Alberta, the University of Saskatchewan, Queen's University, and the University of Toronto.
59 The American Academy of Religion (AAR) being the more national or, at least, North American version.
60 On the Winnipeg IAHR, see Wiebe, "Memory, Text, and Interpretation."
61 For relevant context, see chapter 2 in this volume.
62 Watson, *Religious Studies in the University of Toronto*, 13.
63 Ibid., 16.
64 Ibid., 17–18.
65 On the history of these developments, see ibid., 17–30.
66 Ibid., 31.
67 For example, as Watson notes, the Department of East Asian Studies and Trinity College cross-appointed an instructor in Hinduism and Buddhism. See ibid., 33. This was, moreover, a far cry from anything that John Strachan would have imagined happening in Trinity.
68 Remus, "Religion and Religious Studies in Ontario," 59. See also Wiebe (with Martin), "Documenting the Delusion: A Case Study," 321.
69 Remus, "Religion and Religious Studies in Ontario," 59.
70 Ibid., 59.
71 Ibid., 61; see also Martin and Wiebe, "Documenting the Delusion," 322. For a history of the Centre, see Watson, *Religious Studies at the University of Toronto*, 68–70.
72 Ibid., 70; Martin and Wiebe, "Documenting the Delusion," 323.
73 Neufeldt. *Religious Studies in Alberta*, 2.

74 Qtd. in ibid., 2.
75 Qtd. in ibid., 2.
76 Coward, *Fifty Years of Religious Studies in Canada*, 19; Neufeldt, *Religious Studies in Alberta*, 3.
77 See chapter 1 in this volume.
78 Bowlby with Faulkner, *Religious Studies in Atlantic Canada*, 10.
79 See chapter 1 in this volume.
80 Bowlby with Faulkner, *Religious Studies in Atlantic Canada*, 51.
81 Ibid., 52.
82 It would only become the University of Regina in 1974.
83 Miller, "Religious Studies in Saskatchewan," 83.
84 Ibid., 82; James M. Pitsula, *As One Who Serves*, 265.
85 Miller, "Religious Studies in Saskatchewan," 86–7; Coward, *Fifty Years of Religious Studies in Canada*, 23.
86 Ibid., 25.
87 A separate school in Canada is one that has constitutional status in Alberta, Saskatchewan, and Ontario. Such schools are operated by a civil authority – a "separate" school board – that is elected by Roman Catholics (determined by school tax forms), and takes into consideration Catholic theology, doctrine, and practices. Separate schools do not exist for members of other religious minorities (e.g., Jews, Muslims).
88 Miller, "Religious Studies in Saskatchewan," 104.
89 Sanche, *Heartwood*, 187.
90 Miller, "Religious Studies in Saskatchewan," 105.
91 Ibid., 105.
92 See Bibby, *Fragmented Gods*, 3–12.

Conclusions

1 Even American scholars have begun to question the role this Supreme Court case has played in the American context, arguing that it is more a "myth of origins" than anything else. See, for example, Imhoff, "The Creation Story," 466–97.
2 Coward, *Fifty Years of Religious Studies in Canada*, 212.
3 Anderson, *Guide*, 10.

Bibliography

Abbot-Smith, G. "Frederick Julius Steen." In *Leaders of the Canadian Church*, ed. William Bertal Heeney. Toronto: Ryerson Press, 1943.

Adams, Charles J. "The Development of Islamic Studies in Canada." In *The Muslim Community in North America*, ed. Earle H. Waugh, Baha Abu-Laban, and Regula B. Qureshi, 185–201. Edmonton: University of Alberta Pres, 1983.

Adams, F.D. *A History of Christ Church Cathedral*. Montreal: McGill University Press, 1941.

Aitken, Ellen, and Arvind Sharma, eds. *The Legacy of Wilfred Cantwell Smith*. Albany: SUNY Press, 2017.

Akins, T.B. *A Brief Account of the Origins, Endowment, and Progress of the University of King's College, Windsor, Nova Scotia*. Halifax: MacNab and Sons, 1865.

Alexander, William Hardy. *The University of Alberta: A Retrospect 1908–1929*. Edmonton: University Printing Press, 1929.

Allen, Richard. "The Social Gospel and the Reform Tradition in Canada, 1890–1928." *Canadian Historical Review* (1968): 381–99.

Allen, Robert C. *The British Industrial Revolution in Global Perspective*. Cambridge: Cambridge University Press, 2009.

Alles, Gregory D., ed. *Religious Studies: A Global View*. New York and London: Routledge, 2008.

Anderson, Alan B. *Settling Saskatchewan*. Regina: University of Regina Press, 2013.

Anderson, Charles P. *Guide to Religious Studies in Canada / Guide des sciences religieuses au Canada*. N.p: Corporation for the Publication of Academic Studies in Religion in Canada, 1972.

Anderson, Fred. *Crucible of War: The Seven Years' War and the Fate of Empire in British North America, 1754–1766*. New York: Vintage, 2000.

Andrews, Michal B., Edward A. Holdaway, and Gordon L. Mowatt. "Postsecondary Education in Alberta since 1945." In *Higher Education in*

Canada: Different Systems, Different Perspectives, ed. Glen A. Jones, 59–92. London and New York: Routledge, 1997.

[Anonymous]. "Review of *Elements of Natural Philosophy* by James Beaven D.D." *The English Review* 15 (1851): 192.

– "Review of *Elements of Natural Philosophy* by James Beaven D.D." *The Gentleman's Magazine and Historical Review* 35 (1851): 70.

Arnal, William E., Willi Braun, and Russell T. McCutcheon, eds. *Failure and Nerve in the Academic Study of Religion: Essays in Honor of Donald Wiebe*. Sheffield: Equinox, 2012.

Babcock, Douglas R. *Alexander Cameron Rutherford: A Gentleman of Strathcona*. Calgary: University of Calgary Press, 1989.

Badertscher, John M., Gordon Harland, and Roland E. Miller. *Religious Studies in Manitoba and Saskatchewan: A State-of-the-Art Review*. Waterloo: Wilfrid Laurier University Press, 1993.

Bailey, Alfred G. "Early Foundations, 1783–1829." In *The University of New Brunswick Memorial Volume*, ed. Alfred G. Bailey, 15–21. Fredericton: University of New Brunswick Press, 1950.

Baird, A.G. "The History of the University of Manitoba." In *Manitoba Essays*, ed. R.C. Lodge, 10–52. Toronto: Macmillan, 1937.

Bangarth, Stephanie. "'We Are Not Asking You to Open Wide the Gates for Chinese Immigration': The Committee for the Repeal of the Chinese Immigration Act and Early Human Rights Activism in Canada." *Canadian Historical Review* 84.3 (2003): 395–422.

Barman, Jean. *The West Beyond the West: A History of British Columbia*, 3rd ed. Toronto: University of Toronto Press, 2007.

Barton, Carlin A., and Daniel Boyarin. *Imagine No Religion: How Modern Abstractions Hide Ancient Realities*. New York: Fordham University Press, 2016.

Baugh, Daniel. *The Global Seven Years War 1754–1763: Britain and France in a Great Power Contest*. London: Routledge, 2011.

Bell, David. *Loyalist Rebellion in New Brunswick: A Defining Conflict for Canada's Political Culture*. Halifax: Formac, 2013.

Bensen, Roy C. "Karma and Transmigration." *Canadian Journal of Religious Thought* 8.3 (1931): 210–15.

Bibby, Reginald W. *Fragmented Gods: The Poverty and Potential of Religion in Canada*. Toronto: Irwin, 1987.

Biggar, Henry Percival, ed. *The Voyages of Jacques Cartier*. Toronto: University of Toronto Press, 1993.

Boone, Kathleen C. *The Bible Tells Them So: The Discourse of Protestant Fundamentalism*. Albany: SUNY Press, 1989.

Boorman, Sylvia. *John Toronto: A Biography of Bishop Strachan*. Toronto: Clark, Irwin, 1969.

Bothwell, Robert. *The Penguin History of Canada.* Toronto: Penguin, 2006.

Bounadère, René. *Aperçu historique sur les petits séminaires de la Province du Québec.* Québec: Les Presses de l'Université Laval, 1945.

Bowlby, Paul W.R., with Tom Faulkner. *Religious Studies in Atlantic Canada: A State-of-the-Art Review.* Waterloo: Wilfrid Laurier University Press. 2001.

Boyden, Joseph. *Louis Riel and Gabriel Dumont.* Toronto: Penguin, 2010.

Brennan, J. William. "'The Autonomy Question' and the Creation of Alberta and Saskatchewan, 1905." In *The New Provinces: Alberta and Saskatchewan, 1905–1980,* ed. Howard Palmer and Donald Smith, 43–63. Vancouver: Tantalus Research, 1980.

Buckner, Philip. "Whatever Happened to the British Empire?" *Journal of the Canadian Historical Association* 4.1 (1993): 3–32.

Bulman, Raymond E. "The Historical Context." In *From Trent to Vatican II: Historical and Theological Investigations,* ed. Raymond F. Bulman and Frederick J. Parrella, 3–18. Oxford and New York: Oxford University Press, 2006.

Bultmann, Rudolf. "Jesus and the Eschatological Kingdom." In *Rudolf Bultmann: Interpreting Faith for the Modern Era,* ed. Roger A. Johnson, 91–127. Minneapolis: Fortress Press, 1965.

Bumstead, J.M. *A History of the Canadian Peoples.* Oxford: Oxford University Press, 2004.

– *Lord Selkirk: A Life.* Winnipeg: University of Manitoba Press, 2008.

– *St. John's College: Faith and Education in Western Canada.* Winnipeg: University of Manitoba Press, 2006.

Bureau, Gilles. "Le Petit Séminaire de Québec 1668–2008." *L'Abeille* 55.2 (2008): 17–20. Québec: Amicale du Petit Séminaire de Québec.

Burkinshaw, Robert K. *Pilgrims in Lotus Land: Conservative Protestantism in British Columbia, 1917–1981.* Montreal and Kingston: McGill–Queen's University Press, 1995.

Burwash, N. "Origin and Development of the University of Toronto." In *The University of Toronto and Its Colleges, 1827–1906,* ed. W.J. Alexander, 9–38. Toronto: The University Library, 1906.

Cairns, A.C. "The Governments and Societies of Canadian Federalism." *Canadian Journal of Political Science* 10.4 (1977): 695–726.

Calderola, Carlo. "The Social Credit in Alberta, 1935–1971." In *Society and Politics in Alberta,* ed. C. Calderola, 33–48. Agincourt: Methuen, 1979.

Calvin, D.D. *Queen's University at Kingston: The First Century of a Scottish-Canadian Foundation, 1841–1941.* Kingston: The Trustees of the University, 1941.

Campbell, Michel. "Notes sur la conjoncture des sciences religieuses au Canada français depuis 1967." In C. Anderson, *Guide to Religious Studies in Canada / Guide des sciences religieuses au Canada,* 21–39. N.p.: Corporation for the Publication of Academic Studies in Religion in Canada, 1972.

Campey, Lucille H. *The Scottish Pioneers of Upper Canada, 1784–1855: Glengarry and Beyond*. Toronto: Natural Heritage, 2005.

Capps, Walter H. *Religious Studies: The Making of a Discipline.* Minneapolis: Fortress, 1995.

Carpenter, Joel A. "Fundamentalist Institutions and the Rise of Evangelical Protestantism, 1929–1942." *Church History* 49.1 (1980): 62–75.

Charlebois, Peter. *The Life of Louis Riel.* Toronto: New Canada Publications, 1975.

Chidester, David. *Empire of Religion: Imperialism and Comparative Religion.* Chicago: University of Chicago Press, 2014.

– *Savage Systems: Colonialism and Comparative Religion in Southern Africa.* Charlottesville: University of Virginia Press, 1996.

Christian, William, and Colin Campbell. *Political Parties and Ideologies in Canada: Liberals, Conservatives, Socialists, Nationalists*, 2nd ed. Toronto: McGraw-Hill Ryerson, 1983.

Clarke, Brian, and Stuart Macdonald. *Leaving Christianity: Changing Allegiances in Canada since 1945.* Montreal and Kingston: McGill–Queen's University Press, 2017.

Clifford, N. Keith. "The History of Protestant Theological Education in Canada." *Sessions d'etude: Société canadienne d'histoire d'Église catholique* 56 (1989): 85–95.

– "Religion and the Development of Canadian Society: A Historiographical Analysis." *Church History* 38.4 (1969): 506–23.

– "Universities, Churches, and Theological Colleges in English-Speaking Canada: Some Current Sources of Tension." *Studies in Religion / Sciences religieuses* 19.1 (1990): 3–16.

Cochrane, Rev. Wm., ed. *The Canadian Album: Men of Canada; or, Success by Example in Religion, Patriotism, Business, Law, Medicine, Education and Agriculture.* Brantford: Bradley, Garretson and Co, 1895.

Combs, Eugene. "Learned and Learning: CSSR/SCER, 1965–1975." *Studies in Religion / Sciences religieuses* 6.4 (1977): 357–63.

Conrad, Margaret R. *A Concise History of Canada.* Cambridge: Cambridge University Press, 2012.

Conrad, Margaret R., and James K. Hiller. *Atlantic Canada: A History*. Oxford and Toronto: Oxford University Press, 2006.

Conway, John S. "The Universities and Religious Studies." *Canadian Journal of Theology* 5.4 (1959): 269–72.

Cook, Tim. *Vimy: The Battle and the Legend.* Toronto: Penguin Canada, 2017.

Corbett, E.A. *Henry Marshall Tory: A Biography* [1954]. Edmonton: University of Alberta Press, 1992.

Coward, Harold. *Fifty Years of Religious Studies in Canada: A Personal Retrospective.* Waterloo: Wilfrid Laurier University Press, 2014.

Damer, Eric, and Herbert Rosengarten. *UBC: The First 100 Years*. Vancouver: UBC Press, 2009.

Davidson Richard. "The Living Truth." *Canadian Journal of Religious Thought* 1.2 (1924): 156–63.

Davis, Charles. "The Reconvergence of Theology and Religious Studies." *Studies in Religion / Sciences religieuses* 4.3 (1974–5): 205–21.

– "Wherein There Is No Ecstasy." *Studies in Religion / Sciences religieuses* 13.4 (1984): 393–400.

Dawson, John William. *Acadian Geology: The Geological Structure, Organic Remains, and Mineral Resources of Nova Scotia, New Brunswick, and Prince Edward Island*, 2nd ed. London: Macmillan and Company, 1878.

– *Facts and Fancies in Modern Science: Studies of the Relations of Science to Prevalent Speculations and Religious Belief*. Philadelphia: American Baptist Publication Society, 1882.

– *The Origin of the World, According to Revelation and Science*. New York: Harper and Brothers, 1877.

Denison, John D. "Higher Education in British Columbia, 1945–1995: Opportunity and Diversity." In *Higher Education in Canada: Different Systems, Different Perspectives*, ed. Glen A. Jones, 31–58. London and New York: Routledge, 1997.

Desrosiers, Yvon. "Notes épistémologiques sur la religiologie." In *Sciences sociales et églises. Questions sur l'évolution religieuse au Québec*, ed. P. Stryckman and J.P. Rouleau, 61–8. Montreal: Bellarmin, 1980.

Dewolf, Mark, and George Flie. *All the King's Men: The Story of a Colonial University*. Halifax: Alumni Association of the University of King's College, 1972.

Dow, John. *This Is Our Faith: An Exposition of the Faith of the United Church of Canada*. Toronto: United Church of Canada, 1943.

Dubuisson, Daniel. *The Western Construction of Religion: Myths, Knowledge, and Ideology*, trans. Willard Sayers. Baltimore: Johns Hopkins University Press, 2003.

Durkheim, Émile. *The Elementary Forms of the Religious Life*, trans. Joseph Ward Swain. New York: The Free Press, 1915.

Eagle, John A. *The Canadian Pacific Railway and the Development of Western Canada*. Montreal and Kingston: McGill–Queen's University Press, 1989.

Earl, David W.L. *The Family Compact: Aristocracy or Oligarchy?* Toronto: C. Clark, 1967.

Eccles, W.J. *The Canadian Frontier, 1534–1760*, rev. ed. Albuquerque: University of New Mexico Press, 1983.

[Editors]. "The End of an Episode." *Canadian Journal of Religious Thought* 9.4 (1932): 247.

– "Preface to *On the Significance of Niebuhr's Ideas of Society*." *Canadian Journal of Theology* 7.2 (1961): 99.

– "The Purpose of the Journal." *Canadian Journal of Religious Thought* 1.1 (1924): 1–5.

– "The Purpose of the Journal: An Editorial." *Canadian Journal of Theology* 1.1 (1955): 1–2.

– "Religious Education and the Public School." *Canadian Journal of Religious Thought* 1.4 (1924): 273.

– "A Theological Need." *Canadian Journal of Theology* 2.3 (1956): 125–8.

– "Theological Scholarship." *Canadian Journal of Theology* 1.3 (1955): 139–40.

Elliot, David R. "Anti-Semitism and the Social Credit Movement: The Intellectual Roots of the Keegstra Affair." *Canadian Ethnic Studies / Études ethniques au Canada* 1.1 (1985): 78–89.

– "The Devil and William Aberhart: The Nature and Function of His Eschatology." *Studies in Religions / Sciences religieuses* 9.3 (1980): 325–37.

Elliot, David R., and Iris Miller. *Bible Bill: A Biography of William Aberhart.* Edmonton: Reidmore Books, 1987.

Fahey, Chris. *In His Name: The Anglican Experience in Upper Canada, 1791–1854.* Ottawa: Carleton University Press, 1991.

Fairweather, Rev. Eugene R. "Editorial: Canadian Journal of Theology, 1955–1970." *Canadian Journal of Theology* 16.3–4 (1970): 127–8.

Fennell, William O. "The Canadian Theological Society: An Anniversary Retrospective." *Studies in Religion / Sciences religieuses* 14.4 (1985): 409–13.

Fielding, Charles R. *Education for Ministry.* Dayton: American Association of Theological Schools, 1966.

– "Twenty-Three Theological Schools: Aspects of Canadian Theological Education." *Canadian Journal of Theology* 12 (1966): 229–37.

Firth, Frances A. "King's College, Fredericton: 1829–1859." In *The University of New Brunswick Memorial Volume*, ed. Alfred G. Bailey, 22–32. Fredericton: University of New Brunswick Press, 1950.

Fitzgerald, Timothy. *The Ideology of Religious Studies.* Oxford and New York: Oxford University Press, 2000.

Flatt, Kevin N. *After Evangelicalism: The Sixties and the United Church of Canada.* Montreal and Kingston: McGill–Queen's University Press, 2013.

Fleming, Sandford. *Report and Documents in reference to the Canadian Pacific Railway.* Ottawa: MacLean, Roger and Co., 1880.

Forbes, Hugh Donald. "Trudeau as the First Theorist of Canadian Multiculturalism." In *Multiculturalism and the Canadian Constitution*, ed. M. Temelini, 27–42. Vancouver: UBC Press, 2007.

Foster, George Burman. *The Function of Religion in Man's Struggle for Existence.* Chicago: University of Chicago Press, 1909.

Fraser, Brian G. *The Study of Religion in British Columbia: A State-of-the-Art Review.* Waterloo: Wilfrid Laurier University Press, 1995.

Frei, Hans. *The Eclipse of Biblical Narrative: A Study in Eighteenth and Nineteenth Century Hermeneutics.* New Haven: Yale University Press, 1974.

Friedland, Martin L. *The University of Toronto: A History*. Toronto: University of Toronto Press, 2002.

Friesen, G. "The Evolving Meanings of Region in Canada." *Canadian Historical Review* 82.3 (2001): 529–45.

Frost, Stanley Brice. *James McGill of Montreal*. Montreal and Kingston: McGill–Queen's University Press, 1995.

– *McGill University: For the Advancement of Learning*, vol. 1: *1801–1895*. Montreal and Kingston: McGill–Queen's University Press, 1980.

Gidney, R.D. "Centralization and Education: The Origins of an Ontario Tradition." *Journal of Canadian Studies* 7.4 (1972): 33–48.

Gifford, W.A. "Christianity in the British Isles before Augustine." *Canadian Journal of Religious Thought* 1.2 (1924): 144–55.

Grant, George Monro. *Advantages of Imperial Federation*. Toronto: C. Blackett Robinson, 1891.

– *Ocean to Ocean: Sandford Fleming's Expedition through Canada in 1872*. Toronto: Rose Belford, 1973 [repr.].

– *The Religions of the World in Relation to Christianity*. New York: Anson D.F. Randolph and Co., 1895.

Grant, George P. "The Academic Study of Religion in Canada." In *Scholarship in Canada, 1967: Achievement and Outlook*, ed. R.H. Hubbard, 59–68. Toronto: University of Toronto Press, 1968.

– *Lament for a Nation: The Defeat of Canadian Nationalism* [1965]. Montreal and Kingston: McGill–Queen's University Press, 2005.

Grant, John W. "Asking Questions of the Canadian Past." *Canadian Journal of Theology* 1 (1955): 98–104.

– *The Canadian Experience of Church Union*. Richmond: John Knox Press, 1967.

– *Moon of Wintertime: Missionaries and the Indians of Canada in Encounter since 1534*. Toronto: University of Toronto Press, 1984.

Grant, William Lawson, and Frederick Hamilton. *George Monro Grant*. Toronto: Morang and Co., 1905.

Greenlee, James G. *Sir Robert Falconer: A Biography*. Toronto: University of Toronto Press, 1988.

Greer, Allan. *The People of New France*. Toronto: University of Toronto Press, 1999.

Greer, Allan, ed. *The Jesuit Relations: Natives and Missionaries in Seventeenth-Century North* America. Boston: Bedford/St. Martin's, 2000.

Gregor, Alexander D. "Higher Education in Manitoba." In *Higher Education in Canada: Different Systems, Different Perspectives*, ed. Glen A. Jones, 114–36. London and New York: Routledge, 1997.

Guenther, H.V. "Buddhist Metaphysics and Existential Mysticism." *Studies in Religion / Sciences religieuses* 1.4 (1971–2): 291–7.

Gunkel, Hermann. *The Legends of Genesis*, trans. W.H. Carruth. Chicago: Open Court, 1901.

Gwynne-Timothy, J.R.W. *Western's First Century*. London: University of Western Ontario Press, 1978.

Harris, Cole. "Locating the University of British Columbia." *BC Studies* 32 (1976–7): 106–25.

Harris, Robin S. *A History of Higher Education in Canada, 1663–1960*. Toronto: University of Toronto Press, 1976.

Havard, Gilles. "'Protection' and 'Unequal Alliance': The French Conception of Sovereignty over Indians in New France." In *French and Indians in the Heart of North America, 1630–1815*, ed. Robert Englebert and Guillaume Teasdale, 113–38. East Lansing and Winnipeg: Michigan State University Press and University of Manitoba Press, 2013.

Hawkins, Freda. *Canada and Immigration: Public Policy and Public Concerns*, 2nd ed. Montreal and Kingston: McGill–Queen's University Press, 1988.

– *Critical Years in Immigration: Canada and Australia Compared*. 2nd ed. Montreal and Kingston: McGill–Queen's University Press, 1991.

Hayes, Alan L. *Anglicans in Canada: Controversies and Identity in Historical Perspective*. Champaign: University of Illinois Press, 2004.

Hayes, Geoffrey, Andrew Iarocci, and Mike Bechtold, eds. *Vimy Ridge: A Canadian Reassessment*. Waterloo: Wilfrid Laurier University Press, 2007.

Henderson, J.L.H. "The Founding of Trinity College, Toronto." *Ontario History* 44 (1952): 7–14.

Hill, Brad Sabin. "Early Hebrew Printing." *Studia Rosenthaliana* 38–9 (2005–6): 306–47.

Hodgins, J. George. *Documentary History of Education in Upper Canada from the Passing of the Constitutional Act in 1791 to the Close of Rev. Dr. Ryerson's Administration of the Education Department in 1876*. Toronto: Warwick Brothers and Rutter, 1894.

Horn, Michiel. *Academic Freedom in Canada: A History*. Toronto: University of Toronto Press, 1999.

– "Frank Underhill's Early Drafts of the Regina Manifesto, 1933." *Canadian Historical Review* 54.5 (1973): 393–418.

Howard, Richard B. *Upper Canada College, 1829–1979: Colborne's Legacy*. Toronto: Macmillan Canada, 1979.

Hughes, Aaron W. *Abrahamic Religions: On the Uses and Abuses of History*. Oxford and New York: Oxford University Press, 2012.

– *Comparison: A Critical Primer*. Sheffield: Equinox, 2017.

– *Rethinking Jewish Philosophy: Beyond Universalism and Particularism*. Oxford and New York: Oxford University Press, 2014.

Hughes, Edward J. *Wilfred Cantwell Smith: A Theology for the World*. London: SCM Press, 1985.

Ignatieff, Michael. *True Patriot Love: Four Generations in Search of Canada.* Toronto: Penguin Canada, 2009.

Imhoff, Sarah. "The Creation Story, or How We Learned to Stop Worrying and Love *Schempp.*" *Journal of the American Academy of Religion* 84.2 (2016): 466–97.

Introvigne, Massimo. *The Plymouth Brethren.* Oxford and New York: Oxford University Press, 2018.

Irving, John A. *The Social Credit Movement in Alberta.* Toronto: University of Toronto Press, 1959.

Johns, Walter Hugh. *A History of the University of Alberta, 1908–1969.* Edmonton: University of Alberta Press, 1981.

Johnston, Charles M. *McMaster University*, vol. 1: *The Toronto Years.* Toronto: University of Toronto Press, 1976.

– *McMaster University*, vol. 2: *The Early Years in Hamilton, 1930–1957.* Montreal and Kingston: McGill–Queen's University Press, 2015.

Jones, Glen A. "Higher Education in Ontario." In *Higher Education in Canada: Different Systems, Different Perspectives*, ed. Glen A. Jones, 138–60. London and New York: Routledge, 1997.

Jordan, Louis H. *Comparative Religion: Its Genesis and Growth.* Edinburgh: T. and T. Clark, 1905.

Jordan, W.G. "The Higher Criticism in Canada." *Queen's Quarterly* 36.1 (1929): 31–46.

Kaell, Hillary, ed. *Everyday Sacred: Religion in Contemporary Quebec.* Montreal and Kingston: McGill–Queen's University Press, 2017.

Kazimi, Ali. *Undesirables: White Canada and the Komagata Maru – An Illustrated History*. Vancouver: Douglas and McIntyre, 2011.

Keirstead, W.D. "University of New Brunswick Past and Present." *Dalhousie Review* 22 (1943): 344–54.

Kelley, Ninette, and Michael Trebilcock. *The Making of the Mosaic: History of Canadian Immigration Policy*, 2nd ed. Toronto: University of Toronto Press, 2010.

Kelley, Robert. *The Transatlantic Persuasion: The Liberal-Democratic Mind in the Age of Gladstone*. New York: Alfred A. Knopf, 1969.

Kerr, Don. "Building the University of Saskatchewan, 1907–1930." *Prairie Forum* 5 (1980): 157–81.

King, Carlyle. *The First Fifty: Teaching, Research, and Public Service at the University of Saskatchewan, 1909–1959*. Toronto: McClelland and Stewart, 1959.

Kinsley, David R. "'The Taming of the Shrew': On the History of the Goddess Kālī." *Studies in Religion / Sciences religieuses* 1.4 (1971–2): 328–38.

Klostermaier, Klaus K. "Hindu–Christian Dialogue: Its Religious and Cultural Implications." *Studies in Religion / Sciences religieuses* 1.2 (1971): 83–97.

Krikorian, Jacqueline D., David R. Cameron, Marcel Martel, Andrew W. McDougall, and Robert C. Vipond, eds. *Roads to Confederation: The Making of Canada, 1867*. 2 vols. Toronto: University of Toronto Press, 2017.

Lacroix, Benoit. "Les origines ou la naissance des sciences humaines de la religion au Québec (1940–1969)." In *L'enseignement et la recherche dans le secteur des sciences humaines de la religion*, ed. N. Ryan. Québec: Ministère de l'Éducation, 1969.

Lam, Vincent. *Tommy Douglas*. Toronto: Penguin, 2011.

Lamb, W. Kaye. *History of the Canadian Pacific Railway*. New York: Macmillan, 1977.

Lanctot, Gustave. *A History of Canada*, vol. 3: *From the Treaty of Utrecht to the Treaty of Paris, 1713–1763*, trans. Margaret M. Cameron. Cambridge, MA: Harvard University Press, 1965.

Langton, John. "The University of Toronto in 1856." *Canadian Historical Review* 5.2 (1924): 132–45.

Lapointe, Richard, and Lucille Tessier. *The Francophones of Saskatchewan: A History*. Regina: Campion College and University of Regina Press, 1988.

Laporte, Jean-Marc. "Editorial." *Toronto Journal of Theology* 1.1 (1985): 1–2.

Larouche, Jean-Marc, and Guy Ménard, eds. *L'étude de la religion au Québec. Bilan et prospective*. Québec: Les Presses de l'Université Laval, 2001.

Lee, Robert C. *The Canada Company and the Huron Tract, 1826–1853*. Toronto: Natural Heritage Books, 2004.

Levine, George. "Defining Knowledge : An Introduction." In *Victorian Science in Context*, ed. Bernard Lightman, 15–23. Chicago: University of Chicago Press, 1997.

Lovick, L.D., ed. *Tommy Douglas Speaks*. Lantzville: Oolichan Books, 1979.

MacKinnin, Ian F. "'Formgeschichte' and the Synoptic Problem: Present Position." *Canadian Journal of Religious Thought* 9.3 (1932): 190–6.

MacKirdy, Kenneth A. "The Formation of the Modern University, 1859–1906." In *The University of New Brunswick Memorial Volume*, ed. Alfred G. Bailey, 33–46. Fredericton: University of New Brunswick Press, 1950.

Macklem, Patrick, and Douglas Sanderson, eds. *From Recognition to Reconciliation: Essays on the Constitutional Entrenchment of Aboriginal and Treaty Rights*. Toronto: University of Toronto Press, 2016.

Macleod, Rod. *All True Things: A History of the University of Alberta, 1908–2008*. Edmonton: University of Alberta Press, 2008.

MacNeill, H.L. "Buddha as Pragmatist." *Canadian Journal of Religious Thought* 6.5 (1929): 335–44.

– "The Course of Buddhism in India." *Canadian Journal of Religious Thought* 6.1 (1929): 47–54.

– "Paul: The First Christian Protestant." *Canadian Journal of Religious Thought* 5.3 (1928): 199–208.

MacPherson, John. "A History of the Canadian Society of Biblical Studies." In *Canadian Biblical Studies*, 1–16. Ed. Norman E. Wagner. Waterloo: Canadian Society of Biblical Studies, 1967.

MacRae, J.D. "The New Tide in China." *Canadian Journal of Religious Thought* 1.6 (1924): 515–20.

Maheux, A. "Pourquoi l'Université en 1852?" *Revue de l'Université Laval* 5 (1951): 381–7.

Manson, William. "Foundations Which Are Not Removed." *Canadian Journal of Religious Thought* 1.1 (1924): 16–23.

– "From an Expositor's Notebook." *Canadian Journal of Religious Thought* 2.1 (1925): 164–6.

Margoshes, Dave. *Tommy Douglas: Building the New Society*. Lantzville: XYZ, 1999.

Markell, H.K. *The Faculty of Religious Studies, McGill University, 1948–1978.* Montreal: McGill University, 1978.

Martin Luther H., and Donald Wiebe. "Documenting the Delusion: A Case Study." In *Conversations and Controversies in the Scientific Study of Religion: Collaborative and Co-authored Essays by Luther H. Martin and Donald Wiebe*, ed. L.H. Luther and D. Wiebe, 319–30. Leiden: Brill, 2016.

Masters, D.C. *Protestant Church Colleges in Canada: A History*. Toronto: University of Toronto Press, 1966.

– "The Rise of Liberalism in Canadian Protestant Churches." *CCHA Study Sessions* 36 (1969): 27–39.

– *The Winnipeg General Strike*. Toronto: University of Toronto Press, 1950.

McCurdy, John F. *Aryo-Semitic Speech: A Study in Linguistic Archaeology* [1881]. Eugene: Wipf and Stock, 2004.

McCutcheon, Russell T. *The Insider/Outsider Problem in the Study of Religion: A Reader.* New York: Continuum, 1999.

– *Manufacturing Religion: The Discourse on Sui Generis Religion and the Politics of Nostalgia*. Oxford and New York: Oxford University Press, 1997.

McDougall, John. *In the Days of the Red River Rebellion: Life and Adventure in the Far West of Canada (1868–1872)* [1903]. Toronto: Briggs, 2017.

McIntire, C.T. "Unity among Many: The Formation of the United Church of Canada, 1899–1930." In *The United Church of Canada: A History*, ed. Don Schweitzer, 3–38. Waterloo: Wilfrid Laurier University Press, 2012.

McLelland, Joseph C. "Editorial." *Studies in Religion / Sciences religieuses* 6.5 (1976–7): 483–4.

McMurrich, J. Playfair. "Evolution and Religion." *Canadian Journal of Religious Thought* 1.6 (1924): 463–72.

Menkis, Richard. "'The Voice of the Minister Heard in Words of Exhortation and Instruction': Abraham de Sola and the Jewish Sermon in Victorian Montreal, and Beyond." *Jewish History* 23.2 (2009): 117–47.

Mercer, Samuel A.B. "An Expedition to Abyssinia." *Canadian Journal of Religious Thought* 7.5 (1930): 371–5.

Micklem, Nathaniel. "Religions and Religion." *Canadian Journal of Religious Thought* 5.1 (1928): 23–7.

Miller, James R. *Residential Schools and Reconciliation: Canada Confronts Its History*. Toronto: University of Toronto Press, 2017.

Mills, David. *The Idea of Loyalty in Upper Canada, 1784–1850*. Montreal and Kingston: McGill–Queen's University Press, 1988.

Moir, John S. *A History of Biblical Studies in Canada: A Sense of Proportion*. Chico: Scholars' Press, 1982.

Moore, George Foot. "Fate and Free Will in the Jewish Philosophies According to Josephus." *Harvard Theological Review* 22.4 (1929): 371–89.

Morton, Arthur S. *A History of the Canadian West to 1870–71; Being a History of Rupert's Land (the Hudson's Bay Company's Territory) and of the North-West Territory (including the Pacific Slope)*, 2nd ed., ed. Lewis G. Thomas. Toronto: University of Toronto Press, 1973.

– *Saskatchewan: The Making of a University*. Toronto: University of Toronto Press, 1959.

Morton, Desmond. *A Short History of Canada*, 7th ed. Toronto: McClelland and Stewart, 2017.

Morton, William L. *One University: A History of the University of Manitoba, 1877–1952*. Toronto: McClelland and Stewart, 1957.

Muir, William R. "Higher Education in Saskatchewan." In *Higher Education in Canada: Different Systems, Different Perspectives*, ed. Glen A. Jones, 93–114. London and New York: Routledge, 1997.

Murray, Jean. "The Contest for the University of Saskatchewan." *Saskatchewan History* 12 (1959): 1–22.

– "The Early History of Emmanuel College." *Saskatchewan History* 9 (1956): 81–101.

Neufeldt, Ronald. *Religious Studies in Alberta: A State-of-the-Art Review*. Waterloo: Wilfrid Laurier University Press, 1983.

Nicholls, William. "Editorial: A New Journal and Its Predecessor." *Studies in Religion / Sciences religieuses* 1.1 (1971): 1–3.

Nongbri, Brent. *Before Religion: The History of a Modern Concept*. New Haven: Yale University Press, 2015.

Paradis, James, and Thomas Postlewait, eds. *Victorian Science and Victorian Values: Literary Perspectives*. New Brunswick: Rutgers University Press, 1985.

Partikan, P., and Louis Rousseau. *La théologie québécoise contemporaine (1940–1973). Genèse de ses producteurs et transformations de son discours*. Québec: Institut supérieur des sciences humaines, 1977.

Patterson, George. *Memoir of James MacGregor, D.D.* Philadelphia: Joseph M. Wilson, 1859.

Patterson, Graeme. "An Enduring Canadian Myth: Responsible Government and the Family Compact." *Journal of Canadian Studies / Revue d'études canadiennes* 12.2 (1977): 3–16.

Peake, Arthur S. "The Alleged Reaction in Old Testament Criticism." *Canadian Journal of Religious Thought* 1.1 (1924): 40–6.

Phelps, Arthur L. "An Approach to Contemporary Poetry." *Canadian Journal of Religious Thought* 1.1 (1924): 24–35.

Pilcher C.V. "Hermann Gunkel on Psalms 42, 43." *Canadian Journal of Religious Thought* 7.4 (1930): 314–19.

Pilon, Henri. "The Founding of the University of Trinity College." *Trinity Convocation Bulletin* 14.2 (1977): 1–11.

Pitsula, James M. *As One Who Serves: The Making of the University of Regina.* Montreal and Kingston: McGill–Queen's University Press, 2006.

Preus, J. Samuel. *Explaining Religion: Criticism and Theory from Bodin to Freud.* New Haven: Yale University Press, 1996.

Price, Percy G. "Japan and the Christian Movement." *Canadian Journal of Religious Thought* 2.6 (1925): 435–9.

Provost, Honorius. "Historique du Séminaire de Québec." *Revue de l'Université Laval* 17 (1963): 591–9.

– "Les Origines éloignées du Séminaire de Québec." *Canadian Catholic Historical Association Report* (1955–6): 25–31.

– *Le Séminaire de Québec. Documents et biographies.* Quebec: Séminaire de Québec, 1964.

Ralston, Helen. "Canadian Immigration Policy in the Twentieth Century: Its Impact on South Asian Women." *Canadian Woman Studies* 19.3 (1999): 33–7.

Rawlyk, George, and Kevin Quinn. *The Redeemed of the Lord Say So: A History of Queen's Theological College, 1912–1972.* Kingston: Queen's Theological College, 1980.

Raymond, W.O. *The Genesis of the University of New Brunswick: With a Sketch of the Life of William Brydone-Jack A.M., D.C.L., President, 1861–1885.* n.p: Forgotten Books, 2009.

Read, Colin, and Ronald J. Stagg, eds. *The Rebellion of 1837 in Upper Canada.* Ottawa: Carleton University Press, 1985.

Remus, Harold. "Religion and Religious Studies in Ontario." In *Religious Studies in Ontario: A State-of-the-Art Review*, ed. H. Remus, W.C. James, and D. Fraiken, 5–92. Waterloo: Wilfrid Laurier University Press, 1992.

Remus, Harold, William C. James, and Daniel Fraikin. *Religious Studies in Ontario: A State-of-the-Art Review.* Waterloo: Wilfrid Laurier University Press, 1992.

Report on the Affairs of British North America (The Durham Report). Ottawa: n.p., 1839. http://www.canadiana.ca/view/oocihm.32374/1?r=0&s=1.

Riddell, J.S. *Methodism in the Middle West.* Toronto: Ryerson Press, 1940.

Robinson, John Beverly. *Canada and the Canada Bill* [1840]. New York: Johnson Reprint, 1967.

Roper, Henry. "The Anglican Episcopate in Canada: An Historical Perspective." *Anglican and Episcopal History* 57.3 (1988): 255–71.

Rose, William J. "Travelling Europe." *Canadian Journal of Religious Thought* 1.1 (1924): 47–55.

Rousseau, Louis. "De fierté, d'espoir et d'inquiétude." In *L'étude de la religion au Québec. Bilan et prospective*, ed. Jean Marc Larouche and Guy Ménard, xiii–xxv. Québec: Les Presses de l'Université Laval, 2001.

– "La religiologie à l'UQAM. Genèse sociale et direction épistémologique." In *Sciences sociales et Églises. Questions sur l'évolution religieuse du Québec*, ed. P. Stryckman et J.P. Rouleau, 73–96. Montréal: Bellarmin, 1980, 73–96.

Rousseau, Louis, ed. *Le Québec après Bouchard-Taylor. Les identités religieuses de l'immigration*. Montreal: Les Presses de l'Université du Québec, 2012.

Rousseau, Louis, and Michel Despland. *Les sciences religieuses au Québec depuis 1972*. Waterloo: Wilfrid Laurier University Press, 1988.

Rousseau, Louis, and Frank W. Remiggi. *Atlas historique des pratiques religieuses. Le sud-ouest du Québec au XIXe siècle*. Ottawa: University of Ottawa Press, 1998.

Rowell, Newton W. "The International Situation and the Christian Ideal." *Canadian Journal of Religious Thought* 1.1 (1924): 6–25.

Ruggles, Richard I. *A Country So Interesting: The Hudson's Bay Company and Two Centuries of Mapping, 1670–1870*. Montreal and Kingston: McGill–Queen's University Press, 2011.

Rushforth, Brent. *Bonds of Alliance: Indigenous and Atlantic Slaveries in New France*. Chapel Hill: University of North Carolina Press, 2014.

Russell, Peter A. "Rhetorics of Identity: The Debate over Division of the North-West Territories, 1890–1905." *Journal of Canadian Studies* 20.4 (1985–6): 99–114.

Ryan, N., ed. *L'enseignement et la recherche dans le secteur des sciences humaines de la religion*. Québec: Ministère de l'éducation, 1969.

Sanche, M. *Heartwood: A History of St. Thomas More College and Newman Center at the University of Saskatchewan*. Saskatoon: St. Thomas More, 1986.

Sandeen, Ernest. *The Roots of Fundamentalism: British and American Millenarianism, 1800–1930*. Chicago: University of Chicago Press, 1970.

Saperstein, Marc. "The Academic Study of Canadian Jewish Preachers." *Jewish History* 23.2 (2009): 107–16.

Saul, John Ralston. *Louis-Hippolyte Lafontaine and Robert Baldwin*. Toronto: Penguin Canada, 2010.

Sauvé, Madeline. *La Faculté de théologie de l' Université de Montréal. Mémoire et histoire, 1967–1997*. St-Laurent: Fides, 2001.

Savoie, Donald J. "All Things Canadian Are Now Regional." *Journal of Canadian Studies* 35.1 (2001): 203–17.

Schneider, Fred D. "The Habit of Deference: The Imperial Factor and the 'University Question' in Upper Canada," *Journal of British Studies* 17.1 (1977): 82–104.

Schul, Joseph. *Rebellion: The Rising in French Canada, 1837*. Toronto: Macmillan Canada, 1996.

Schweitzer, Don. "Introduction." In *The United Church of Canada: A History*, ed. Don Schweitzer, xi-xix. Waterloo: Wilfrid Laurier University Press, 2012.

Scott, Ernest F. "Some Doubts about Psychology." *Canadian Journal of Religious Thought* 1.2 (1924): 97–106.

Scott, J. Brian. "Brandon College and Social Christianity." In *Costly Vision: The Baptist Pilgrimage in Canada*, ed. Jarold K. Zeman, 139–63. Burlington: Welch, 1988.

Shackleton, Doris French. *Tommy Douglas*. Toronto: McClelland and Stewart, 1975.

Sharpe, Eric J. *Comparative Religion*. London: Duckworth, 1975.

Shevell, Martin. "A Canadian Paradox: Tommy Douglas and Eugenics." *Canadian Journal of Neurological Sciences* 39.1 (2012): 35–49.

Silcox, Edwin. *Church Union in Canada: Its Causes and Consequences*. New York: Institute of Social and Religious Research, 1933.

Simmons, Deidre. *Keepers of the Record: The History of the Hudson's Bay Company Archives*. Montreal and Kingston: McGill–Queen's University Press, 2007.

Sinclair-Faulkner, Tom. "Theory Divided from Practice: The Introduction of the Higher Criticism into Canadian Protestant Seminaries." *Studies in Religion / Sciences religieuses* 10.3 (1981): 321–43.

Sissons, C.B. *A History of Victoria University*. Toronto: University of Toronto Press, 1952.

Slater, Robert H.L. "Christian Attitudes to Other Religions." *Canadian Journal of Theology* 2.4 (1956): 215–24.

– *Paradox and Nirvana: A Study of Religious Ultimates with Special Reference to Burmese Buddhism*. Chicago: University of Chicago Press, 1950.

Smith, George Terence. "Federation and Fullness: A History of the Early Years of Federation at the University of Toronto from the Viewpoint of the Three Denominational Colleges." EdD, University of Toronto, 1997.

Smith, Jonathan Z. *Imagining Religion: From Babylon to Jonestown*. Chicago: University of Chicago Press, 1982.

Smith, Wilfred Cantwell. "A Human View of Truth." *Studies in Religion / Sciences religieuses* 1.1 (1971): 6–24.

Smyth, James. "The Faith of Modern Man." *Canadian Journal of Religious Thought* 1.1 (1924): 61–70.

Spragge, George W. "John Strachan's Contribution to Education 1800–1823." *Canadian Historical Review* 22.2 (1941): 147–58.

Stagg, J.C.A. *The War of 1812: Conflict for a Continent*. Cambridge: Cambridge University Press, 2012.

Stanley, George F.G. *Birth of Western Canada: History of the Riel Rebellions*. Toronto: University of Toronto Press, 1960.

Stebner, Eleanor J. "The 1930s." In *The United Church of Canada: A History*, ed. Don Schweitzer, 39–56. Waterloo: Wilfrid Laurier University Press, 2012.

Stevens, G.R. *History of the Canadian National Railways.* New York: Macmillan, 1973.

Strachan, John. *Church University of Upper Canada: Pastoral Letter from the Lord Bishop of Toronto.* Toronto: A.F. Plees, 1842.

Stroumsa, Guy G. *A New Science: The Discovery of Religion in the Age of Reason.* Cambridge, MA: Harvard University Press, 2010.

Strykman, Paul. "Présentation." In *Sciences sociales et Églises. Questions sur l'évolution religieuse du Québec*, ed. P. Stryckman and J.P. Rouleau, 13–18. Montréal: Bellarmin, 1980.

Sylvester, James Joseph. *The Collected Mathematical Papers of James Joseph Sylvester.* 4 vols. Cambridge: Cambridge University Press, 1904–12.

Taylor, Alan. *The Civil War of 1812: American Citizens, British Subjects, Irish Rebels, and Indian Allies.* New York: Vintage, 2010.

Taylor, K.W. "Racism in Canadian Immigration Policy." *Canadian Ethnic* Studies 23.1 (1991): 1–20.

Temelini, Michael. "Multicultural Rights, Multicultural Virtues: A History of Multiculturalism in Canada." In *Multiculturalism and the Canadian Constitution*, ed. M. Temelini, 43–60. Vancouver: UBC Press, 2007.

Thomas, C.E. "The Early Days of King's College, Windsor, Nova Scotia." *Canadian Church Historical Society Journal* 6 (1964): 30–45.

Thomas, Ernest. "The Significance of Political Groups." *Canadian Journal of Religious Thought* 1.1 (1924): 71–81.

Thomas, Lewis G. "The Church of England and Higher Education in the Prairie West before 1914." *Journal of the Canadian Church History Society* 3 (1956): 1–11.

– *The Liberal Party in Alberta: A History of Politics in the Province of Alberta, 1905–1921.* Toronto: University of Toronto Press, 1959.

Thomson, D.E. "McMaster University, 1887–1906." *McMaster University Monthly* 16 (1906): 20–8.

Topping, Ryan. "Catholic Studies in Canada: History and Prospects." *Études d'Histoire Religieuse* 76 (2010): 45–60.

True, Micah. *Masters and Students: Jesuit Mission Ethnography in Seventeenth-Century New France.* Montreal and Kingston: McGill–Queen's University Press, 2015.

Trumbell, Charles G. *The Life Story of C.I. Scofield* [1920]. Eugene: Wipf and Stock, 2007.

Truth and Reconciliation Committee of Canada. *The Final Report of the Truth and Reconciliation Commission of Canada*, vol. 4: *Canada's Residential Schools: Missing Children and Unmarked Burials.* Montreal and Kingston: McGill–Queen's University Press, 2015.

Tulchinsky, Gerald. "'Said to Be a Very Honest Jew': The R.G. Dun Credit Reports and Jewish Business Activity in Mid-19th-Century Montreal." *Urban History Review* 18.3 (1990): 200–9.

United Church of Canada. "The Basis of Union" [1925]. http://www.united-church.ca/sites/default/files/resources/basis-of-union.pdf, General Precepts.

Vining, C.A.M., ed. *Woodstock College Memorial Book*. Toronto: Woodstock College Alumni Association, 1951.

Voisine, Nive. *Histoire de l'Église catholique au Québec (1608–1970)*. Montréal: Fides, 1971.

Vroom, F.W. *King's College: A Chronicle, 1789–1939*. Halifax: Imperial Publishing Co., 1941.

Waardenburg, Jacques. *Classical Approaches to the Study of Religion: Aims, Methods, and Theories of Research*. The Hague: Mouton, 1973.

Wallace, W. Stewart. *The Family Compact: A Chronicle of the Rebellion in Upper Canada*. Toronto: Brook, 1915.

Wasserstrom, Steven M. "Islamicate History of Religions." *History of Religions* 27.4 (1988): 405–11.

Watson, Gordon. *Religious Studies in the University of Toronto: A History of Its Foundation to Celebrate the 20th Anniversary of the Center for the Study of Religion, 1976–1996*. Toronto: Department for the Study of Religion, 1997.

Wayland, Sarah V. "Immigration, Multiculturalism and National Identity in Canada." *International Journal of Group Rights* 5.1 (1997): 33–58.

Welch, Jr., Claude R. "New Building Will House Church Study." *Harvard Crimson*, 20 November 1959. http://www.thecrimson.com/article/1959/11/20/new-building-will-house-church-study.

Wevers, John W. "Canadian Universities and the Teaching of Religion." *Canadian Journal of Theology* 2.3 (1956): 151–62.

Whidden, H.P. "What Is a Liberal Education?" *Canadian Journal of Religious Thought* 1.1 (1924): 36–9.

Whitaker, Reg. *Canadian Immigration Policy since Confederation*. Ottawa: Canadian Historical Association, 1991.

Wiebe, Donald. "The Failure of Nerve in the Academic Study of Religion." *Studies in Religion / Sciences religieuses* 13.4 (1984): 401–22.

– "Is a Science of Religion Possible?" *Studies in Religion / Sciences religieuses* 7.1 (1978): 5–17.

– "Memory, Text, and Interpretation: A Critical Appreciation of IAHR International Congresses – 1975–2010." In *The Academic Study of Religion and the IAHR: Past, Present, and Prospects*, ed. Tim Jensen and Armin Geertz, 253–82. Leiden: Brill, 2015.

– *The Politics of Religious Studies: The Continuing Conflict with Theology in the Academy*. New York: Palgrave Macmillan, 1999.

Wilson, Alan. *The Clergy Reserves of Upper Canada*. Ottawa: Canadian Historical Association, 1969.

Index

www.ingramcontent.com/pod-product-compliance
Lightning Source LLC
LaVergne TN
LVHW090157080826
844660LV00013B/844/J

* 9 7 8 1 4 8 7 5 0 4 9 7 7 *